Oklahoma Notes

Basic-Sciences Review for Medical Licensure
Developed at
The University of Oklahoma, College of Medicine

Suitable Reviews for:
United States Medical Licensing Examination
(USMLE), Step 1
Federation Licensing Examination (FLEX)

Oklahoma Notes

Behavioral Sciences

Third Edition

Ronald S. Krug
Alvah R. Cass

Springer-Verlag
New York Berlin Heidelberg London Paris
Tokyo Hong Kong Barcelona Budapest

Ronald S. Krug, Ph.D.
Department of Psychiatry and Behavioral Sciences
College of Medicine
Health Sciences Center
The University of Oklahoma
Oklahoma City, OK 73190
USA

Alvah R. Cass, M.D.
Clinical Associate Professor of Family Medicine
The Department of Family Medicine
Health Sciences Center at Syracuse
SUNY Syracuse
Syracuse, NY 13210
USA

Library of Congress Cataloging-in-Publication Data
Krug, Ronald S.
    Behavioral sciences / Ronald S. Krug, Alvah R. Cass, — 3rd ed.
      p. cm. — (Oklahoma notes)
    Includes bibliographical references.
    ISBN 0-387-97782-1, — ISBN 3-540-97782-1
      1. Psychology—Outlines, syllabi, etc. 2. Developmental psychology—Outlines,
syllabi, etc. 3. Psychology, Pathological—Outlines, syllabi, etc. 4. Psychiatry—
Outlines, syllabi, etc. 5. Medical care—Outlines, syllabi, etc. I. Cass,
Alvah R. II. Title. III. Series.
    [DNLM: 1. Behavior—outlines. 2. Delivery of Health Care—outlines.
3. Psychology, Social—outlines. 4. Psychopathology—outlines. WM 18 K94b]
BF141.K78 1992
362.2'076—dc20
DNLM/DLC
for Library of Congress   92-2155

Printed on acid-free paper.

© 1992, 1989, and 1987 Springer-Verlag New York, Inc.
All rights reserved. This work may not be translated or copied in whole or in part without the written permission of the publisher (Springer-Verlag New York, Inc., 175 Fifth Avenue, New York, NY 10010, USA), except for brief excerpts in connection with reviews or scholarly analysis. Use in connection with any form of information storage and retrieval, electronic adaptation, computer software, or by similar or dissimilar methodology now known or hereafter developed is forbidden.
The use of general descriptive names, trade names, trademarks, etc., in this publication, even if the former are not especially identified, is not to be taken as a sign that such names, as understood by the Trade Marks and Merchandise Marks Act, may accordingly be used freely by anyone.
While the advice and information in this book is believed to be true and accurate at the date of going to press, neither the authors nor the editors nor the publisher can accept any legal responsibility for any errors or omissions that may be made. The publisher makes no warranty, express or implied, with respect to the material contained herein.

Production managed by Christin R. Ciresi; manufacturing supervised by Jacqui Ashri.
Camera-ready copy prepared by the authors.
Printed and bound by Edwards Brothers, Inc., Ann Arbor, MI.
Printed in the United States of America.

9 8 7 6 5 4 3 2 1

ISBN 0-387-97782-1 Springer-Verlag New York Berlin Heidelberg
ISBN 3-540-97782-1 Springer-Verlag Berlin Heidelberg New York

Preface to the *Oklahoma Notes*

In 1973, the University of Oklahoma College of Medicine instituted a requirement for passage of the Part 1 National Boards for promotion to the third year. To assist students in preparation for this examination, a two-week review of the basic sciences was added to the curriculum in 1975. Ten review texts were written by the faculty: four in anatomical sciences and one each in the other six basic sciences. Self-instructional quizzes were also developed by each discipline and administered during the review period.

The first year the course was instituted the Total Score performance on National Boards Part I increased 60 points, with the relative standing of the school changing from 56th to 9th in the nation. The performance of the class since then has remained near the national candidate mean (500) with a range of 467 to 537. This improvement in our own students' performance has been documented (Hyde et al: Performance on NBME Part I examination in relation to policies regarding use of test. J. Med. Educ. 60:439–443, 1985).

A questionnaire was administered to one of the classes after they had completed the Boards; 82% rated the review books as the most beneficial part of the course. These texts were subsequently rewritten and made available for use by all students of medicine who were preparing for comprehensive examinations in the Basic Medical Sciences. Since their introduction in 1987, over a quarter of a million copies have been sold. Assuming that 60,000 students have been first-time takers in the intervening five years, this equates to an average of four books per examinee.

Obviously these texts have proven to be of value. The main reason is that they present a *concise overview* of each discipline, emphasizing the content and concepts most appropriate to the task at hand, i.e., passage of a comprehensive examination over the Basic Medical Sciences.

The recent changes in the licensure examination structure that have been made to create a Step 1/Step 2 process have necessitated a complete revision of the Oklahoma Notes. This task was begun in the summer of 1991; the book you are now holding is a product of that revision. Besides bringing each book up to date, the authors have made every effort to make the texts and review questions conform to the new format of the National Board of Medical Examiners tests.

I hope you will find these review books valuable in your preparation for the licensure exams. Good Luck!

Richard M. Hyde, Ph.D.
Executive Editor

Preface

There are five separate sections to this book arranged in a logical sequence. Section One covers *normal* phenomenology of human behavior, including issues of learning and growth and development. Section Two addresses the *theories* of human development (which have implications for problem behavior) as well as the *psychosocial issues* in health care delivery. The latter are those issues which are *not clearly psychopathology,* but represent problems in health care delivery which physicians encounter in the normal practice of medicine. Section Three is an overview of *psychopathology* in both children and adults, and Section Four deals with the diagnosis and intervention issues involved in various forms of psychopathology and problems of living. Section Five is the overview of the different *systems of health care delivery* and the *incidence/prevalence* of different health care problems.

This is a review text and should not be substituted for more complete texts. The authors do not recommend that this book be used as a course text except to those academic offerings that are specifically directed to an overview of the behavioral sciences.

To use this book effectively, the beginning student should start at the first chapter and progress through the text in a systematic fashion. For the more advanced student the basic information in Sections One and Two might be skipped and they can proceed directly to Sections Three and Four.

The authors believe that this text would be helpful in preparation for licensing examinations, including *National Boards, Parts One and Two (NBME I & II),* the *Medical Sciences Knowledge Profile (MSKP),* the *Foreign Medical Graduate Examination in the Medical Sciences (FMGEMS),* the *Federation Licensure Examinations, Parts One and Two (FLEX I & II);* and most specifically the new single path to licensure, the *United States Medical Licensing Examination (USMLE).*

The authors wish to gratefully acknowledge the efforts of L. Blaine Shaffer, M.D., for his work in selecting appropriate questions for the sections of the text, and Ms. Susan Jordan, for her invaluable assistance in the preparation of the manuscript.

Ronald S. Krug
Alvah R. Cass

Contents

Preface to the *Oklahoma Notes*	v
Preface	vii
Introduction	xi

Section One: Review of Basics of Human Behavior ... 1

I. Assumptions	4
II. Definitions and Concepts	4
III. Affect and Emotional States	9
IV. Memory	15
V. Consciousness	17
VI. Orientation	18
VII. Perception	19
VIII. Thinking	21
IX. Learning	22
X. Intelligence, Mental Retardation, and Aging Effects	27
XI. Growth and Development	32
XII. Neurophysiologic Considerations	44
XIII. Neurotransmitter and Behavior Correlates	46
XIV. Selected Psychophysiologic Topics	50
Examination Questions and Answers	58

Section Two: Theories, Psychosocial Issues ... 67

I. Theories	70
II. Sexuality	77
III. Substance Abuse	84
IV. Alcoholism	92
V. Aging	97
VI. Death and Dying/Grief and Bereavement	98
VII. Attitudes	101
VIII. Prejudice	102
IX. Subculture Parameters	103
X. Psychological Assessment	107
XI. Divorce	114
XII. Suicide, Homicide, and Other Forms of Violence	115
XIII. Social Stress and Physical Concomitants	122
Examination Questions and Answers	123

Section Three: Psychopathology ... 130

I. Assumptions and Rationale	131
II. Defense Mechanisms	131
III. Differential Diagnosis Flow Chart	135
IV. Major Categories of Psychopathology	136

V. Cross Theoretical Comparisons	155
VI. Special Problems of Children	158
VII. Incidence/Prevalence Statistics of Emotional Illness	167
Examination Questions and Answers	169

Section Four: Diagnosis and Intervention — 178

I. Mental Status Examination, Interviewing	179
II. Major Treatment Modalities	182
III. Group Methods	197
IV. Environmental Manipulations	198
V. Medical Legal Issues	200
Examination Questions and Answers	203

Section Five: Introduction to Health Care Systems — 211

I. Introduction	215
II. The Health of the Nation	216
III. Health Manpower	239
IV. Ambulatory Care: Traditional Models	244
V. Ambulatory Care: Alternative Models	249
VI. Institutions for Health Care	257
VII. Financing Patient Care	266
VIII. Regulation and Quality Assurance	295
IX. Comparative Models of Health Care Systems	306
X. Final Comments	313
XI. Selected Bibliography	313
Examination Questions and Answers	316

Introduction

All conditions of human behavior, both "normal" and "abnormal" can be understood. It can be understood if you look at it in a matrix of an *organism* which has *needs* and has the *capability to learn*. To understand it, you must place it into a context of development and learning and *set aside* preconceived notions from movies, television, and sensational novels. Those media have taken one aspect of a human being's life and concentrated on it with no history, leaving the impression that there is something magical in human behavior. For example, if what you are doing right now—looking at a sheet of paper with black markings on it—were taken out of context and you and your behavior were placed into the midst of a culture in which they did not understand writing, but yet it was explained to them that you were getting ideas and knowledge from that sheet of paper, it would seem quite abnormal, magical, and without basis or logic to that particular culture.

Below is an overview statement of the Behavioral Sciences. This is a skeleton and an orientation on which you can build knowledge, as well as a map in case you get lost. It can assist you in finding your way back.

  I. Birth: Until the fetus is born, the fetus has been cared for with or without the cooperation of the world as a whole. That is, the fetus has a constant supply of food, it is warm, its elimination functions are taken care of, etc. When the child is born it is suddenly and abruptly dependent upon the "good will" of others for satisfaction of basic biological needs.
 II. There may be any number of intervening variables at this point which may lay the groundwork for the child's development.

   A. The mother's health, her intelligence level, her own "psychopathological state," etc.
   B. Environmental Variables: the climatic temperature, relative food supply, the socio-economic status (SES) of the family into which the child was born, the presence or absence of wars, the presence or absence of disease, the educational opportunities available, etc.
   C. Cultural Beliefs: whether the baby (boy or girl) is circumcised early in its life, whether the child is fed on his demand versus a preordained schedule, the race of the child in relation to the predominant race in the culture, etc.

III. Assume there is a normal unfolding developmental course for all humans. Assume also that accompanying that normal unfolding developmental course are some basic biological needs that, if not satisfied, will destroy the person and/or the species.
IV. Assume that psychopathology is an end result of the basic needs not being appropriately met. This can be due to internal physiologic conditions of the organism or the external world.

A. If the organism does not get enough satisfaction of a need, it may not have enough "nourishment" to "grow" to the next stage of development.
B. If the organism receives too much "nourishment," it may "decide" that "it doesn't want to grow" to the next stage.
C. Consider the following chain of events:

1. The child's basic biological needs are either not met or met in such a way that the child's normal reactions to the presence of the basic biological needs are "different."
2. The child from birth (through the handling process, the way the parents attend to or ignore the child) gets a sense of its value or place in the world.
3. As the child gains symbols and language, the child learns to assign symbols, thoughts, perception, feelings, interpretations, etc., to various needs that he has. The symbols, etc., may be appropriate or not.
4. The end result may be that the child ends with a mental set, a "perception" of the world, a "learned" way of defending against anxiety (the threat of injury or death). That "set" may be adaptive or not.
5. The resultant pattern that is seen may be a "normal" pattern, a Personality Disorder pattern, a Psychotic Anxiety Disorder, Psychophysiologic Reaction, etc.

V. Assume that emotions are signals that the basic biological needs are or are not being "appropriately" satisfied.
VI. Because human beings are a special type animal, we have abilities which are cognitive-symbolic capacities.

A. These cognitive-symbolic abilities do not appear and develop totally until the organism is a few years old.
B. Before the organism can deal in cognitive-symbolic capabilities (at a very early age), basic biological needs of the organism (whether they are satisfied or not) get manifested only in emotions and in nonverbal behavior.
C. With the acquisition of cognitive and symbolic skills, basic biological needs get manifested not only behaviorally, but also symbolically in consciousness, orientation, memory, thoughts and perceptions.

VII. Depending upon various environmental, parental, "genetic," biological time of frustration, etc., variables, we are able to label ("diagnose") certain gross classifications of pathological behavior.
VIII. With the above understanding of how a person becomes "psychopathologic" we attempt to intervene in that process by a number of therapeutic modalities.

SECTION ONE: REVIEW OF BASICS OF HUMAN BEHAVIOR

I. **ASSUMPTIONS** **4**

II. **DEFINITIONS AND CONCEPTS** **4**

    A. Motivation
    B. Frustration
    C. Psychological stress
    D. Conflict
    E. Emotions
    F. Functional
    G. Acute versus chronic
    H. Affect

III. **AFFECT AND EMOTIONAL STATES** **9**

    A. General Information
    B. Fear
    C. Anxiety
    D. Tension
    E. Anger
    F. Sadness
    G. Disgust
    H. Shame
    I. Guilt

IV. **MEMORY** **15**

    A. Definition
    B. Mechanisms of Memory
    C. Phenomenology of Memory and Forgetting

V. **CONSCIOUSNESS** **17**

    A. Definition
    B. Special states of consciousness

VI. **ORIENTATION** **18**

    A. Orientation to time
    B. Orientation to place
    C. Orientation to person
    D. Orientation to present situation

VII. PERCEPTION 19

      A. Definition
      B. Neurophysiological considerations

VIII. THINKING 21

      A. Definition
      B. Phenomenology

IX. LEARNING 22

      A. General Considerations
      B. Terms
      C. Types of Learning
      D. Applied Learning

X.   INTELLIGENCE, MENTAL RETARDATION AND 27
     AGING EFFECTS

      A. Definition
      B. Verbal versus Performance
      C. Nature versus Nurture
      D. Intelligence Quotients
      E. Commonly used Intelligence Tests
      F. Mental Retardation
      G. Aging, Intelligence and Performance

XI. GROWTH AND DEVELOPMENT 32

      A. Preface and Theories
      B. Prenatal Influences
      C. Birth and Neonate
      D. Infancy
      E. Preschool
      F. School-age
      G. Adolescence
      H. Addendum: Child abuse, maternal deprivation,
          parental discipline, socio-economic status (SES).

XII. NEUROPHYSIOLOGIC CONSIDERATIONS 44

      A. Limbic System
      B. Reticular Activating System

XIII. NEUROTRANSMITTERS AND BEHAVIOR CORRELATES 46

      A. Definition
      B. General Classes of Neurotransmitters
      C. Neurotransmitter Correlates of Behavioral Pathology

XIV. SELECTED PSYCHOPHYSIOLOGIC TOPICS 50

      A. Sensory Deprivation
      B. EEG Waves and Epilepsy
      C. Sleep
      D. Circadian Rhythms
      E. Cortical Lesions and Behaviors
      F. Chronic Pain
      G. Immune System Correlates

EXAMINATION QUESTIONS AND ANSWERS 58

SECTION ONE: REVIEW OF BASICS OF HUMAN BEHAVIOR

I. **ASSUMPTIONS**

   A. Each human is a <u>biological</u> system who has physiologic needs. This person is immersed in an environmental system. This person possesses certain symbolic and communicative skills through which the physiologic needs can learn to be met.

   B. Each person in the process of utilization of the symbolic and communicative skills to meet these physiologic needs also develops unique psychological needs.

   C. In trying to meet physical and psychological needs, each person encounters other people who are trying to get their own unique needs met.

II. **DEFINITIONS AND CONCEPTS**

   A. <u>Motivation</u>: Energy which moves man to activity for meeting physical and psychological needs. That is, his <u>drives</u> (tension state) and his <u>impulses</u> (unexpected urges over which the person has little or no control).

   B. <u>Frustration</u>: When goal-directed behavior (or motivation to fulfill physiologic needs) is blocked, we call this a state of frustration. One can always assume there will be affect accompanying this state of frustration.

   C. <u>Psychological Stress</u>

   1. **Loss (or threat of loss) of objects** - e.g., oxygen, water, food, teeth, mother, wife, job, or a "A" in a given course in school.

   2. **Injury (or threat of injury)** - e.g. a storm, a knife held in the hand of a threatening person, surgery, an accident, an illness, a verbal insult.

   3. **Frustration of drive** - e.g. the blocking of the drive to get and eat food, to have an adequate living space, for sexual expression, etc.

   These three classes of psychological stress are also accompanied by feeling states.

Different persons' reactions to stress are different. A reaction to stress is dependent on such things as:

    a. The person's cultural background.
    b. Their physiologic/biologic condition at the time of stress.
    c. Their unique personality.
    d. The implications or meanings of the stress.
    e. The mechanisms available to assist in management of the stress.

4. **Psychosocial stress** and physiological concomitant.

    a. With stress, think of Cannon's fight or flight reaction.

        These include: (basically a sympathetic reaction)

            Increased respiration
            Decreased CO_2
            Increased muscle tone
            Increased gut motility
            Increased heart rate and blood pressure
            Increased piloerection
            Increased perspiration on hands and feet
            Dry mouth
            Dilated pupils

    b. If it's inter-personal, the stress is dealt with through fight or flight and the reactions return to normal.

    c. If it's intra-personal, it's difficult to fight or fly away from yourself; therefore, physiologic reactions aren't dismantled quickly and can become chronic. Selye is the important name.

D. <u>Conflict</u>

1. When two or more drives are aroused simultaneously (e.g. study for an exam or go to a party) or when two or more incompatible responses to a given drive are aroused simultaneously (love and hate for a parent).

2. Emotion frequently accompanies a conflict state.

3. Conflict by definition denotes a struggle <u>within</u> an individual. Therefore pure stress as defined in 3 above does not necessarily lead to conflict. You can be hungry without being in conflict.

4. There are 3 basic types of conflict:

   a. **Approach-approach** to two different <u>desirable</u> objects: no problem develops. When you select or move towards one, the other diminishes in intensity of desirability. E.g., if one is asked out for a date by two equally attractive persons, as soon as one moves towards person 1, person 2 doesn't seem as attractive.

   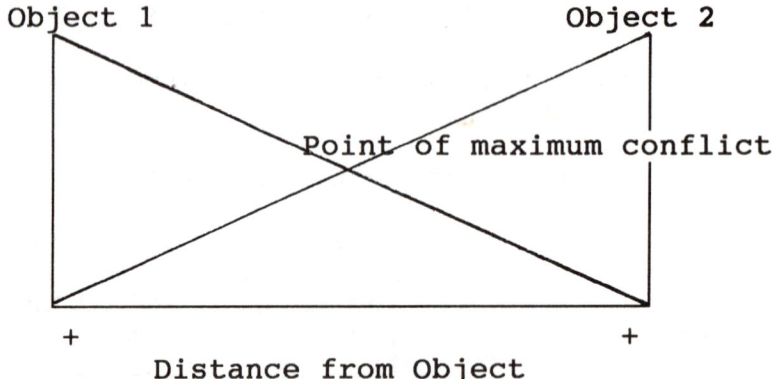

   b. **Avoidance-avoidance** of two different <u>undesirable</u> objects: problem develops. As you avoid or move away from one and towards the other, the other becomes more intensely negative; therefore, you reverse yourself and go back to the first one avoided which in turn begins to become more negative as you approach it, so you vacillate between the two equally negative choices, again and again and again. E.g., being asked out by two equally unattractive persons. As you get closer to person one, person 2 doesn't appear as unattractive.

   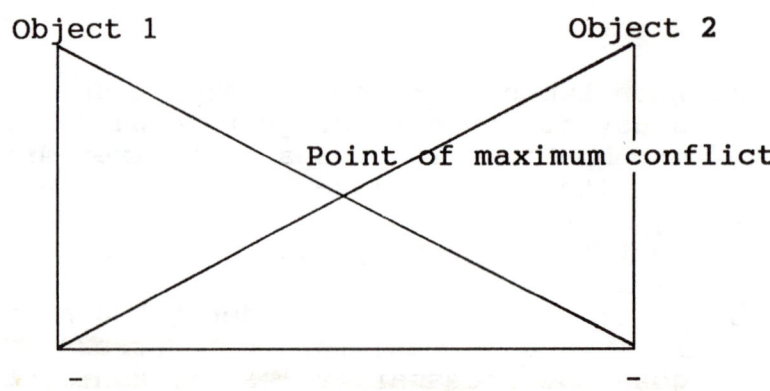

c. <u>Approach-avoidance</u> of the same object: problem develops. At first, the object seems very positive and attractive. However, as you approach the object, the avoidance (e.g., negative aspects of the object) become more intense. This is the classic conflict in which an abused wife finds herself with regard to leaving the abusing husband. Leaving seems very attractive (positive gradient); however, as she gets closer to leaving, the insecurity and fears associated with trying to survive and raise children by herself increase in intensity and she begins to say it's less difficult to take the abuse than to face the insecurity and lack of protection of the husband.

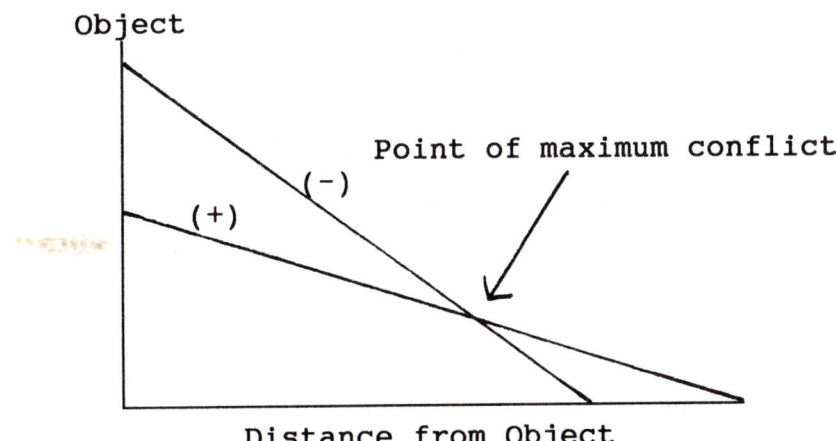

E. <u>Emotions</u>: Accompaniments of, and signal the immediate disruption of, a dynamic steady state in the human organism. By dynamic steady state is meant:

1. <u>Dynamic</u>: interactive or adaptive or adjusting.

2. <u>Steady state</u>: implies that the person is in a homeostatic condition of constantly adjusting.

3. When this is disrupted, emotions signal the change from the steady state. Obviously, these can be small adjustments and often are unnoticed by the person. They can be positive (e.g. love) and they can be negative (e.g. sadness). They can be large adjustments and noticed vividly. Again, these large adjustments can be positive (inheriting a million dollars) or negative (your child suddenly dying in your arms). Both large and small adjustments are important since small

unnoticed ones can build into a large one (e.g. small cumulative pressures may precipitate a heart attack).

4. The author Plutchik has given a classification of emotions which is helpful. Understand that primary emotions are states in the organism which are associated with adaptive behaviors that are related to basic biological processes.

Primary Emotions	Adaptive Behaviors
Acceptance	Incorporation
Disgust	Rejection
Fear (anxiety)	Protection
Anger	Destruction
Joy	Reproduction
Grief or sorrow (sadness)	Deprivation
Anticipation (expectancy)	Exploration
Surprise	Orientation

F. **Functional**: This term means that you **can't see the "cause" with a light microscope**. It is also liberally interpreted to mean that there is **no organic cause** for the disease. The symptoms with which the person presents constitute **emotionally induced illness**. **Functional does not mean malingering, nor does it mean lying**. **50-70% of all illness is emotionally related**.

G. <u>Acute vs. Chronic in Behavioral Sciences</u>

1. **Acute** means **reversible**. It does not mean recent onset (e.g. getting intoxicated on marijuana leads to Acute Brain Syndrome).

2. **Chronic** means **non-reversible** (e.g. a frontal lobectomy leads to a chronic brain disorder).

H. Affect: It is important to differentiate between the concepts of affect and emotion.

1. **Affect**: Refers to the state of the person that is more **persistent, more pervasive, less directly reflected in physiological responses, more generalized in ideational content**. **Affect is more a life style**.

2. **Emotion**: Is essentially the **reverse of affect**. That is, it is **more transient, less pervasive, more directly reflected in physiological responses, and more specific in ideational content**. It is that which is experienced by the organism (subjective evidence) or that which is communicated to others.

III. AFFECT AND EMOTIONAL STATES

A. General information.

1. Disturbance in affect can be manifested in emotion, behavior, thinking or somatic responses.

2. Definitions

   a. Flattening of Affect: very little display of emotion, even on topics where one usually expects an emotional display.

   b. Inappropriate Affect: the display of emotion is different from that expected with a given topic.

   c. Emotional Lability: emotional responses in excess of what is usually anticipated even with minor stimuli. This also refers to a rapid alteration in the emotions which are displayed such as crying versus laughing.

   d. Denial of Affect or Repression of Affect: subjective awareness is missing even when objective evidence suggests the contrary.

B. Fear as an emotion

1. Fear as an emotion is related to an object.

2. The object is seen as threatening, in fantasy or fact.

3. Protective behavioral responses accompany the feeling of fear.

C. Anxiety as an emotion

1. Because anxiety plays such a central role in all theories of human behavior (pathology as well as medical management of the physically ill patient), you should understand this concept very well before proceeding with any of the remaining material.

2. Definition of **anxiety as an emotion**

   a. Usually related to underlying affect anxiety or fear.

   b. Anxiety may be viewed as repressed (forgotten) fear. In this instance, the person cannot relate the anxiety to an object.

c. Anxiety as an emotion is experienced subjectively, but it is not linked to an object. In those psychopathologic conditions regarded as the Anxiety Disorders in the Diagnostic and Statistical Manual of Mental Disorders, Edition III, Revised (DSM-III-R), the patients appear with massive anxiety, BUT doesn't know what is frightening them. The naive health care person insists on asking the patient what is so scary, and the patient CAN'T, not won't tell the examiner.

3. Subjective vs. objective evidence of fear-anxiety

   a. Subjective anxiety: With fear the object is named. The irrationality of fear or the magnitude of the threat causes the patient distress. With anxiety, the object is not named, or the object named under examination turns out to be an instance of displacement (the inappropriate object). Remember, subjective evidence refers to the patient's verbal report. The report indicates some degree of awareness.

   Subjective evidence of anxiety includes statements like: "I'm scared, I'm nervous, etc." Subjective evidence of anxiety can also be inferred from statements like: "I'm shaky, I've got butterflies in my stomach, My knees are weak, etc."

   b. Objective evidence: This refers to evidence observed by another person, for example, a physician.

   General objective signs of anxiety include eyebrows raised; eyelids wide open; pupils dilated with a fixed stare; mouth open in a round or rectangular distribution, lips trembling, dry mouth with licking of lips; face generally white with a cold sweat; head fixed and pulled back; tendency to inspiration and yawning; the body trembling with frequent body shifts, guarding gestures and trivial hand occupation; speech is trembling, hesitant, blocked or rapid and disjointed, and speaking is at the height of inspiration; feet placed one in front of the other to "get away fast."

4. Some special aspects of anxiety to which you should pay particular attention. Understand these relationships:

   a. Anxiety and Performance: There is a curvilinear relationship between anxiety and ANY performance (be it sex, be it learning new skills, driving a car, etc.). This is expressed by the following graph.

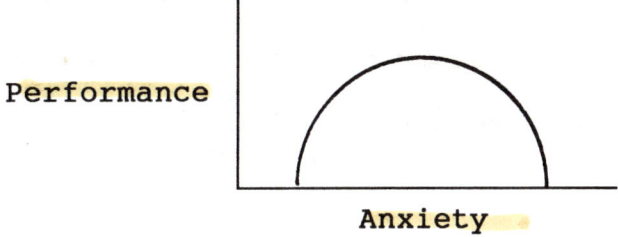

Up to a certain amount, anxiety increases performance. After that point more anxiety leads to a decrement in performance.

b. Anxiety and feared object: The closer one gets to a feared object (physically/psychologically), the more anxiety.

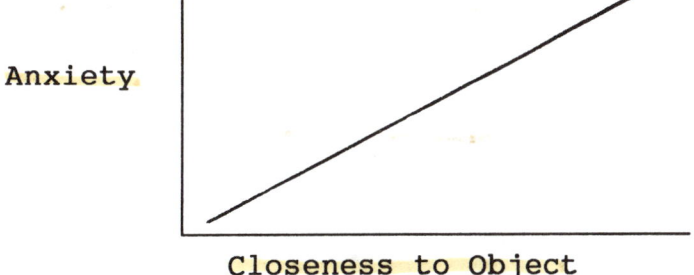

Remember: The anxious person has repressed what the real feared object is. You can get a clue to what is frightening the person by observing the different levels of anxiety as the person deals with different things. The closer they are to the feared object the more anxious they'll be; however, they predictably will not be aware of the relationship.

c. Psychophysiologic responses to anxiety

Most authors write about anxiety as an epinephrine-like response and suggest gross overactivity of the sympathetic nervous system. Below is a list of common somatic manifestations of anxiety.

(1) Excessive perspiration: particularly in the axilla and on the palms. This sweating forms the basis of the Galvanic Skin Response (the GSR).

(2) **Skeletal muscle tension**: tension headache, constriction in the back of the neck or chest, quavering voice, backache.

(3) **Hyperventilation syndrome**: dyspnea, dizziness, and paresthesia of the fingers and toes, often resulting in carpopedal spasm. Feeling of needing <u>more</u> oxygen when, in fact, already has too much.

(4) **Functional gastrointestinal disorders**: abdominal pain, anorexia, nausea, diarrhea, constipation, "butterflies" in the stomach.

(5) **Cardiovascular irritability**: transient systolic hypertension, premature contraction, tachycardia, fainting.

(6) **Genitourinary dysfunction**: urinary frequency, dysuria, impotence, pelvic pain in women, frigidity.

(7) **Pupils dilate**.

d. <u>Common situations provoking anxiety</u>

(1) **Anticipatory**: e.g. stage fright, in small amounts can improve performance, but large amounts are incapacitating.

(2) **"Castration"**: in psychoanalytic theory, this is part of the Oedipal complex. It is the anxiety associated with the fear father will castrate the son for "loving" the mother. In the adult, generalizes to any authority figure.

(3) **Separation**: Anxiety associated with impending or feared loss of a person whom one "needs" (e.g., first day at school for both parents and children).

(4) **Signal**: Psychoanalytic concept meaning the anxiety is a signal of danger approaching the "ego" from the instinctual drives. If the course of action required for the satisfaction of "id" based drives is unacceptable to the ego, anxiety arises and leads to establishment of defense mechanisms (e.g., sex drive increases, the person only has same sex persons available. Anxiety over sexual impulse associated with same sex person arises and the defense mechanism of denial is brought into

play--that is, "I don't have homosexual impulses!").

- (5) **Stranger:** That reaction demonstrated by infants when an unfamiliar (or not usual) person comes into contact with the child. Around the 6th-8th month, lasting until the 11th or 12th month.

D. <u>Tension</u> as an emotion:

1. Distinguish tension from anxiety or fear. It is partially compensated anxiety. That is, the individual experiences anxiety but feels he can cope with anxiety or at least tolerate it.

2. There is good evidence that appropriate tension enhances performance and problem solving under certain circumstances.

E. <u>Anger</u> as an emotion

1. Anger is a "<u>drive discharge emotion</u>." The emotion allows discharge of the underlying drive and satisfaction of the need.

2. Underneath the emotion of anger is usually hostility or aggression. Most frequently anger as an emotion is the response to frustration. When a person is seeking needs that are not met by others or by the environment, the person is frustrated, leading to anger, which is the effort to "force" the object to supply "needs" and hence alleviate anxiety.

3. Psychophysiologic Considerations: anger in general tends to result in a norepinephrine-like response.

    a. Diencephalic-Limbic System-Cortical Influences

    b. Rage reactions occur after intercollicular section. Nociceptive stimulation in the most posterior and lateral portions of the hypothalamus and in other areas of the limbic system as well.

    c. Seemingly, there is a tendency for modifying influences from the forebrain or from the rostral thalamic nuclei.

d. **Temporal Lobe** Neocortical Paleocortical Influences.

      (1) Nature of Temporal Lobe Epilepsy attacks is forced activity and violent behavior if the forced activity is blocked.

      (2) Kluver-Bucy Syndrome includes absence of fear responses and hypersexuality.

   e. Apparently in all cultures, males are more aggressive than females. This may represent differences in central nervous system structure/function; and, may be tied to differential androgen levels.

4. General objective signs of anger

   Eyebrows are frowning or "knitted"; eyelids are tensely narrowed; pupils are constricted in a glare; mouth is open with a tense grin with lips retracted or compressed and teeth clenched; face is red, veins distended, masseter prominent, and nostrils widened; head is jutted forward towards an object with jutting jaw; respiration is expiratory in nature; the body muscles are tense, with fist clenched in quick forceful gestures, and feet are planted side by side firmly on the floor. Speech is controlled, precise, forceful, and loud during expiration and very controlled.

F. Sadness as an emotion

   1. Underlying affect is usually grief.

   2. Sadness as an emotion is usually a response to loss or threatened loss of a significant object (person, job, retirement, etc..)

   3. It is important not to confuse sadness or uncomplicated grief with depression. Depression is a psychiatric syndrome and needs appropriate treatment. Sadness needs expression.

   4. General objective signs of sadness: tears with red eyes; downcast eyes; flacid muscles of the face and extremities; mouth is downturned at the corners; head and shoulders droop; speech is at the end of expiration and very soft; a great deal of sighing; legs usually "sag" apart.

G. **Disgust** as an emotion

1. Disgust is the emotion related to trying to get rid of something on the inside that is noxious or toxic to the person.

2. The facial expression of someone who has put something in their mouth that is distasteful or spoiled is similar to that of the person who is disgusted with something they have just encountered.

H. **Shame** as an emotion

1. Shame usually denotes blame of self from the environment, e.g. "It's your fault that your child was born with an arterio-venous malformation and died."

2. We tend to learn shame in the presence of others' disgust.

I. **Guilt** as an emotion

1. Guilt usually denotes blame of self by the self.

2. Sadness plus anger turned inward, e.g., "It's my fault my child was born with an arteriovenous malformation and died."

3. If we listen to others tell us we should be ashamed of a given behavior long enough, we will then begin to shame ourselves and feel guilty.

IV. **MEMORY**

A. Definition: The ability upon demand to bring to awareness past events and experiences, and the associated affect.

B. Mechanisms of Memory

1. Certainly the **limbic circuit** is involved. The **hippocampus, dorsal medial nucleus,** and the **mamillary bodies** are integral parts of the anatomic/physiologic substrate of memory.

2. Possible roles for RNA and DNA in the formation and storage of memory traces.

3. Types of memory based on length of time involved.

    a. **Immediate memory:** 0 to about 15 minutes. Also called **short term memory** (STM).

b. Recent memory: within the last two weeks. Also called intermediate memory.

c. Remote memory: two years or more. Also called long term memory (LTM).

4. Note that memory traces are formed in short-term memory; and, with "reinforcement" (emphasis, repetition, etc.) are "transferred" to recent or remote memory.

5. The neurotransmitter Acetylcholine (ACH) appears to be of central importance in memory functioning.

C. Phenomenology of Memory and Forgetting

1. Forgetting: usually not a passive process but rather an active phenomenon with a "dynamic" basis.

2. Some special causes of memory disturbances:

a. Hypermnesia: unusual memory for detail in selected areas.

b. Amnesia: loss of memory - for past experiences:

(1) Patchy or lacunar amnesia

(2) Anterograde (forgetting of material following a significant life event)

(3) Retrograde amnesia (loss of memory for materials preceding a significant life event)

(4) Paramnesia or distortion of memory (retrospective falsification, confabulation)

3. Some general comments with regard to memory deficits:

a. In general, memory defect is psychogenic if there is no disturbance of consciousness and no intellectual impairment.

b. Short-term memory (STM) is particularly disrupted with bilateral lesions of the hippocampus and/or mammillary bodies, e.g., Korsakoff's Syndrome.

If motivation and attention is good and STM is impaired - it's suggestive of organic involvement.

c. Long-term memory (LTM) is rarely defective unless accompanied by psychosis or there is extensive dementia.

d. If organic memory loss occurs, recovery is typically gradual and from the extremes to the precipitating event.

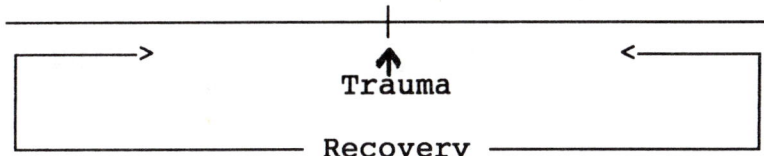

e. If a person has memory loss:

(1) Abrupt return of the lost memory generally implies psychologically based etiology.

(2) Gradual return of the lost memory generally implies organic etiology.

(3) Organic memory loss is characterized when:

(a) Immediate memory goes first.
(b) Recent memory goes next.
(c) Remote memory is last to go.

f. Deep anesthesia may not render the person totally amnestic for the events that occur during the anesthetic state.

V. CONSCIOUSNESS

A. Definition: the awareness of self (this includes both body and mental content) and the environment; and the relationship of self to the environment.

B. Special states of consciousness:

1. The following tend to be "organic" in nature.

   a. Fluctuating levels of attention are normal phenomena but may be accentuated with certain forms of pathology, particularly of an organic nature.

   b. Confusion states are very typical of organic brain syndromes.

   c. Clouding of consciousness: typical of organic brain syndromes.

d. <u>Stupor</u>: sensibilities are deadened and the individual has little appreciation of surroundings. Usually organic.

e. <u>Coma</u>: no awareness of surroundings, usually organic.

Note: confusion states, clouding of consciousness, stupor and coma are quite common sequelae of traumatic head injury or concussion.

2. The following tend to be "functional" in nature.

   a. <u>Fugue</u>: a state during which the person, for a certain period of time seemingly acts in a conscious way (perhaps traveling, buying food and, in general, conducting self in a natural manner). Afterwards he has no conscious recall for the period of time or behavior. The person may seem to possess all his facilities to the casual observer but, upon questioning, may reveal complete or partial amnesia for certain experiences.

   b. <u>Dream state or twilight state</u>: used to describe a state between stupor and fugue. That is, the patient will seem to the observer to be in an abnormal state; however, he responds somewhat appropriately to the environment. Again, with termination of this state, amnesia for this state is common.

   c. <u>Somnambulism</u>: Sleepwalking. Is similar to fugue with the exception that it begins from a state of sleep.

VI. **ORIENTATION**

A. <u>Orientation to Time</u>: Is a person aware of his position in linear time, both the name of the day as well as the date, year, month?

B. <u>Orientation to Place</u>: Is the person aware of self in terms of geographic location? Sometimes as a portion of orientation to place, the person may display <u>derealization</u>.

   <u>Derealization</u>: Both <u>Jamais vu</u>, which means the person is in a familiar surrounding but suddenly feels as if he has never been there before; and <u>Deja vu</u>, in which the person is in a totally unfamiliar situation and suddenly it seems as if he has been there before or done that thing before, are examples of disturbances in orientation to place.

C. <u>Orientation to Person</u>: is the individual aware of self as a person? Does he know his name? Does he know his date of birth? Other examples include:

   1. **Depersonalization**: the body as a whole or parts of the body seem unreal or dissociated.

   2. **Anosognosia**: not being aware that one is ill.

   3. **Autotopagnosia**: not knowing or correctly locating one's own body parts.

D. <u>Orientation to Present Situation</u>: is the person aware of the relationship of his person with the present place in time and what the person's purpose in being there is?

<u>Note</u>: disturbance in orientation usually implies an organic basis to the "peculiar" behavior. The organicity may be an induced, acute, toxic state (e.g. grass/alcohol) or a traumatic chronic brain disease (e.g. massive head injury in a vehicular accident).

VII. PERCEPTION

A. <u>Definition</u>: Perception is not equivalent to sensation. We don't experience pure sensation frequently. The closest is awakening in the night from an unusual noise we do not know. <u>Perception is best defined as the integration of that noise or sensory stimuli into some framework which has meaning based upon past experiences</u>.

B. <u>Neurophysiological Considerations of Perception</u>:

   1. The arrival of impulses by the demonstration of <u>evoked responses</u> at the cortex does not guarantee perception. <u>This arrival of impulses only allows one to know the neurologic path is intact.</u>
      Auditory evoked response can be a differential diagnostic tool to separate a deaf child from other type problems, e.g. autism.

   2. All exteroceptive inputs are not necessarily processed into perceptions. E.g., the Reticular Activating System has an inhibitory function on many incoming stimuli.

   3. Exteroceptive stimuli are not essential for a perception. For example, imagination, dreaming, etc.

   4. The perception of present events is strongly influenced by past experiences. E.g., <u>we see what we believe</u>.

5. Phenomenology of perception which may be "psychopathological."

   a. Illusions: Misinterpretations of real sensory data. For example, in a dark room one may have concern about there being a mouse in the room, and when coming into the room, perceive a "thing" on the floor as being a mouse. When examined carefully it may turn out to be a wadded-up piece of paper.

   b. Hallucinations: Internal images may be projected onto the world. These are labeled hallucinations. They are perceptions the person has when there is not sufficient external stimulation to warrant their occurrence. Hallucinations may occur in any sensory modality.

      (1) Visual hallucinations are characteristic of acute brain syndromes. Sometimes, they occur in acute schizophrenia.

      (2) Auditory hallucinations are characteristic of schizophrenia.

      (3) Olfactory hallucinations frequently occur as the "aura" of a psychomotor or temporal lobe epilepsy ("Uncinate fits"). Sometimes, they occur in schizophrenia.

      (4) Gustatory hallucinations are relatively rare, although they frequently represent the aura of a convulsive disorder.

      (5) Tactile hallucinations are more common than realized. They are especially characteristic of acute brain syndromes secondary to toxic conditions, and particularly of that type known as delirium tremens or alcohol withdrawal delirium. FORMICATION is the feeling of "bugs crawling on the skin".

      (6) Hypnagogic: hallucinations occurring when going into sleep.

      (7) Hypnopompic: hallucinations when coming out of sleep.

      Hypnagogic and hypnopompic hallucinations are considered to be "normal" hallucinations; i.e., they do not signify pathology.

VIII. THINKING

A. **Definition**: A process whereby we conceptualize, construct, manipulate, and communicate symbols. Others view it as a form of problem solving behavior which involves the correlations and integration of cortical events in time and space.

B. Phenomenology of Thinking

1. Disorders of **Association of thought**.

    a. **Loosening of associations** A—> D—> F—> B—> G—> etc. Also called predicate logic: e.g. Jesus Christ was a man with a beard, I am a man with a beard, I am Jesus Christ.

    b. **Tangential**: Thoughts go off on a tangent from the goal direction. E.g. "Governor, are we going to discontinue farm aid?" Answer: "The farmer's plight is a concern of ours."

    c. **Circumstantial**: All details of the circumstances surrounding the event are given before coming to the point.

    d. **Perseveration**: Repetition of a given behavior/response in inappropriate circumstances.

2. Disorders of **Thought Rate**

    a. Pressure of speech, flight of ideas.

    b. Retardation/blocking/inhibition of thinking.

3. Disorders of **Thought Content**

    a. **Delusions**: A false, fixed belief system in the absence of substantiating evidence. For example, delusions of grandeur, persecution, self-accusation.

    b. **Obsessions** or **ruminations**: e.g., obsessive thoughts of "How bad I am."

    c. **Concrete** versus abstract or symbolic: e.g., "what brought you to see me?" "A car."

    d. **Autistic**: narcissistic/egocentric, emphasizes subjective, and does not have regard for reality versus logical or rational. Autistic thought process often is characterized by a personal and private understanding of the world.

e. *Ideas of reference*: events (e.g., a television program) are interpreted as having special personal meaning for the individual.

IX. **LEARNING**

   A. General Considerations

   1. **Definition:** A "relatively permanent change in a behavioral tendency that occurs as a result of reinforced practice." Learning is always inferred from performance or behavior and may lead to more effective behavior OR to maladaptive behavior.

   2. **Range:** Learning enters all aspects of human behavior from the simplest reflex to the complex behavior of a physician.

   3. "**Reinforced**" practice is central to learning. Reinforcement refers to the rewards and/or punishments that strengthen the behavioral tendency.

   B. Terms used in learning.

   1. **Acquisition:** changing the probability of a response occurring.

   2. **Generalization:** transfer of a response from one stimulus to a similar one without practice.

   3. **Discrimination:** learned response to a given stimulus but not others.

   4. **Primary reinforcers:** rewards or punishments relatively independent of previous learning (food, sex, pain).

   5. **Secondary reinforcers:** learned rewards or punishments (money, grades, praise, shame).

   6. **Positive reinforcers:** reinforcement comes from getting this, e.g. money.

   7. **Negative reinforcers:** reinforcement comes from stopping this, e.g. nagging. Stopping the behavior is the reinforcer.

   8. **Punishment:** An aversive event that suppresses behavior.

   9. **Extinction:** weakening or disappearance of a response with non-reinforced practice (e.g. "learned helplessness": why try? I never get rewarded.).

10. **Learning without awareness:** individual does not have to attend to acquire the behavior.

C. <u>Types of Learning</u> Ordered by Complexity and Chronology of Appearance

1. **Instinct:** inborn predisposition to behave in a specific way when appropriately stimulated. Usually species specific--<u>not learned</u>! Note the question of a maternal instinct in humans. Instincts can be controlled but they can't be eliminated.

2. **Imprinting:** early learned attachments formed <u>automatically</u> in accord with **hereditary predispositions**. <u>Role of reward is minimal</u>. Most consider it an innate mechanism released by a set of stimuli, often visual (Lorenz). Takes place in the **first hours of life and probably extends to about six months**. Proven in subhuman animals; hypothesized in humans, again, as a mechanism to promote "Mother-Child" bonding. Note its presence in the form of child delivery being promoted by Le Boyer. This mother-child bonding appears to be important for forming close adult relationships later in life.

3. **Classical conditioning** (<u>Stimulus substitution</u>): most typically associated with **sympathetic and para-sympathetic responses**. <u>Pavlov</u> popularized with the demonstration of conditioning of salivary response. He presented a dog with meat powder (unconditioned stimulus-UCS) and salivation (unconditioned response-UCR) occurred. He rang a bell (conditioned stimulus-CS) just before the meat was presented. Repeated <u>pairings</u> of bell and meat occurred. Eventually the bell elicited the conditioned response (salivating) in the absence of the meat powder.

```
UCS---------------------------->UCR
Meat--------------------------->Salivation

CS----------------------------->CR
Bell--------------------------->Salivation
```

a. The basic principles of classical conditioning have been demonstrated to hold from the smallest one cell organisms to man.

b. Generally operates only on reflexive/autonomic behaviors.

c. Classical conditioning is thought to be the basic process by which certain early fears and emotional reactions are learned. Some workers in psychosomatic medicine believe the groundwork for psychosomatic diseases is laid in the early infant by this process. Also, office based hypertensive reading may be classical conditioning.

4. **Operant Instrumental Conditioning (Skinner)**

   a. <u>General Considerations</u>: The operant is a behavior resulting in a reinforcement. The organism emits a response (rat bar press) which results in an <u>environmental event</u> (delivery of food pellet) which is a <u>rewarding</u> consequence. Or, in the case of using negative reinforcement, the employee does what his supervisor is "nagging" him to do, leading to the supervisor stopping the nagging. In this sense the environment "controls" behavior. Operant conditioning is the more general case of learning, and, affects all behavior including autonomic nervous systems.

   b. <u>Biofeedback</u>: is a direct outgrowth of operant conditioning and has been applied to a variety of medical problems. In biofeedback, individual is given reinforcement for emitting some type of physiologic response, e.g. heart rate, EEG alpha, etc. The reinforcements for humans can be as simple as "keeping a light one", a smile or a frown.

   c. <u>Schedules of reinforcement</u>: whereas in classical conditioning every response is reinforced (UCS), in operant conditioning three types of partial reinforcement are often used.

      (1) <u>Ratio</u>: reinforcing every <u>n</u>th response

      (2) <u>Interval</u>: reinforcing at given time intervals.

      (3) <u>Fixed or variable</u> schedules of either of the first two can be used.

	Fixed (rapid acquisition)	**Variable** (resistant to extinction)
Ratio	Reward every 3rd response. E.g., nurse doesn't answer patient's buzzer til 3rd ring.	Sometimes reward the third response, then the fifth, then the second, etc., e.g., a slot machine payoff.
Interval	Reward every fourth hour. E.g., Morphine every 6 hours.	Sometimes rewards after three, then five, then two hours. E.g., PRN valium.

      (4) Note: Schedules of partial reinforcement are typical of what humans experience. Partial reinforcement is more resistant to extinction than "always reinforce" schedules. A fact in animals which may help explain gambling and drug taking behavior in the human.

      (5) Note: "Always reward" is necessary to get the response to occur. After response is established, partial reinforcement results in extreme stability of the response.

      (6) In operant conditioning, partial or intermittent reinforcement results in greater resistance to extinction; in classical conditioning it hastens extinction.

      (7) Shaping of behavior: in operant conditioning the response is frequently "shaped" by reinforcing successively closer approximations of the behavior desired.

      (8) Immediacy of reinforcement: the closer the reinforcement to the operant, the better the learning.

  5. **Cognitive Learning Theories**

    a. Emphasize changes in the brain, e.g. insight, plans, thinking. Focuses on understanding: e.g. follow a map to get to a location; reason our way to conclusions not previously familiar to us; learning higher mathematics.

    b. Usually implies <u>full attention and awareness</u>.

    c. May use data learned by other learning methods, e.g. operant conditioning to execute the understanding.

6. Social Learning Theories

    a. Combine all of the above with emphasis on imitation, modeling and reciprocal human interactions. E.g., learning to drive.

    b. Major questions today are influence of television violence on real aggressive social behavior, and advertisement of recreational chemical use on real substance abuse.

        Major findings are that one may try a behavior through models (real or TV); however, it won't become permanent unless there is reinforcement for the behavior from the environment.

D. <u>Applied data about learning and forgetting</u>:

1. <u>Massed or crowded practice is inefficient</u>. Many spaced periods of practice are more efficient to learning than one massively long one.

2. <u>Retention</u> is improved by more strongly fixing the data in the memory the <u>first</u> time. Best methods for this are:

    a. <u>Do periodic reviews WITH ACTIVE RECALL of the material, not just reading it over.</u>

    b. <u>Overlearn it the first time</u>.

    c. Make it logical, <u>not rote memory</u>. This is the basis of mnemonic aids to memory.

3. **Part versus whole learning.**

    a. Whole learning is more advantageous with higher intelligence.

    b. Whole learning is more advantageous with distributed practice.

    c. Unified meaningful material favors whole learning.

4. **Forgetting**: these three work in combination with each other.

   a. Time decay

   b. Spontaneous and progressive change in the memory trace

   c. Inhibition

   (1) Retroactive inhibition: new learning interferes with old.

   (2) Proactive inhibition: old learning interferes with new.

X. INTELLIGENCE, MENTAL RETARDATION, AND AGING EFFECTS

   A. Definition: Intelligence is a concept defined as "the aggregate or global capacity of the individual to act purposefully, to think rationally, and to deal effectively with his environment." (Wechsler). This capacity to learn is a product of genetically and biologically determined qualities of the central nervous system and his (early) environmental influences.

   B. At least 2 different areas of intelligent behavior have been distinguished: verbal and performance.

   Wechsler expanded the measurement of intelligence by constructing a test with two main dimensions: a Verbal Scale, based on language skills; and, a Performance Scale based largely on perceptual-motor and non-verbal skills. To exemplify, it would be expected that lawyers do well on the Verbal Scale while engineers do well on the Performance Scale.

   C. The Nature vs. Nurture Issue

   1. Nature: Note while the following are data with regard to intelligence, the research strategies employed are those used to study genetic bases of many different types of human behavior.

      a. Twin studies consistently show the concordance rate of IQ's is distributed:

         Monozygotic > Dizygotic > Siblings

      This holds true even for twins reared apart.

b. Adopted childrens' IQ correlates higher with biological parents' IQ than with adoptive parents' IQ.

c. Racial differences remain a controversy. Probably differences observed are an effect of standardization of tests on samples that don't include representative subcultural groups.

   (1) WAIS and WISC appear to be biased towards white middle class.

   (2) BITCH (Black Intelligence Test of Cultural Homogeneity) is characteristically failed by non-black samples or blacks strongly integrated into white culture.

2. Nurture

   a. Social, cultural, interpersonal deprivation is correlated with low IQ scores.

   b. Rural, isolated, and mistreated children have lower IQ scores than matched city, stimulated, well treated children.

   c. Genetic effects are more apparent in children raised in a favorable environment. <u>Unfavorable environment effects mask the genetic differences.</u>

   d. There is a high positive correlation between IQ scores and education.

D. **Intelligence Quotients (IQ):** There are two general methods for assessing Intelligence or IQ.

1. **Mental Age Concept:** Divide the mental age (derived from a standardized test) by the chronological age and multiply the result by 100. For example, if a child with a chronological age of 12 scored a mental age of 12 on a given test, then the child would have a calculated IQ of 100 (12/12 x 100). If a 10 year old obtained a mental age of 12, his IQ would be 120 (12/10 x 100). If his chronological age were 15 and his mental age was 12, his IQ would be 80 (12/15 x 100).

2. **Deviation IQ Concept:** For each age range the mean score of a sample, selected to be representative of the general population at that age range, is set at 100 with a standard deviation (a measure of variability) of 15. Scores for individuals are in terms of deviations from the mean. Note that in this method of test development,

in constructing the norms, a group of older people in their 80's who perform much more poorly in their on a given test than a group of 20 year olds will, by definition, have the same mean IQ of 100.

E. Commonly Used Intelligence Tests

   1. Deviation IQ Tests

      a. Wechsler Adult Intelligence Scale-Revised (WAIS-R)

         (1) **Verbal Scales** (Yield a Verbal Intelligence Quotient or **VIQ**): each subscale ordered from easy to hard items.

             Information--tests general fund of acquired knowledge

             Comprehension--social awareness and social reasoning

             Arithmetic--rapid mental calculation

             Similarities--abstraction of commonalities between two objects, e.g., orange and banana

             Digit span--repeat a series of spoken numbers, forward and/or backward. Series get progressively longer.

             Vocabulary--standard vocabulary test

         (2) **Performance Scales:** (Yield a Performance Intelligence Quotient or **PIQ**). All are timed tests.

             Digit symbol--coding numbers into symbols

             Picture completion--identify an important part of a picture is missing

             Block design--reproduce a visual design with colored blocks

             Picture arrangements--order pictures of social situations to make a meaningful story

             Object assembly--similar to a jigsaw puzzles

(3) A **Full-Scale Intelligence Quotient (FSIQ)** can be calculated to reflect the overall adaptive functioning of the person.

(4) By comparing the VIQ and PIQ scores, if the difference is great (e.g., 10-15 points) one can infer diagnostic impressions. Examples follow:

- (a) If **VIQ>PIQ** suspect **dysfunction of the nondominant (right) hemisphere** since spatial relations and picture/figure recognition tends to be located there.

- (b) If **PIQ>VIQ** suspect **dysfunction of the dominant (left) hemisphere** since language tends to be located there.

- (c) If **both VIQ & PIQ** are down relative to education and professional achievement; and, there is **no suggestion of an organic process, suspect depression.**

b. Wechsler Intelligence Scale for Children-Revised (WISC-R): ages **6--16 years**.

(1) Verbal scales: Same as WAIS except **digit span is optional**.

(2) Performance scales: Same as WAIS except a new scale--MAZES (paper and pencil mazes) can be substituted for coding.

c. Wechsler Preschool and Primary Scale of Intelligence (WPPSI): ages **4-6.5 years**.

(1) Similar to WAIS and WISC but simpler.

(2) Three different scales replace four standard Wechsler Scales.

- 1) Digit span replaced by "**Sentences**"

- 2) Picture arrangement replaced by "**Animal House**"

- 3) Object assembly and coding replaced by "**Geometric Designs**"

2. Mental Age IQ Tests

   a. The most reliable and valid mental age IQ test of importance is the Stanford-Binet. Usually used with age ranges three to about twelve years old.

3. Both types of measurements give IQ scores which reflect relative standing in groups. The following are important to remember:

   a. Intelligence tests measure only certain selected aspects of behavior.

   b. IQ's are obtained by different methods on different tests.

   c. IQ's are reported in terms of a number; there is an error of measurement so that plus or minus 5 IQ points is usually a safe estimate. For example, an IQ of 100 is probably anywhere from 95-105. While this is not too important in the average range of intelligence, when near borderline or mental defective levels, it can have important consequences for the child.

   d. Group intelligence tests from schools can be very misleading. We are estimating intelligence from performance. A person can perform poorly for a variety of reasons -- illness, lack of interest, motivation, etc., are among some of the more common.

   e. Individually administered intelligence tests are usually reliable and valid measures of intelligence if given by trained persons.

   f. Intelligence can be underestimated by intelligence tests (due to interfering factors) but seldom "overestimated." In other words, if one obtains a high IQ it is unlikely that he achieved it because of some extraneous factor, whereas with low IQ's, the factors mentioned previously could be present.

   g. Intelligence and emotional disturbance: No necessary relation. High and low intelligence people both develop psychopathology.

F. Mental Retardation

   1. For more complete discussion of Mental Retardation see Section Three below.

2. Three aspects comprise this syndrome diagnosis.

LDP

- It is a developmental problem.
- Low intelligence.
- Poor social adaptation.

3. Many more persons have lower intelligence than the bell-shaped curve would predict, due to the many diseases and states of health of the mother which can adversely affect the fetus.

4. Mental retardation is classified as follows by DSM-III-R:

   a. Mild mental retardation: IQ = 50-55 to
      (educable mentally handicapped)   approx. 70

   b. Moderate mental retardation: IQ = 35-40 to
      (trainable for personal hygiene   50-55
      and minimal academics)

   c. Severe mental retardation: IQ = 20-25 to
      (custodial)   35-40

   d. Profound mental retardation: IQ = below 20-25
      (custodial)

G. Aging, Intelligence and Performance

1. Cross-sectional studies (studying of different decades at the same time) report most abilities decline as a function of age. Complicating factor here is education level of different decades differs (the average older person has lower education.)

2. Longitudinal studies (studying same populations over the years) show much less decline in abilities.

   Studies of performance on the Army Alpha over 40 years indicate the verbal abilities show little decline; tests involving speed and perceptual-motor performance decline most. Be able to translate this data into specific WAIS scales.

3. IQ measured at a younger age is not as predictive as that measured later.

XI. GROWTH AND DEVELOPMENT

A. Preface and Theories: In general, development proceeds as:

1. Positive change in the organism.

2. Decentration: moving from focus on self to extension to others.

3. Change from globality to differentiation.

4. Effective handling of conflict which is essential for developmental growth.

5. **Freudian psychosexual theory** in brief (explained in detail in next chapter):

    a. Intrapsychic structures of the individual's mind (the Id, Ego, and Superego) become more differentiated from one another.

    b. The conscious ego becomes more the executive of the mind.

    c. Development proceeds so more areas of sensual and social gratification are added with each stage of development until a complex series of sensual zones and social modes in the genital period are able to interact with the world.

6. **Erikson's psychosocial theory** in brief (explained in detail in next chapter):

    a. Conceptualizes development as the resolution of a series of developmental conflict states.

    b. In each conflict, there is a positive and a negative pole e.g. trust versus mistrust.

    c. The task is to resolve the conflict toward the positive pole e.g. develop a basic sense of trust.

    d. If a developmental conflict stage is poorly resolved, it forms a weak base on which later stages are built. Just as with a tower of blocks, if a lower one is not square, other perfect square ones placed on top of the defective one will form a tower that leans and is subject to less stability than a perpendicular one.

7. **Piagetian cognitive theory** in detail.

    a. The structure of the cognitive mind is determined by four factors:

        (1) biological maturation

        (2) social transmission i.e. others actively teach the child.

(3) the **equilibration process**: **assimilation** (of information from the environment) and **accommodation** (mind structures are forced to change in part by the mass of information that has been assimilated not being able to be understood and managed by the extant cognitive structure).

(4) **active experience** of the individual with his environment.

b. The development is through a series of stages. **The sequence of stages is fixed. The time of appearance can be different** due to social environmental issues: e.g., a given socio-economic status (SES) may decrease the opportunity for access to, and stimulation from a diversified environment.

   (1) **Sensorimotor stage** (**birth to about 18** months). Employs **senses**, **reflexes** and **motor activity** to interact with the world. Out of sight = out of mind. With practice, infant becomes more well organized. By the end of this stage, the infant has moved from reflex activity to intentional purposeful coordinated movements.

   (2) **Preoperational stage** (about **18 months to 7 years**). Relies on **perception** and **intuition** (e.g. a sponge that looks like a rock is a rock). No conservation of identity of an object (e.g. if one of two objects with the same mass is changed in shape to make it look different, it's not the same volume anymore.) **Focuses on one dimension at a time**.

   (3) **Concrete operations stage** (about **7 to around 11-13 years**). **Can abstract the commonality from observed things**. Can add and subtract elements but conserve the essence of each element. Toward the end of this stage, the child can **begin to have reversibility of thought**.

   (4) **Formal operations stage** (begins about 11-13 years). Conceptual deductive thinking is possible. Objects need not be present to conceptualize about them. Cognitive reasoning is possible. Reversibility and conceptual projection into the future is possible.

8. **Learning theorists** in brief:

   a. Conceptualize development as effective habit formation.

   b. Effective generalization and discrimination of these habits define proper development.

   c. Situationally determined behaviors are a focal point for learning theorists.

B. Prenatal Influences

   1. The **fetus is affected by the emotional state of mother and adrenergic type substances transmitted from the mother to the child in the prenatal period.**

      Highly nervous mothers are likely to produce infants with sleep disorders, irritability, hyperactivity, feeding disorders, and prematurity.

   2. **Malnutrition of the mother**, especially **protein deficiency**, effects the **brain size** and **weight of the infant**.

      a. **Protein deficiency** appears to be very important. Is correlated with **prematurity** which in turn is correlated with **mental retardation**, mental illness, **birth defects**, and **failure to thrive**.

      b. In cultures where nutrition is seriously impaired (e.g., Bangladesh War, Ethiopian famine, Gulf War) it can lead to a syndrome known as Kwashiorkor with severe retardation and often failure to thrive (brittle hair and protruding stomach).

      c. In animal studies, malnutrition effects can be seen one to two generations later.

C. Birth and Neonate

   1. Any **depressant** medication administered to the mother at birth may affect **nutritive sucking** and **attention** of the infant for **ten days or more** after the birth of the child.

   2. The **newborn** normally sleeps **sixteen hours a day** and **eight of these are in Rapid Eye Movement (REM) sleep** (perhaps essential for early neurological development). This R.E.M. sleep is reduced by almost **80%** in adult life. An infant's activities are directly related to

its sleep state (drowsiness, awake, etc.). The first signs of voluntary activity of the infant probably come from his auditory and visual pursuit activities.

3. **Premature children** (under **2500 grams** and **34 weeks**) have normatively greater physical, mental and emotional problems. Many problems of prematurity are not associated with prematurity per se, but the complications of prematurity which involve low birth weight, toxemia, maternal bleeding, infections, etc.

4. The neonate generally:

    Can fixate on objects.

    Prefers a large, patterned object over a smaller pattern.

    Has functional memory by **2 weeks** of age.

    Prefers a curved body position over a straight one.

    Has innate "hard wired" facial expression, which can be later modified by training.

5. **Neonate's major reflexes**

    a. Babinski: scratch on lateral aspect of a sole of foot (heel to toe), leads to **dorsiflexion of the great toe** and **fanning of other toes**. Normally disappears at **12 to 18 months**.

    b. Crossed extensor: extend one leg by pressure on the knee, stimulate sole of foot of extended limb, and other leg will extend and slightly abduct. Normally disappears about **2 months**.

    c. Deep tendon reflexes: **sudden stretching of striated muscle**. Jaw jerk, biceps, triceps, knee and ankle are usually tested.

    d. Eye blink: **touching eyelashes, tapping the bridge of the nose or any intense visual or auditory stimulation** leads to blinking of the eyes in the normal infant.

    e. Grasp: from about 1 month to 5 or 6 months, **pressure on the palm leads to grasping**.

    f. Moro: sudden movement of infant's head and neck results in rapid abduction of arms and opening hands. Thumb and forefinger form a "c". Normally disappears about 4-6 months. Sometimes called the "startle" reflex.

    g. **Suck**: stimulate the perioral or oral area and infant will turn head toward stimulation and start sucking behaviors.

D. **Infancy**

1. In the **Piagetian scheme**, the infant is in the **sensory motor stage**. His senses and motor activities are his main structure for interacting with the world.

2. Infant tests are valuable in assessing **gross** disturbances but are relatively ineffective in predicting. The **Denver Developmental Test**, the **Bayley**, and the **Cattell Test** are three **measures of infant intelligence**.

3. **Freud** described the infant in the **oral stage** of development as receptive and symbiotic with his mother, and in **Erikson's** terms the infant's task is to develop a sense of **basic trust**.

    The infant needs to know that things in its environment are affected by the infant's actions (contingency). Around the sixth month, the infant needs to develop an attachment (a positive relationship) with at least one person to effectively proceed with development.

4. Social Behavior Development

    a. **Social smiling** appears as an approximate response to a stimulus at about **two months**.

    b. **Babbling** appears at about **six to eight months**.

    c. **Stranger anxiety**: fear response to a "non-mother" person normally is present between **eight and eleven months** (indicates object-constancy has developed).

    d. **Separation anxiety**: fear response to separation from "mothering" person. Normally present between **11-13 months**. Infant hasn't learned to trust that mother will return.

    e. **Words as meaningful symbols** begin to appear at about **12 months**, (1-3 years is a normal range).

f. Toilet training can only be effected after sphincter control is attained between 1.5 and 2.5 years, although most Americans begin it between 9-14 months.

g. Males are held more, show more gross motor activities, cry more; and show overall growth lags in walking, talking, bone ossification, and most areas of development. More aggressive.

h. Later infancy: correlating with serious toilet training, the infant begins establishing a sense of autonomy (Freud's anal stage; Erikson's stage of Autonomy versus Shame and Doubt). "Terrible twos", representing normal negativism and testing limits of autonomy. The child is saying "I am not you!"

i. Demand feeding schedules produce better attachments between mother and child if the mother is not exceptionally nervous.

j. Sensory stimulation in the first six months of life is thought to be essential to adequate neurological development.

k. Gender identity (internal feeling of sexual role: feeling male or female), established by 2-3 years. Apparently determined by physiology of the child and response of significant care-takers, e.g., differences in the "roughness" with which they handle the child.

l. Normal Motor Development   Weeks

   Chin up   3
   Chest up   9-10
   Sit alone momentarily   24
   Knee push/swim   24
   Stand with help   30
   Sit alone for about 1 minute   32
   Motor progress on stomach   37
   Scoot backward   40
   Stands holding onto furniture   42
   Walk when led   46
   Pull to stand   47
   Stand alone   62
   Walk alone   64

E. Preschool Child - Approximately 2 to 5 years old

1. The preschool child: characterized by rapid advances in language (2 years old = 200 words; 3 years old = 500 words, 4 years old = 1500 words) and abstraction; peer

involvement in parallel play; evolution of defense mechanisms; and in Piagetian scheme a reliance on perception and intuition in thought processes (pre-operational stage).

2. The preschool years are a time of moving beyond **gender identity** into **gender identification** (the public display of sexual role) with the appropriate sex role. Learned from role models.

3. Children tend to **test parents' limits** with extreme behaviors.

4. In terms of **health care, the child most fears:**

   a. Mutilation, often interpreted as punishment.

   b. Loss of parents.

   To facilitate care, let the child rehearse the procedure and allow the parents to be present and contribute to the care as much as possible.

5. Major emphasis in **preschool education** has focused on increasing cognitive capacities and intelligence levels. These have been implemented by techniques which include Headstart efforts for low socio-economic children, "Sesame Street" type programs, and emphasis on social skill improvement such as a delay of gratification and concentration/attention. There is suggestion that children who are **withdrawn and less aggressive lose the most IQ points** during this preschool period.

6. In later preschool period the individual child in Erikson's system should be acquiring a basic sense of initiative (the phallic stage of development in Freudian theory).

F. The School Age Child (6 to 12 years)

1. The school age child is in the stage of concrete operation (Piaget), until early teens. Can abstract commonalities from objects, and conservation has been accomplished. Pure abstract discussions and reversibility of thinking are still difficult. For Erikson, the child's needs are a basic sense of industry and adequacy in peer relationships (Freud's latency stage).

2. Females are more verbal than males. Adjustment factors relate directly to family and peers.

3. A firm understanding of death isn't achieved until about 8-10 years of age.

   Children do become depressed and commit suicide, although they often envision it as "going to sleep."

4. Initially there is an eager anticipation toward beginning school (the first two years), and slowly many children decrease their favorable attitude towards the school and teachers. Each year of school seems to bring increased amounts of emotional disturbance in children. There appears to he a high degree of cross generalization between the child's attitude towards his parent and his teacher.

5. The child's confidence in peer groups and his readiness and completion of previous tasks (e.g. autonomy, trust, delay of gratification, etc.) are important factors in school performance. Handicaps to adequate school performance include learning or perceptual problems, hyperactivity, and visual or physical problems which create difficulty for a child to learn.

6. Socially, studies indicate that males, children from the lower classes, and children from minority groups have a more difficult time adjusting to the white middle class school situation.

7. The appearance of sexual exploration and masturbatory activity is normal in preschool and childhood years. Unless it creates a public disturbance, it is seen as part of normal development.

8. The generation gap appears larger for families whose parents have more authoritarian/non-rational approaches with children.

G. Adolescence (12-14 years to 16-18 years)

1. The major task of adolescence is solidifying identity (Erikson's stage of Identity versus Role Confusion) and obtaining emotional support outside the primary family as preparation to coupling, intimacy, and permanent pairing.

2. The adolescent must develop a realistic sense of his own identity, be what he is, and like what he is (acquire self-esteem). A high incidence of physical complaints and anxiety are indices of poor self-esteem.

3. Adolescent adjustment factors are stable geographic setting, parents, and peers.

4. The onset of adolescence in heralded by the onset of puberty. Reflected in females by increase of breast size and the body taking on a feminine shape, and in males by growth of testes.

5. Early attachment and marriage in adolescent years has a good chance of ending in divorce. 50% of teenage marriages occurred because of pregnancy. 1/3 of all teenage marriages end in divorce within four years after the marriage has begun.

6. Pregnancy in teens

   a. Correlates: poor supervision; child abuse; wanting a "living doll" to love and be loved by; poor home life.

   b. National data suggest that in 14 year old girls:

      (1) 4 out of 10 will become pregnant in their teen years.
      (2) Of these, 2 of 10 will give birth.
      (3) 3 of 20 will have an abortion.

   c. One pregnancy in teen years leads to increased probability of pregnancy occurring again.

   d. Teens have the highest rate of birth complications.

   e. Pregnancy in teenage years leads to a three fold likelihood of being on welfare; and, major problems getting off welfare.

   f. Adolescent fathers eventually tend to have more children, are confined to lower SES, have higher divorce rates, and wives with more OB problems and risks.

H. Growth and Development Addendum

   1. Child Abuse

      a. Includes (1) purposeful physical and emotional harm, (2) sexual abuse, and (3) neglect.

      b. All states have laws against it. The physician is protected for legitimate report of suspicion.

      c. Neglect can lead to retarded growth.

      d. Three general groups of parents who abuse:

(1) Parents with **continual and pervasive hostility/aggression** which is sometimes focused and sometimes directed at the world in general.

(2) Parents with characteristics of **rigidity, compulsiveness, lack of warmth, lack of reasonableness and minimal pliability in thinking and belief.** Considerable rejection of the child is noted. They feel self-righteous and defend their right ot act as they did in abusing thier child.

    (a) Child buys in by saying was bad and deserved it. "It was the only way."

    (b) The self righteousness and the child buying into the delusional system tends to stabilize the abuse across generations.

(3) **Strong feelings of passivity and dependence.** Many are unassuming, reticent and very unaggressive. Often **competed with the child for the love and attention of their spouse.** Generally depressed, moody, unresponsive and unhappy. They are immature people.

e. Characteristics of parents:

(1) Abnormal preoccupied aversion to care of child's basic needs (e.g. diapering)

(2) Likely were abused themselves as children; however, not all abused children become abusers as adults.

(3) Perceive child as ungrateful/to blame for family problems/"doing things to parent", e.g. "that kid won't let me sleep."

(4) Socially isolated from environment (e.g., unlisted phone).

(5) **Reported** cases tend to be lower in SES.

(6) See child as different: e.g., ugly/pretty/dumb/smart/etc.

f. Broken bones in the first ten months of life are rare. If present, suspect child abuse. Infants who are at high risk for abuse:

(1) Parents abuse substances.

        (2) Child is ill or irritable.
        (3) "Different".
        (4) Unwanted pregnancy.
        (5) Hard to raise.

    g. <u>Community</u>: not supportive of family; less belief in child's rights; minimal community services; disorganized.

    h. <u>Culture</u> similar to the community.

2. "Maternal" Deprivation

    a. Institutionally reared children appear less developed, probably because of lowered stimulation. Appear permanently impaired in ability to form "bonding" with others throughout their lives.

    b. Severe maternal deprivation (including institutionally reared children) can lead to a syndrome known as <u>marasmus</u> where the child refuses to eat or involve self with the world and often die (Spitz). Condition can be prevented by physical bonding.

    c. A "hard to raise" child can lead mother to withdraw which in turn can lead to decreased "bonding."

3. Parent-Child Relations and Resultant Child Personality Development

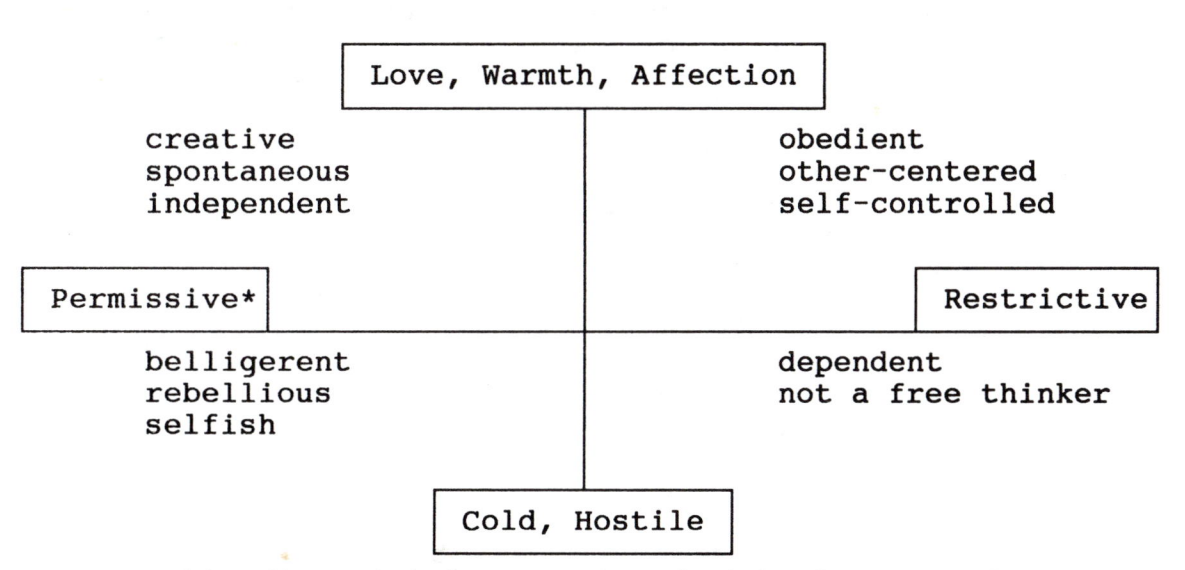

```
                    ┌─────────────────────────┐
                    │ Love, Warmth, Affection │
                    └─────────────────────────┘
        creative              │         obedient
        spontaneous           │         other-centered
        independent           │         self-controlled
┌─────────────┐               │                    ┌─────────────┐
│ Permissive* │───────────────┼────────────────────│ Restrictive │
└─────────────┘               │                    └─────────────┘
        belligerent           │         dependent
        rebellious            │         not a free thinker
        selfish               │
                    ┌─────────────────────────┐
                    │      Cold, Hostile      │
                    └─────────────────────────┘
```

* This dimension is associated with allowance for rough and tumble behavior.

4. Socio-economic status (SES) and Child Rearing

   a. Low SES correlates with the most disparity in roles. E.g., "A man doesn't change diapers"; "a woman's place is in the home."

   b. Low SES has a positive correlation with:

      (1) Offspring with congenital malformations.
      (2) Birth injuries of the child.
      (3) Children with respiratory and/or digestive disorders.
      (4) Premature death of the parents.
      (5) More restrictive, stereotypic, and demanding role behavior.

XII. NEUROPHYSIOLOGIC CONSIDERATIONS

   A. Limbic System

      1. The limbic system is comprised of the phylogenetically old cortex and its associated structures; the hippocampus, fornix, mammillary bodies, anterior thalamic nuclei, cingulate gyrus, septal nuclei and amygdala.

      2. This system is arranged into circuits; and, influences behavioral expression regulated by the hypothalamus.

      3. The functional regulative activities of the limbic system include: modulation and coordination of the central processes of emotional elaboration; motivation; establishment of conditioned reflexes; and memory storage.

      4. There are rich connections between limbic system and neocortex. The frontal lobes are the major neocortical representatives of the limbic system. They monitor and modulate limbic mechanisms.

      5. The neocortex receives data from the external world through sense organs. Perception is in the neocortex. However, perceptions lack emotional coloring without the limbic system.

      6. Behaviors associated with the limbic system

         a. Apparently there is a satiety center. Destruction of this center leads to hyperphagia.

         b. Lesions of the ventral-medial nucleus of the hypothalamus results in overeating and obesity.

c. There is apparently a thirst center; destruction of this center leads to loss of the urge to drink fluids.

d. Kluver-Bucy Syndrome: first established in monkeys where previously aggressive and vicious animals, after removal of the temporal lobe and amygdala, became tame and submissive. They also displayed visual agnosia, hyper-sexuality, and a tendency to oral exploration. Since establishment of the Kluver-Bucy Syndrome in animals in 1937, it has been identified in humans as a correlate of insult to the amygdala.

e. Simulation of the septal brain area has demonstrated a pleasure or reward center. Electrical stimulation has halted epileptic seizures; dulled cancer pain; brought relief from anger; and, produced sexual pleasure accompanied by feelings of intoxication and about to remember something interesting. Animals will seek self stimulation of this site.

B. Reticular Activating System (RAS)

1. The brain stem reticular formation and its thalamic projections are some of the oldest parts of brain involved with behavior.

2. It consists of a network of nerve cells located in the lower brain stem at a point where all sensory and motor impulses pass on the way in and out of the brain.

3. It appears the RAS alerts the brain to complete wakefulness so that it can deal with stimuli necessary to survival. The "Paul Revere" of the CNS.

4. The RAS facilitates and inhibits a great range of data. The fact that a sleeping mother wakes to the crying of her baby but not to louder noises is connected with functioning of the RAS.

5. Regarding voluntary and involuntary motor performances, the RAS influences excitability of afferent relays in the spinal cord.

6. **The orienting response.** RAS modulates and inhibits transmission of impulses peripherally or at the first central synapse of the major different pathways. Thus it functions as a selective filter of incoming information; e.g., during attention focusing, the RAS may exclude irrelevant sensory input.

Facilitation of ascending spinothalamic impulses by the RAS initiates and maintains the aroused state with its associated waking, e.g. patterns of low voltage, fast activity on the EEG.

7. **Sleep.** Reduction of reticular activity is associated with sleep. Earlier concepts of sleep as a passive phenomenon secondary to reduced afferent input have given way to the hypothesis that sleep is an active process.

8. **Psychotic behaviors.** Researchers have associated insufficient functioning of RAS with schizophrenia. It is proposed that lesions of the RAS have a wider effect than do lesions elsewhere, since they involve the filter system through which the entire CNS is alerted to the task of integrating activity.

   Other data associating psychotic-like behavior with RAS include the fact that drugs which control psychoses are effective in the limbic system and reticular formation. They work in the synaptic cleft but do not penetrate the neuron. In this cleft they affect neurotransmitters.

XIII. NEUROTRANSMITTER AND BEHAVIOR CORRELATES

   A. <u>Definition</u>: Neurotransmitters are the mechanisms of (information) transmission in the brain.

   B. <u>There are three general classes of neurotransmitters</u>: biogenic amines, amino acids and peptides.

      1. **Biogenic Amines**

         Are synthesized in the nerve terminals.

         a. <u>Dopamine</u>:

            (1) Major functions appear to be: experience of pleasure; and, to organize thoughts and feelings. <u>Has a very significant role in the mediation of reward</u>.

            (2) Schizophrenia: associated with dopamine **hyperactivity**. The D_2 receptor is specifically implicated. New data on a D_3 receptor has potential implications for schizophrenia.

            (3) Manic states: associated with dopamine **hyperactivity**.

(4) Depressed states: associated with dopamine **hypo**activity.

b. **Norepinephrine**:

   (1) **Major functions appears to be relative activation.**

   (2) central role in **sleep** cycles and arousal;

   (3) involved with **anxiety and pain.**

   (4) Also appears to be important in **anxiety** disorders

   (5) **MHPG** (metabolite of norepinephrine) is **lowered** in urine of persons with **severe depressive disorders**.

   (6) **MHPG in CSF** is **decreased** in some persons who have attempted **suicide.**

c. **Serotonin**:

   (1) Major general functions associated with regulation of **mood, sleep, pain, perception, aggression, memory, appetite, blood pressure, heart rate** and **respiration.**

   (2) **Dorsal raphe nucleus** contains almost all of the brain's serotonergic cell bodies.

   (3) Some correlates with **schizophrenic** states.

   (4) **Depressed states**: associated with **lowered** serotonin levels.

   (5) **5-HIAA** (metabolite of serotonin): associated with **suicide attempts** in depressed persons.

   (6) 5-HIAA concentrations also **lowered** in persons who demonstrate **aggressive and violent behaviors.**

   (7) Associated with **anxiety**, including the **obsessive-compulsive** disorders.

   (8) Lowered levels associated with **sleep reduction.**

d. **Histamine**

   (1) Histamine cells are present in the hypothalamus.

   (2) Major association is with the sleep-wake cycle.

   (3) Abnormalities in the histaminic system have been observed in schizophrenic patients.

e. **Acetylcholine**

   (1) Major functions appears to be associated with sleep, aggression, memory and cognition.

   (2) Implicated in mood disorders. Overactivity of cholinergic pathways associated with depression.

   (3) Correlations with sleep problems.

   (4) Degeneration of cholinergic neurons (nucleus basalis of Meynert) is observed in Alzheimer's disease, Down's syndrome and Parkinson's disease.

   (5) Blockade of cholinergic receptors can result in delirium.

2. **Amino Acids**

   a. **Gamma-aminobutyric acid (GABA)**

   (1) Major activity is mediating presynaptic inhibition through modulation of the chloride ions. Leads to calming effect.

   (2) Account for 60% of synapses in the human brain.

   (3) Decreased GABA activity is associated with development of anxiety and some forms of epilepsy.

   (4) Correlations with Tardive Dyskinesia.

   (5) Suggestions that underactivity may be correlated with schizophrenias.

b. **Glutamic acid**

   (1) Has an **excitatory function** and is correlated with **epilepsy** and **degenerative diseases** of the central nervous system.

3. **Peptides**

   a. Major correlate is with the **control of stress and pain.**

   b. Synthesized in cell body and transported down the axon to the terminal.

   c. Some correlates with **mood disorders** (particularly Somatostatin; Substance P and Vasopressin).

   d. **Enkephalins and endorphins** have been correlated with schizophrenia (particularly Cholecystokinin--CCK; and Neurotensin).

   e. Some correlations with **alcoholism.**

C. <u>Neurotransmitter Correlates with Behavioral Pathology</u>

	Schizo-phrenia	Aggress. Violence	Sleep Prob's	Pain	Anxiety	Mood Dis.
Dopamine	X	X	X			X
Norepine-phrine	X	X	X	X	X	X
Serotonin	X	X	X	X	X	X
Acetyl-choline		X	X			X
GABA	X				X	X
Peptides	X	X	X	X	X	X

XIV. SELECTED PSYCHOPHYSIOLOGIC TOPICS

A. <u>Sensory Deprivation</u>: Involves placing a person in a situation where visual, auditory, temperature, tactile, and gustatory senses are held constant. The subject gets no sensory input of change. This effectively removes all perceptual frameworks into which the person can integrate ongoing internal processes.

   1. With relatively short periods of deprivation (1 hour):

      a. Profound anxiety and fear develop.
      b. Depression and/or hostility appear.
      c. Sometimes auditory and visual hallucinations occur.
      d. Depressed level of consciousness and/or attention observed.
      e. **EXTREME** stimulus hunger develops.

   2. Note the similarity of sensory deprivation and:

      a. Monotonous activity e.g., night driving alone with no radio.

      b. Isolation used in "brain-washing" to make one open to ideas, etc. (stimulus hunger); or, compliance via profound fear.

B. <u>Electroencephalograph (EEG) wave classification and Epilepsy</u>

   1. **Delta:** 4 (CPS). Associated with sleep, some types of brain dysfunction, and some deep meditation states.

   2. **Theta:** 4-8 CPS. Associated with sleep, deep relaxation, some lighter meditation states.

   3. **Alpha:** 8-12 CPS. Characteristic of awake and resting state.

   4. **Beta:** >12 CPS. Attentive and focused.

   5. NOTE:

      a. EEG tracings are greatly affected by level of arousal, drug states, and integrity of the brain.

      b. EEG slowing often found in metabolic problems, e.g., hypothyroidism.

6. Epilepsy and EEG characteristics:

   a. <u>Grand Mal or Generalized Seizure</u>: Tonic, then clonic movement; loss of consciousness; incontinent, consciousness clouded after ictus. EEG = high voltage spike--fast activity.

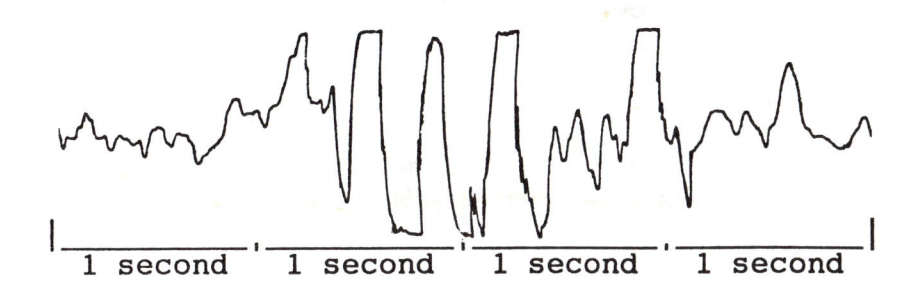

   |_____|_____|_____|_____|
      1 second   1 second   1 second   1 second

   b. <u>Petit Mal</u>: Short lapses of consciousness, maybe muscle tone loss, abrupt return of awareness after ictus with minimal clouding of consciousness. EEG = 3/second spike & dome formation.

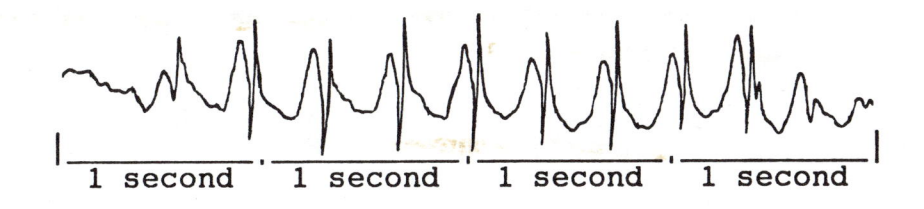

   |_____|_____|_____|_____|
      1 second   1 second   1 second   1 second

   c. <u>Psychomotor (Temporal lobe)</u>: Non-goal directed purposive activity; e.g., lip smacking, walking, automatism; but, not integrated goal directed behavior like play a piano piece or committing a complicated murder. EEG = spikes (sometimes slow) in the temporal lobes, particularly anterior.

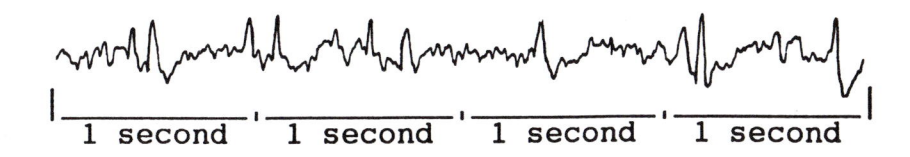

   |_____|_____|_____|_____|
      1 second   1 second   1 second   1 second

d. <u>Jacksonian</u>: "march" or spread of muscle group activity; e.g. finger, hand, forearm, shoulder, etc. EEG = focal slow, fast or spiking around central sulcus.

e. <u>Partial seizure</u>: when only one part of the brain is involved.

f. If consciousness impaired, is called partial complex seizure.

g. If spreads to a generalized seizure, is called secondary generalized epilepsy.

C. <u>Sleep</u>:

1. Stages and EEG equivalents: one complete cycle (Stages 1, 2, 3, and 4 and REM) lasts an average of 90 minutes.

2. Recent work has demonstrated the presence of structures in the lower pons and medulla that are responsible for initiating or maintaining sleep through synchronization of cortical rhythms. Presumably act through inhibition of the midbrain reticular system. Cortex isn't necessary for sleep.

   a. Stage 1: Low voltage-mixed frequency but most predominant is Theta (4-8 cps). (Similar to experienced meditators.)

   b. Stage 2: Between 1 and 3 and 4 (Spindles 12-14/second here, and random spikes.)

   c. Stages 3 and 4: Slow wave -- mainly Delta (less than 4 cps). High amplitude. Very deep sleep.

   Stages 1, 2, 3, and 4 are sometimes referred to as non-REM sleep.

   d. <u>REM (rapid eye movement)</u>:

   (1) Background EEG same as Stage 1 except bursts of REM.

   (2) Behavioral concomitants: a) vivid **visual dreams** like hallucinations. Non-visual dreams occur in other stages and resemble thoughts running through mind; b) **erections** in men and vasocongestion in women; c) **torso muscles** in state of total relaxation except for some

finger, toe, limb twitches. Maybe facial grimace.

- (3) In the autonomic nervous system, all measures except electrodermal activity are at their highest and lowest producing the greatest variability.

- (4) In REM the lateral geniculate of the thalamus receives volleys of information from the pons. From the thalamus the information travels to the cortex. Another path goes from the pons to the medulla and spinal cord. Nerve tissue shows peak growth patterns with such stimulation.

e. At all age groups after two years of age, REM constitutes about 20-25% of sleep. Early in infancy REM constitutes between 50% (age 1-3 months) and 40% (3-5 months) of sleep.

3. Sleep correlates:

a. Daytime wakefulness is more dependent upon uninterrupted periods of sleep than total amount.

b. Sleep deprivation has a cumulative effect.

c. Age issues

- (1) Sleep becomes progressively fragmented over the course of a lifetime in that there is an increase in the amount of waking time and the number of awakenings after sleep onset.

- (2) The percent of REM is highest in infants

- (3) Children: rarely awaken in the night and get more REM in the last 2\3 of the night.

- (4) Young adults get deep sleep early on with less later in the night. REM increases as the night goes on.

- (5) In the elderly there is an equal distribution of REM throughout the night; however, the major problem is an increased number of awakenings and a decrease in slow wave sleep. This results in lighter sleep with more awakenings.

d. Deep sleep is associated with serotonin levels; and wakefulness is associated with norepinephrine levels.

e. With **sedative-hypnotic medication and alcohol REM is reduced**; but in the chronic user on withdrawal, one sees a **rebound phenomenon** with more than average REM.

4. Unusual behavioral sleep states and the sleep cycle.

   a. <u>Sleep walking (**somnambulism**)</u>:

      (1) **1-6%** of population
      (2) **Males more than females**
      (3) Occurs in **NON REM** period

   b. <u>Night terrors</u>:

      (1) More frequent in **children**
      (2) Characterized by anxiety, **high ANS discharge**, motility, verbalizations
      (3) **Stage 4** concomitant
      (4) **Not remembered the next day**
      (5) Upsets others because of the terror

   c. <u>Narcolepsy</u>:

      (1) **Sudden irresistible sleep.**
      (2) REM sleep onset is rapid and instantaneous.
      (3) **Cataplexy**: sudden loss of muscle tone with emotion. Occurs in **66-95%** of narcoleptics.
      (4) Recent data suggest this may be an **auto-immune disorder**.
      (5) May affect as many as 250,000 Americans.
      (6) Treatment is to **take naps during the day**; budget time; **stimulant medication** for the narcolepsy and **tricyclic antidepressants** for the cataplexy (**suppresses** REM).

   d. <u>Nightmares</u>: During **REM**.

   e. <u>Insomnia</u>: Correlated with **depression**; and have **less REM**.

   f. <u>Enuresis</u>:

      (1) **Non-REM**
      (2) Stage 4, 2, or 1
      (3) Occurs in the **first 1/3 of the night**

D. <u>Circadian rhythms</u>: Rhythmic activity of the body which appears cyclic in nature.

1. Regulators

   a. Endogenous--In total isolation from atmospheric and other influences known to affect these rhythms, they still exist even though they may not be as regular, e.g., menstruation.

   b. Exogenous:

      (1) Light-dark cycle is the major one.
      (2) Chemicals: alcohol, stimulants, etc.
      (3) Stress (e.g. crowding), emotional upset, etc.

2. Major rhythms:

   a. Sleep
   b. Menstrual
   c. Liver enzymes for metabolism
   d. Cell reproduction and sensitivity (e.g., utility for cancer poisons and antidotes)
   e. Sleep cycle (90 minute distribution)
   f. Body temperature (high in afternoon; lowest in morning)
   g. Heart rate

E. <u>Cortical lesions and behavior</u>:

1. Aphasia--<u>left</u> hemisphere dysfunction (even for most left handed persons.)

   a. Prerolandic (frontal) lesions affect speech fluency. Is called motor, Broca's or expressive aphasia.

   b. Postrolandic (temporal-parietal) lesions affect comprehension of speech. Is called sensory, Wernicke's or receptive aphasia.

   c. Conduction aphasia is due to lesions that interrupt the <u>connections</u> between the speech fluency and speech comprehension centers. The person has both fluency and comprehension; the defect is in the repetition of words.

   d. Transcortical aphasia can be either deficits in fluency or comprehension. The name comes from the pathology which is infarctions at the border zone between the middle cerebral artery and either the anterior or posterior cerebral artery.

e. Global aphasia is described as the patient behaviorally losing all speech function. Usually caused by lesions in the internal carotid or near the origin of the middle cerebral artery.

2. **Visual-spatial disorders**--<u>right</u>, postrolandic hemisphere

3. **Motor/sensory dysfunction**--<u>contralateral</u> motor/sensory strip

4. <u>Visual field</u> impairment is contralateral to the cortical dysfunction. 1/2 visual field impairment is called homonymous hemianopsia.

5. **Astereognosis**: can't perceive identity of object held in the hand. <u>Contralateral</u> parietal dysfunction.

6. **Bilateral hippocampal lesions** --> memory and learning defects.

7. **Frontal lobe lesions** result in the following:

   (1) Clinically, they are socially inappropriate, and they can't stop a behavior, thought or intent.

   (2) Psychologically, they have very poor ability to abstract, and their speech is separated from their action.

   (3) Have difficulty generating plans and actions; can't sequence components of actions; can't monitor their behavior against environmental goal shifts; and can't correct a course of activity already in progress.

8. **Concussion** with unconsciousness: later the patient often develops: seizures; personality changes; memory problems.

F. <u>Chronic pain</u> frequently is correlated with the following

1. a true physiologic substrate
2. a psychological component: e.g., "a real man can handle this."
3. social control of self and others: e.g., a rationale for not going to the party.
4. holding onto a lost one by developing symptoms similar to those of the lost one: e.g., developing chest pain like those which the loved father had prior to an MI.

G. <u>Immune system</u> functioning is influenced by

   1. stress, e.g., examinations.
   2. onset of a mental disorder, e.g., depression.
   3. grieving over loss, e.g., spouse's death or divorce.

EXAM QUESTIONS - SECTION ONE

Each of the questions or incomplete statements is followed by five suggested answers or completions. Select the one that is BEST in each case and fill in the blank containing the corresponding number on the answer sheet.

1. As opposed to the concept of emotion, all of the following are characteristic of the concept of affect EXCEPT:

    1) Persistent
    2) Pervasive
    3) Less directly reflected in physiological responses
    4) More generalized in ideational content
    5) More likely to be subjectively felt

2. The patient states: "I feel uptight about my new job." This is an example of:

    1) Objective evidence of anxiety
    2) Subjective evidence of anxiety
    3) Inappropriate affect
    4) Repression of affect
    5) A drive discharge emotion

3. All of the following are examples of psychophysiologic responses to anxiety EXCEPT:

    1) Excessive perspiration
    2) Tension headaches, constriction in the chest, backache
    3) Aphasia, apraxia, and a right homonymous hemianopsia
    4) Dyspnea, dizziness, and paresthesia
    5) Transient systolic hypertension, premature contractions, and tachycardia

4. Mr. Smith presents at the Emergency Room after being involved in a traffic accident. He has sustained a severe head injury. Which of the following states of consciousness would NOT be expected as a normal sequela of his concussion?

    1) Confusion state
    2) Fugue state
    3) Clouding of consciousness
    4) Stupor
    5) Coma

5. A student did poorly on an examination which was given in a specific room. The student is afraid he will fail the course. On the next occasion he walks into the room, he experiences fear. This is an example of:

   1) Classical conditioning learning
   2) Social learning
   3) Cognitive learning
   4) Inhibition learning
   5) Fixed schedule learning

6. In learning theory, grades in an academic course would be an example of:

   1) Acquisition
   2) Generalization
   3) Primary reinforcers
   4) Secondary reinforcers
   5) Ratio reinforcement

7. The IQ is most characteristically expressed by which of the following formulas?

   1) $\frac{\text{Mental Age (MA)}}{\text{Chronological Age (CA)}} \times 100 = IQ$

   2) $\frac{CA}{MA} \times 100 = IQ$

   3) $\frac{\text{Social Age (SA)}}{CA} \times 100 = IQ$

   4) $\frac{CA}{SA} \times 100 = IQ$

   5) $\frac{SA}{MA} \times 100 = IQ$

8. Regarding IQ tests, all of the following are correct statements EXCEPT:

   1) Intelligence can frequently be overestimated.
   2) Reliability and validity correlate with tester training.
   3) Group intelligence tests can be very misleading.
   4) IQ's are obtained by different methods in different tests.
   5) A usual safe estimate is the IQ $\pm$ 5 points.

9. In the Freudian scheme of Growth and Development, as the organism matures, there is greater executive control of the "mind" by the:

   1) Id processes
   2) Assimilation processes
   3) Superego processes
   4) Accommodation processes
   5) Ego processes

10. Regarding parameters of the birth process and the neonate, which of the following is NOT a correct statement:

    1) Any depressant administered to the mother may effect nutritive sucking of the neonate for 10 days or more.
    2) Premature neonates do not differ significantly from full-term neonates regarding incidence of physical, mental, or emotional problems.
    3) The newborn normally sleeps 16 hours a day, 8 of which is REM sleep.
    4) A neonate's activity level is directly related to his state of drowsiness/awakeness.
    5) The first signs of voluntary activity of the neonate probably come from his auditory and visual pursuit activities.

11. In the preschool child (age 2-5 years old), all of the following statements are true EXCEPT:

    1) There are rapid advances in language and abstraction.
    2) There is development of identification with appropriate sex role.
    3) Preschool educational programs emphasize mainly social skill improvement.
    4) Preschool children who are less behaviorally aggressive tend to gain more in IQ points.
    5) In Erikson's system, during the preschool period, the major task is to acquire a basic sense of initiative.

12. All of the statements below regarding adolescence (age 13-18) are true EXCEPT:

    1) In Erikson's framework, the basic task to be resolved is to develop affiliation with others.
    2) 50% of teenage marriages occur because of pregnancy.
    3) One-third of teenage marriages end in divorce within 4 years.
    4) A high incidence of physical complaints and anxiety indicate poor self-esteem.
    5) Must maintain a sense of identity in the frame of rapid changes.

13. Which of the following is not a symptom of the Kluver-Bucy Syndrome?

    1) Increased REM sleep
    2) Visual agnosia
    3) Hypersexuality
    4) Submissiveness
    5) Oral exploration

14. The reticular activating system:

    1) Has no inhibitory function.
    2) Functions only above the upper motor neuron.
    3) Can selectively filter incoming stimuli.
    4) Does not contribute to sleep.
    5) Is a relatively new portion of the CNS.

15. Mr. Josephson, an alcoholic, states he drinks to "relax." To assist in his therapy, Mr. Josephson is trained to produce large amounts of theta and alpha waves on the EEG, a condition association with a very relaxed state. This was accomplished by biofeedback training. This type of training is an example of:

    1) Classical conditioning learning
    2) Cognitive learning
    3) Operant conditioning learning
    4) Generalization learning
    5) Extinction learning

16. In terms of etiology, anxiety is usually viewed as repressed or forgotten:

    1) Fear
    2) Guilt
    3) Sorrow
    4) Grief
    5) Anger

17. All of the following are true statements about the memory process EXCEPT:

   1) Long-term memory is rarely defective in organicity unless accompanied by psychosis.
   2) If memory loss occurs, recovery is typically from the extremes of loss to the precipitating event.
   3) Short-term memory is particularly disrupted with bilateral lesions of the hippocampus and/or mammillary bodies.
   4) In general, memory defect is psychogenic if there is no disturbance of consciousness and no intellectual impairment.
   5) If there is short-term memory loss and motivation, and attention is good, it is suggestive of psychogenic involvement.

18. If an unmarried woman is in a situation where she wants to have a sexual relationship and, at the same time, she wants to remain a virgin until she is married, she is considered to be in a state of:

   1) Frustration
   2) Conflict
   3) Lability
   4) Chronicity
   5) Denial

19. In speaking of orientation, four spheres are usually examined. All of the following are included EXCEPT:

   1) Relationship of self to a place in time
   2) Awareness of self as a person
   3) Knowledge of geographic location
   4) Awareness of internal affective state
   5) Knowledge of present situation in time

20. A patient presents to the Emergency Room with the complaints that six months earlier he took LSD and had not ingested any since that time. His presenting complaints at this time revolve around walls not maintaining their perpendicular, assuming a waving shape, and objects in the environment which he knows to be stationary appearing to move. This man is experiencing:

   1) Delusions
   2) Illusions
   3) Autisms
   4) Concretisms
   5) Confabulations

21. All of the following are characteristics of the phenomenology of thinking EXCEPT:

    1) Concrete vs. Abstract
    2) Autistic vs. Logical
    3) Tangential vs. Goal-directed
    4) Delusional vs. Realistic
    5) Disassociated vs. Integrated

22. The advantage to the deviation IQ score is that:

    1) It is the only acceptable way to measure social behavior.
    2) It is the only method to assess verbal IQ separate from performance IQ.
    3) It is the only method that allows you to take the standard deviation statistic into consideration.
    4) It is the only method that directly relates to school performance.
    5) It is the only method that equates for age differences and absolute performance levels.

23. According to the Diagnostic and Statistical Manual of Mental Disorders, Edition III, Revised (DSM-III-R), an IQ of 65 classifies a person as:

    1) Borderline mental retardation
    2) Mild mental retardation
    3) Moderate mental retardation
    4) Severe mental retardation
    5) Profound mental retardation

24. Which of the following is NOT expected after one hour of sensory deprivation?

    1) Anxiety
    2) Depression
    3) Hostility
    4) Fugue
    5) Hallucinations

25. A 35-year-old white female appears in the Emergency Room presenting the argument that the day of Armageddon and the end of the world is at hand. She presents evidence of this in the form that a yellow light on a stop light has burned out signaling the warning is over and the end is near. This is an example of:

    1) Affect disturbance
    2) Circumstantiality
    3) Predicate logic
    4) Tangential thinking
    5) Ambivalent thinking

26. The implications of the limbic system for human behavior include a primary involvement in all of the following behaviors **EXCEPT**?

    1) Memory storage
    2) Emotional elaboration
    3) Motivation
    4) Conditional reflexes
    5) Cognitive learning

27. Regarding the anatomy, physiology and biochemistry of memory, which of the following has the most responsibility for memory.
    1) Dopamine system
    2) Epinephrine system
    3) Histamine system
    4) Nigro-striatal system
    5) Limbic system

28. Luigi Provasano is a 65-year-old male who has recently come to Oklahoma City from Naples, Italy, to live with his son. His son, Stephano, brings him to your office. As you talk with Luigi, you note he refers to presently being in Florence, but when you call his attention to this he denies it. Your conclusion is:

    1) Disorientation to place
    2) Disorientation to time
    3) Disorientation to person
    4) Disorientation to internal affective state
    5) Normal inattention to detail

29. With regard to Luigi Provasano in Question 28 above, your best assessment of etiology would be:

    1) Cultural
    2) Functional
    3) Normal variant
    4) Organic
    5) Psychogenic

30. Which of the following neurotransmitter systems is most involved in schizophrenia?

    1) Acetylcholine
    2) Dopamine
    3) Endorphin
    4) Epinephrine
    5) Histamine

EXAM QUESTIONS - SECTION ONE

Answer Key

1.	5	11.	4	21.	5
2.	2	12.	1	22.	3
3.	3	13.	1	23.	2
4.	2	14.	3	24.	4
5.	1	15.	3	25.	3
6.	4	16.	1	26.	5
7.	1	17.	5	27.	5
8.	1	18.	2	28.	1
9.	5	19.	4	29.	4
10.	2	20.	2	30.	2

SECTION TWO: THEORIES, PSYCHOSOCIAL ISSUES

I. **THEORIES** **70**

    A. Psychoanalytic
    B. Transactional Analysis
    C. Erikson's Theories of Psychosocial Tasks
    D. Piaget

II. **SEXUALITY** **77**

    A. General Terms and Concepts
    B. Masturbation
    C. Heterosexuality
    D. Miscellaneous Facts
    E. Normal Sexual Dysfunctions
    F. Anatomic/physiologic Variations
    G. Different Sexual Preferences and Life Styles
    H. Paraphilias
    I. Incest

III. **SUBSTANCE ABUSE** **84**

    A. Addictions
    B. General Background Information
    C. Narcotics Addiction and Drug Abuse
    D. Treatment of Chemical Dependence
    E. Neonatal Addiction
    F. Toxicology
    G. Major Medical Problems
    H. Confidentiality

IV. **ALCOHOLISM** **92**

    A. Definition
    B. Statistics
    C. Pharmacologic Aspects
    D. Teenage Use
    E. Female Use
    F. Cultural Factors
    G. Major Physical Illnesses Associated with Alcoholism
    H. Alcohol Induced Organic Mental Disorders
    I. Withdrawal
    J. Treatment

V.   AGING 97

   A.   Statistical Data
   B.   Physiologic State
   C.   Biologic Changes in Mental Functioning
   D.   Total State of Person
   E.   Cognitive and Performance Changes
   F.   Successful Aging

VI. DEATH AND DYING/GRIEF AND BEREAVEMENT 98

   A.   Death and Dying
   B.   Grief and Bereavement

VII. ATTITUDES 101

   A.   Components
   B.   Changing Attitudes

VIII. PREJUDICE 102

   A.   Definition
   B.   Age of Formulation
   C.   Prejudicial Personality
   D.   Mechanisms of Prejudice

IX. SUBCULTURE PARAMETERS 103

   A.   Definition of Minorities
   B.   Subgroup Effects
   C.   Socio-economic Status (SES)
   D.   Community Organization and Mental Health
   E.   Small Group Relations
   F.   Sick Role

X.   PSYCHOLOGICAL ASSESSMENT 107

   A.   Statistical Basis of Psychological Assessment and Prediction
   B.   Research Design Concepts
   C.   Major Categories of Psychological Tests

XI.   DIVORCE 114

        A.   Statistics
        B.   Reactions of Parents and Children
        C.   Etiologies
        D.   Marital Success

XII.   SUICIDE, HOMICIDE, AND OTHER FORMS OF VIOLENCE 115

        A.   Suicide
        B.   Mechanisms of Violence
        C.   Homicide
        D.   Spouse Abuse
        E.   Rape

XIII.   SOCIAL STRESS AND PHYSICAL CONCOMITANTS 122

        A.   Life Stress Social Readjustment Scale
        B.   Consequences of Scores

EXAMINATION QUESTIONS AND ANSWERS 123

SECTION TWO: THEORIES, PSYCHOSOCIAL ISSUES

I. THEORIES: Are complimentary, not contradictory.

Freud = **intrapersonal**; **Erikson** = **interpersonal**; **Piaget** = **cognitive**.

A. Psychoanalytic (Freud, et. al.). There are overlapping subtheories although presented here as distinct entities.

1. **Instinct Theory**: Drive theory. Drive is the psychological parallel of an instinct, defined as a biological urge. A drive has two components: the **aim** to satisfy the instinct; and the **object** which will satisfy the instinct.

    a. Pleasure principle: people seek pleasure and avoid pain.

    b. Libido: "Psychic energy." This word has been misinterpreted to be sexual energy. While psychic energy can take a sexual form, libido is more than sexual.

    c. Stages:

    (1) **Oral** (0-18 months)
    (2) **Anal** (18 months to approximately 3 years)
    (3) **Phallic Urethral** (3 years to approximately 7 years)
    (4) **Latency** (7 years to approximately 12 years)
    (5) **Genital** (approximately 12 years through adolescence)

    d. Oedipal (males) or Electra (females) Complex: (part of the Phallic stage) the way Freud conceptualized movement through various stages of development. Based on the Grecian myth of Oedipus. It says the child develops a love relationship with the parent of the opposite sex and wishes to get "rid of" the parent of the same sex. That is, the child is trying to take on an adult role too soon with an inappropriate person. Simultaneously, the child understands it is too small to adequately battle the parent of the same sex; therefore the child becomes fearful the parent of the same sex (out of jealousy) will "castrate" (make impotent) for the love attachment to the parent of the opposite sex. The healthy parent helps the child understand that it does not need to take on adult responsibility yet; and, it is permissible for the child to be a child and to "play."

2. **Economic Theory**: Involves distribution of the energy (libido).

   a. **Cathexis**: Positive or negative energy invested in an object.

   b. **Narcissism**: Libidinal energy invested in self. Determined by the first three or four months of life on the basis of how much others attended to the child. If an adequate amount was given the child as an adult will be happy. If the amount was inadequate, the child may be suspicious, distrustful, and unhappy as an adult. A person who is very Narcissistic has invested a large amount of energy in self, i.e., has cathected self as an object.

3. **Topographical Theory**: Refers to unconscious, preconscious and conscious.

   a. **Unconscious**: Material is out of the person's awareness; therefore, the person doesn't know what it is.

   b. **Preconscious**: the person is not presently aware of it, but with focus on the topic, can become aware. E.g., your telephone number is not in your awareness; however, with attention or concentration you can become aware of it.

   c. **Conscious Awareness**: the material of which the person is aware at the present time.

4. **Structural Theory**: the constructs of id, ego, and superego.

   a. **Id**: basically the instinctual drive, e.g., food, sex, etc.

   b. **Superego**: standards a person has, values. Is the conscience.

   c. **Ego**: many functions are in the ego. Mediates between Id and Superego.

      (1) Ego Functions: remember the mnemonic **ROADSIT**

         (a) Reality Testing: ability to separate fact from fantasy.
         (b) Object Relations: ability to establish healthy interpersonal relations.
         (c) Autonomous Functions: memory, perception, movement, IQ, singing, etc.

(d) **Defenses:** (covered in Section Three)
(e) **Synthesis:** ability to integrate components into a statement of "This is who I am."
(f) **Impulse Control:** delay of gratification.
(g) **Thinking:** Thought process and content as in Section I above.

(2) Note: **The stronger the ego, the stronger the person.**

5. **Psychosocial Theory:** reflects the interaction between the person's internal "psychic state" and the social environment. The person who developed **psychosocial theory of psychoanalytic thought is Erik Erikson** (see below).

6. **Adaptational Theory:** examines **functional value of symptoms**.

7. Miscellaneous terms with which you should be familiar:

   a. **Transference:** all aspects of the patient's feelings and behavior toward the therapist/doctor.

   b. **Counter-Transference:** the emotional response of the therapist or doctor to the patient.

   c. **Acting-out:** When the patient has transference to the therapist, the patient, instead of talking to the therapist about the transference, puts the wishes into action with others. E.g., if a female patient has transference to a male therapist, she might indulge in significant "sexual acting-out with a variety of men" in order to avoid talking to the therapist about her feelings towards the therapist.

   d. **Regression:** Under stress the person returns to an earlier maturational level. E.g., if the child were at the Phallic stage, with stress (e.g., tired, ill, birth of another sibling), the child may give up the Phallic stage of adaptation and regress to an Anal stage and begin soiling.

   e. **Fixation:** Arrest of psychosexual development at any stage before complete maturation. Also may be a close, paralyzing attachment to another person, such as mother or father.

```
                                    ┌─── Regression
Maturation ──→
Trauma  ∿→  ×  ↙─── Fixation
```

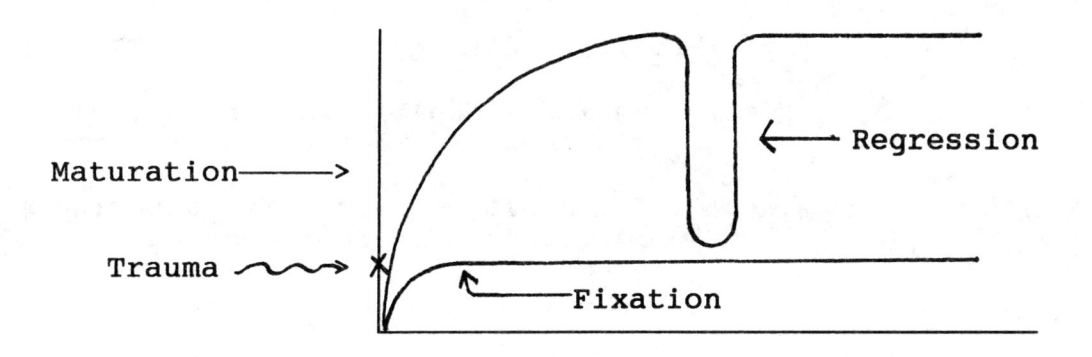

B. <u>Transactional Analysis</u>: (a psychoanalytic type theory)

  1. **Structural analysis:** Ego states of Parent, Adult and Child.

     a. <u>The Child</u> (Id): <u>felt</u> way of life, recognized in self by recognizing feelings, recognized in others by emotions. Two parts: Adapted Child ("Yes sir"); Free Child ("Whee!").

     b. <u>Parent</u> (Superego): <u>Taught</u> attitudes and behaviors from external sources, primarily parents. Two parts: Nurturing Parent (Parental hugs); the Critical Parent ("You should!").

     c. <u>Adult</u> (Ego): <u>Thought</u> way of life. Concerned with reality and objective gathering of information and data processing.

     d. Principles of Structural Analysis

        (1) No ego state is necessarily better than another.

        (2) The question is how appropriate or adaptive a given ego state is in a given circumstance at a given time.

        (3) The **Adult** can check out reality, can turn off either the **Child** or **Parent**, giving control over feelings and beliefs.

        (4) With few exceptions, can't be in 2 ego states at one time.

(5) Problems with ego states from TA standpoint:

    (a) An individual is <u>frozen in a given ego state</u> without ready access to the other two.

    (b) The Adult ego state is <u>contaminated</u> by an intrusion of Parent ego state (<u>prejudice</u>), by Child ego state, (<u>delusions</u>), or by both Parent and Child ego states.

2. <u>Transactional Analysis</u>: The interactions between ego states.

   a. Six classes of transactions. Things people do together.

      (1) **Withdraws:** from social interaction or involvement.

      (2) **Rituals:** a way of introducing self, e.g., "How are you?"

      (3) **Pastimes:** statement with blanks where you simply fill in the blanks e.g., "The weather is _____ today."

      (4) **Games:** a series of transactions leading to a payoff of <u>negative</u> feelings. Maintains Scripts (see below).

      (5) **Activities:** time spent dealing with reality e.g., work.

      (6) **Intimacy:** game-free; trusting; involving recognition and respect of the uniqueness of each person, genuine caring, as well as a mutuality of giving and sharing.

   b. Types of Transactions:

      (1) **Parallel or complimentary:** the ego state of person 1 addresses an ego state of person 2; and the ego state of person 2 responds to the "sending" ego state of person 1. E.g., adult to child<-->child to adult.

      (2) **Crossed transactions:** Person 1 addresses an ego state of person 2, but person 2 responds from a different ego state to person 1; E.g., Person 1: Adult to Adult, Person 2: Parent to Child.

(3) **Ulterior transaction:** involves more than two ego states where a message from the ego state of person 1 is directed to an ego state of person 2, but underneath there is an implied message to another ego state in the second person: i.e., "Would you like to see my etchings?" Message 1 is Adult to Adult; but implied message is Child to Child.

3. **Existential Positions:** Basic personal stance of the person.

   a. I'm ok - you're ok.
   b. I'm not ok - you're ok.
   c. I'm ok - you're not ok.
   d. I'm not ok, you're not ok.

4. **Scripts:** Life plans decided early in childhood.

   a. About age 8 a child begins to answer the questions "Who am I?", "What is the world like?", and "What happens to someone like me in this world?" The answers make up his Script.

   b. Reaffirmed by selective attention/interaction with world.

5. **Important Concepts:**

   a. Strokes: Unit of social recognition. Strokes can be conditional or unconditional, and positive or negative.

   b. Drama Triangle: The three roles are Persecutor, Victim, and Rescuer. Roles are stable, the person who fills a role may change, e.g. a rescuer becomes a victim for rescuing.

C. Erikson's Theory of Psychosocial Tasks

1. In Erikson's theory there are eight tasks which a person must complete in a lifetime to have a totally full, normal life.

2. The Eight Psychosocial Tasks

Stage	Age	Task	Comments
1.	0-18 mos.	Trust vs. Mistrust	Needs handled? Contiguity of own actions established?

"Basically it's safe"

2.	18 mos.- 3 yrs.	Autonomy vs. Shame and Doubt	Once he ventures out, what are his reactions and those of family; can he build a sense of standing on two feet without shame and doubt?

"I am an independent person and can determine some things"

3.	4-6 yrs.	Initiative vs. Guilt	Superego anger: overwhelming fear? Oedipus Complex constructively resolved?

"I can plan and others will not overwhelm all my planning"

4.	6-13 yrs.	Industry vs. Inferiority	School entrance; peer relationships; danger; sense of adequacy especially away from home and with _equals_.

"I have something to offer"

5.	11-20 yrs.	Sense of Identity vs. Role Confusion	Rapid changes, ambiguous period; task: maintain identity and incorporate changes.

"I know me and I can make it as an adult"

6.	20-35 yrs.	Intimacy vs. Isolation	Knows who he is; now must develop affiliation with others; intimacy with them.

"I can share my life and gain support from others"

7.	35-65 yrs.	Generativity vs. Stagnation	Guiding next generation, acquiring personal meaning in life, and making contribution.

"I have meaning and mean something to others"

8.	65-+ yrs.	Integrity vs. Despair	Maintain dignity of personal life.

"I am proud of my life"

D. Piaget

1. Piagetian cognitive theory in detail was presented in Section One. Only the stages are reviewed here.

   a. **The sequence of stages is fixed. The time of appearance can be different** due to social environmental issues:

      (1) Sensorimotor stage (birth to about 18 months). Employs senses, reflexes and motor activity to interact with the world.

      (2) Preoperational stage (about 18 months to 7 years). Relies on perception and intuition (e.g. a sponge that looks like a rock is a rock). No conservation of identity of an object.

      (3) Concrete operations stage (about 7 to around 11-13 years). Can abstract the commonality from observed things. Can add and subtract elements but conserve the essence of each element.

      (4) Formal operations stage (begins about 11-13 years). Conceptual deductive thinking is possible. Objects need not be present to conceptualize about them. Cognitive reasoning is possible.

II. **SEXUALITY**

   A. General Terms and Concepts

   1. Gender = anatomy, physiology, chromosomes

   2. Gender Identity = the **feeling** of "Am I a male or a female?" Established by age 2 or 3. The **private experience** of sex role.

   3. Gender Identification = the masculine or feminine behavior of the person. Learned from role models during preschool, kindergarten, and grade school. Usually in place by puberty. This is the **public expression** of sex role.

   NOTE: Gender, Gender Identity and Gender Identification may match or not. E.g., individual can have male genitalia, a feminine identity, and male identification.

Would look male anatomically and behaviorally, but feel like a female.

B. <u>Masturbation</u>

1. **Estimates:** **60% of women** and **95% of men** have masturbated. **Excessive masturbation (x 3-4/day)** probably is **anxiety release**.

2. **Myths:** will cause warts, weaken body, cause hair to grow on the palms of the hands, and hair will fall out; cause frigidity, impotence, deformities in future children; or exhaust person's "pre-determined allotment of ejaculations" so sex life is shortened, thereby endangering future marital adjustment.

3. **Current opinions regarding masturbation:** Is not harmful. Maximum sexual fulfillment is not intended to be a lonely pursuit; but, there are times in people's lives where loneliness, aloneness, or illness exist and masturbation is only acceptable way to release sexual tensions, and is **NORMAL**. Continues into married life as another form of sexual experience.

C. <u>Heterosexuality</u>

1. **Sexual Response Cycle:**

Phases	Female	Male
① APPETITIVE	— — — INITIAL DESIRE — — —	
② EXCITEMENT	Nipple erection Vaginal lubrication Increased HR & BP Clitoral erection	Nipple erection Penile erection Increased HR & BP
③ PLATEAU	Similar to excitement; cont'd. sexual activity	Same as female

④ ORGASM	Can be multiple
	  Vaginal = Clitoral
	Further increase in
	  HR & BP
		Single (usually)
		Further increase
		  in HR & BP

⑤ RESOLUTION	Quick resolution
	  in 3-10 minutes
		Loses about ½
		  of erection in
		  first 30 min.

D. <u>Miscellaneous facts.</u>

1. **Androgens** tend to increase sex drive in males and females.

2. **Estrogen** in the male tends to induce decreased potency, decreased sex drive and enhancement of breast tissue.

3. **Premarital Intercourse:** Currently, 80% of males and 70% of females report having had intercourse by age 19.

4. The sex "role" is learned and therefore **culture dependent**.

5. **Higher education** tends to blur the role differences.

6. **Lower socio-economic status (SES)** tends to exaggerate distinctiveness of the roles.

7. **Sexual relations during pregnancy** is "up for grabs;" i.e. there is no consistent recommendation among physicians.

    a. Major issue is female's comfort.
    b. Prevent infections.
    c. Unresolved question of orgasm in last few weeks precipitating premature labor.

8. **Sexuality and aging** studies suggest activity in older persons is best predicted by the "pre-aging" sexual activity pattern. Common findings are:

    a. <u>Males</u>: tactile sensitivity decreases, less frequent desire and less insistent desire. Erections take longer to achieve and if loses during intercourse or sex play, may not be able to reachieve it for an hour or so. Full erection may not occur until end of plateau or just before orgasm. Ejaculate decreased in quantity and force of expulsion. Contractions of prostate, penis and rectum are less in frequency and intensity. Resolution is very quick. Refractory period may be hours or days.

    b. <u>Females</u>: lubrication slower and less marked, not as much engorgement of labia; fewer contractions of the vagina and rectum at orgasm; generally faster resolution than with younger females. Walls of vaginal thin out; therefore, after intercourse may experience increased desire to urinate due to the pressure of the penis on the bladder through the thinner walls.

9. In **the sexual interview**, interviewer needs to evaluate "threatening" issues with basic "who, what, when, where, how, and how long" questions. **Never use the WHY question.**

E. "Normal" sexual dysfunctions: If not physiologic in origin, is usually anxiety.

1. Some data for "sexual competence" have come from non-human animal studies (HARLOW). The data imply if monkeys are reared without normal "mother-child" interaction or "peer sex play", are sexually incompetent as adults, even if paired with a sexually experienced partner.

2. Behavioral treatments for "normal" sexual dysfunctions listed below. Success rate (symptom relief) is high (70-100%), and recidivism low (1-5%). Focus on couple's relationship and behavior modification.

3. **Dyspareunia**: Painful intercourse for the female (e.g. tipped uterus, infection, inflammation, depth penetration). Occurs in males as function of infection, irritation, etc..

4. **Vaginismus**: Strong contractions of the walls of the vagina. Impossible to insert a finger or penis. Possibly classically conditioned response to underlying dyspareunia.

5. **Premature ejaculation**: Extravaginal orgasm when intercourse is being attempted; or, lack of voluntary control. Easily treated with the "Squeeze Technique."

6. **General Arousal Dysfunction (in males: Impotence)**: Helen Singer Kaplan called "erectile dysfunction". Most often due to performance anxiety, fatigue, or stress. Other biologic causes: early undiagnosed diabetes; low androgen level; estrogenic medication; hepatic problems; toxicity on alcohol, narcotics, or sedative-hypnotics; neurological diseases; MS; tumors (structural or hormone secreting); operations (e.g. prostatectomy), alpha adrenergic blockade.

7. **General Arousal Dysfunction (in females: Frigidity)**: etiologies similar to that of males. Some find sexuality repugnant or a "duty" (early training?).

8. **Non-orgasm in males and females**: Correlated with emotional issues (fear of failure in men; trust issues in women.)

9. **Drug effects**: Alcohol, sedative-hypnotics, and narcotics decrease sexual behavior; stimulants enhance sexual behaviors; alpha and beta blockers may inhibit certain phases of the sexual response cycle.

F. Anatomic/physiologic variations

1. **XYY syndrome**

    a. Tallness
    b. Poor impulse control
    c. Some difficulty in interpersonal contact
    d. Often: great sexual libido
    e. If criminals: tendency to violence or arson

2. **Klinefelter's Syndrome:**

    a. XXY
    b. After puberty: tall, eunuchoid, thin, small testicles, may have breasts
    c. Almost invariably sterile
    d. Tendency to be emotionally unstable
    e. Tend to be mentally retarded, but not invariably

3. **Testicular Feminization Syndrome:**

    a. Syndrome of androgen insensitivity.
    b. Is extreme form of male pseudohermaphroditism.
    c. Phenotype and sexual identification are female, but no uterus or tubes.
    d. Always sterile.

4. **Turner's Syndrome:**

    a. Only one X chromosome. 45 chromosomes instead of 46.

    b. Signs:

    (1) Cubitus valgus
    (2) Low posterior hairline margin
    (3) Webbed neck
    (4) Short stature
    (5) Ovaries absent --> no puberty development

G. <u>Different Sexual Preferences and Life Styles</u>

1. **Homosexuality:** Vague term, usually referring to people who are sexually **AND** emotionally attracted to persons of the same sex.

    a. Same sex contact is correlated with: availability of the opposite sex; relative stigma of same sex behavior (male vs. female); change in the possibility of expression. I.e., <u>not all same sex behavior is homosexuality</u>.

b. About 10% of adults report they are homosexual. (Of this 10%, 60% are male and 40% are female.)

c. Psychodynamic explanation: For boys: aloof, distant, absent father; overprotective, overindulgent mother, leads to inability to resolve Oedipal conflict and identification with mother. For girls: reverse of this. Research suggests this explanation holds for ego dystonic homosexuals, approximately 20% of the homosexual population.

d. Recent data suggest there may be biochemical, physiologic, anatomic or genetic components for some.

e. Major issues are:

   (1) Blackmail
   (2) Employment compromise
   (3) Discrimination and prejudice
   (4) V.D. considerations because **SOME** have multiple anonymous sexual contacts e.g., gonorrhea, syphilis, & giardia.
   (5) <u>Acquired Immune Deficiency Syndrome-AIDS, now referred to as HIV+ spectrum disease.</u>
   Prevention: partner selection and no exchange of body fluids.

2. Transsexuality (Gender Dysphoria): The **feeling** in a biologically normal person of being a member of the opposite sex (Gender Identity reversal). Seek surgical correction of external appearance to be consistent with internal feelings.

   a. Requirements/precautions before operation:

      (1) Psychological evaluation to establish diagnosis. Requires 1-2 years. To eliminate mental disorders.
      (2) Live/work in other sex role one year before operation.
      (3) Hormone treatments during that or following year.

   b. Approximately 10% of those presenting receive final surgery.

   c. <u>Surgery is not organ transplant</u>. Is restructuring genitals. E.g. creating vaginal labia and vagina in biologic males; creating a penis, scrotum, testes in biologic females.

H. **Paraphilias** or sexual disorders

1. Exhibitionism: prosecuted in males. Male experiencing compulsion to exhibit penis to a child or an adult (or both) for purpose of sexual gratification. No intent of further contact; but intent to elicit a response (e.g., startle) from the other person. Often married and live stable lives.

2. Fetishism: Nonliving object --> sexual arousal (e.g. a shoe).

3. Frotteurism: rubbing against a nonconsenting person.

4. Pedophilia: desire by an adult for sexual gratification with an immature/prepubescent child

5. Sexual Masochism: pain and suffering inflicted on self for sexual excitement.

6. Sexual Sadism: pain and suffering inflicted on another for sexual excitement.

7. Transvestic Fetishism: a fetishistic, pleasurable, sporadic cross-dressing in biologically normal man who doesn't question he is a male. Usually married, heterosexual, and has children.

8. Voyeurism: only prosecuted in males. A sexual situation in which witnessing certain events has become a sexual need and slowly becomes the major outlet for sexual gratification.

9. Other conditions where object is not a living person.

    a. Telephone scatologia (lewdness)
    b. Necrophilia (corpses)
    c. Partialism (exclusive focus on one part of the body, e.g. toes.)
    d. Zoophilia: The preference for animal sexual contact.
    e. Coprophilia (feces)
    f. Klismaphilia (enemas)
    g. Urophilia (urine)

I. Incest

1. Sexual relations between two persons who too closely related by blood to marry. The definition is often extended to stepparent stepchildren dyads. Laws concerning incest vary among states.

2. Most common form of incest is probably siblings. This is most common in families in which children share the same bedroom and poor parental supervision. Usually ignored as "exploration." The most common **reported** form is father-daughter (stepfather-daughter, boyfriend-daughter) incest. Mother-son incest occurs. Was believed the mother had awareness of father-daughter incest; and, through silence or discounting daughter's report, condoned it. New data suggest mothers are usually unaware.

3. Reported to be almost **universally taboo**.

4. Kinsey researchers reported the male incest offender is ineffectual, often drunk, often unemployed man who is deprived of sex. Once the incest taboo is broken, they continue. **Availability and ease of access are the motivating forces. 45% are under the influence of alcohol** at the time of offense.

5. Many documented cases of incest are among the poor. Incest is not confined to the poor. These come to the attention of the courts; more affluent turn up in the mental health professional's office. It is suspected the incidence among all classes of society is nearly equal; however, no good studies. Incest occurs in all races, religions and ethnic groups.

6. The national reported rate is about 20% of American families.

III. SUBSTANCE ABUSE (NOTE: BECAUSE OF ITS IMPORTANCE, ALCOHOLISM WILL BE HANDLED AS A SEPARATE SECTION)

  A. Addictions

    1. Definition: a state of periodic or chronic intoxication, detrimental to the individual and/or society, caused by repeated consumption of a drug with the characteristics of:

        a. habituation: psychological dependence or taking out of habit

        b. tolerance: decreased effect with repeated doses of the same dose level of the drug.

        c. dependence: physiological response to the abrupt termination of drug leads to observable physical signs.

2. **Cross dependence:** two different chemical preparations can substitute for each other, particularly regarding withdrawal.

3. **Cross tolerance:** if tolerant to the effects of one drug, are tolerant to the effects of another.

B. General background information

1. There has never been established an **addictive personality**. The group who abuse chemicals most are the Personality Disorders. However, the vast majority of chemically dependent persons do not fit any behavioral, pathologic or personality category.

2. **Personality variables** of chemically dependent persons (these include persons abusing alcohol).

    a. Low self esteem: don't feel as good as, as pretty as, as athletic as, etc., other persons.

    b. External locus of control: depends on external events to control life, i.e. the bar closes or the bottle is empty.

3. The formula **People + Stress ---> Drug Seeking Behavior** can be utilized to understand etiologic conditions of chemical abuse.

C. Narcotics Addiction and Drug Abuse

1. Drug abuse related agencies.

    a. FDA: Federal Food and Drug Administration. Function is to monitor safety of various chemical preparations

    b. DEA: Drug Enforcement Administration. Responsible for the security of controlled substances.

    c. NIDA: National Institute on Drug Abuse. Provides federal funds for education, research, prevention and treatment.

    d. NIAAA: National Institute on Alcohol Abuse and Alcoholism. Similar to NIDA but for alcohol.

2. Behavioral correlates of different drugs of abuse

   a. <u>Stimulants</u>

   (1) **Amphetamines/methamphetamine:** speed, meth, crystal, white crosses, dexies, black mollies, "Ice" (long acting stimulant: toxic effects can last 20 hours); **Cocaine:** coke, crack, freebase.

   (2) Persons toxic on stimulants are recognizable by their hyperactivity. **Can produce intense euphoria and delusions of grandeur.**

   May demonstrate paranoid characteristics and frequently are misdiagnosed as being agitated schizophrenic or agitated paranoid psychosis.

   (3) Typically deny drugs are the cause of their feeling state. Appropriate treatment usually is to allow the person to "sleep it off" but they may need some medications such as benzodiazepines to "come down."

   (4) In managing a person who is toxic on stimulants, approach them cautiously. They and phencyclidine users, when toxic, can be a danger to others.

   (5) After they "come down" (2-3 days) there is often a refractory depression for 7 days up to 2-3 weeks.

   (6) Overdose can be fatal; withdrawal is not.

   b. <u>Sedative-Hypnotics</u>:

   (1) **Barbiturates:** barbs, downs, red, **Methaqualone:** quays, sopers, ludes, Q's, quaaludes. **Benzodiazepines:** benzo's, tranq's.

   (2) Behavior characteristics: individual looks drunk, but no odor of alcohol (unless using both). Slurred speech, ataxia, impaired social judgement, etc..

   (3) Persons addicted to sedative hypnotics can **die from withdrawal.** Must be medically withdrawn by titrated doses. If not done properly can develop a toxic delirium and withdrawal seizures.

(4) **They also die from overdose.**

(5) There are **synergistic** effects between alcohol and sedative hypnotics The combination can lead to a multiplicative effect. Many accidental overdose deaths are due to this phenomenon.

(6) **ER management:** Clear the airway, support vital signs. Begin titrated withdrawal. Sometimes lavage followed by an activated charcoal bolus is indicated.

c. <u>Narcotics</u>

   (1) <u>Heroin</u> : smack, junk, H, horse, shit, skag.

   (2) 400,000 to 600,000 estimated U.S. addicts. Since Heroin is a Schedule 1 drug (and therefore CANNOT be legally prescribed), prevalence is estimated from overdose deaths, number in treatment, Drug Abuse Warning Network (DAWN).

   (3) 1-2% of any MS-I class will become narcotics addicts.

   (4) In the first 15-20 minutes after injection, toxic persons sometimes manifest semi-somnolent behavior ("on the nod", "kissing the table"). Can be aroused by calling name or shaking them.

   (5) The opiate dependent person **rarely dies from withdrawal. They die from overdose.**

   (6) Best proof of current addiction is development of **narcotic abstinence syndrome:** (piloerection, rhinorrhea, pupillary dilation, diarrhea.) Ancillary signs: "trackmarks"; related diseases.

   (7) Related diseases:

     (a) Hepatitis
     (b) Abscesses
     (c) Pulmonary complications
     (d) Overdose
     (e) Hemorrhoids
     (f) GI tract disturbances, e.g. constipation
     (g) Bacterial endocarditis
     (h) HIV infection

(8) Medical management of overdose includes: **Airway; Vital sign support;** and **Antagonists:** Naloxone (narcan) preferred since it has minimal agonistic properties.

d. <u>Marijuana</u>

(1) grass, pot, joint, weed, hit, number, THC.

(2) Marijuana effects include: euphoria, increased appetite, decreased intraocular pressure, nausea suppression. **Doesn't** dilate pupils.

Also: tachycardia, bronchial dilation, REM sleep suppression , suppression of cell mediated immune response, pain suppression, nausea suppression, and injection of the conjunctiva.

(3) There is significant **impairment of memory**. Apparently hippocampus is major site of action.

(4) Because it is lipophilic, effects can be demonstrated weeks after use is terminated.

(5) IT IS ADDICTIVE.

(6) **The amotivational syndrome** of marijuana tends to develop in some persons. The major motivation in these persons is to get the drug, and all else is secondary. Not correlated to criminal acts or decrease in primary pleasure. They seem to have no energy or drive to accomplish.

e. <u>Tobacco</u>

(1) Only about 25% who try to stop are successful.

(2) Lung cancer occurs in <50% of chronic smokers.

(3) In one large national epidemiologic study, 5 diseases accounted for 39% of deaths of smokers.

   (a) Bronchogenic Carcinoma
   (b) Peptic Ulcer
   (c) Aortic aneurysm
   (d) Acute myocardial infarction
   (e) Centrilobular emphysema

f. Psychedelics

   (1) **Lysergic Acid Diethylamide:** LSD, acid, windowpane, strawberries, orange; **Mescaline:** mesk; **Peyote:** cactus; **psilocybin mushroom:** "shrooms"; STP (serenity, tranquility and peace).

   (2) The toxic and emergent person typically has disorganized thought processes, is fearful ("death trips"), and manifests auditory/visual hallucinations. May manifest signs and symptoms of schizophrenia. Are often difficult to differentially diagnose.

   (3) It is generally accepted that utilization of (neuroleptics) with this group of persons is not recommended because of possible synergistic effects on the cardiovascular and respiratory systems.

g. Phencyclidine (PCP, angel dust):

   (1) The emergency state is characterized by the 4 C's which are dose dependent. These are: Catatonia, Combative, Convulsions, and Coma.

   (2) **Toxicity** is accompanied by vertical and/or lateral nystagmus.

h. Ecstasy (XTC): A psychedelic stimulant. Overdose usually not fatal. Can create management problems similar to crisis on stimulants and psychedelics.

D. Treatment of chemical dependence (includes alcoholism)

   1. Comparative Therapeutic Modalities

	Crisis Intervention	Therapeutic Community	Chemical Blockade
Inpatient			
Intermediate			
Outpatient			

2. Issues of the Therapeutic Community:

   a. less expensive
   b. positive atmosphere
   c. continuity of care
   d. decreased use of the expensive medical personnel
   e. teaches personal responsibility
   f. charismatic leader
   g. total support

3. **Methadone:** Chemical Blockade

   a. Methadone is only useful in treating Opiate addiction. To use Methadone, you must be associated with a licensed program. There are two types of license: Analgesia & Detoxification; and Maintenance

   b. Person who may be placed on Methadone Maintenance must be 18 years of age, have a two year history of narcotic addiction, and be voluntary.

   c. Methadone Maintenance programs are controlled regarding dose level and how many take-home doses the individual may have.

   d. Maintenance programs are oriented toward substituting the chemical for the street opiate until the individual can structure intra- and inter-personal life to not be dependent on chemicals to function. The aim is always to withdraw the persons from the chemical over time.

   e. The withdrawal syndrome from Methadone is similar to that of other opiates. It is slower in onset and lasts longer.

   f. Methadone advantages:

      (1) 1 dose lasts 24-36 hours.
      (2) It's a legal drug.
      (3) Blocks narcotic hunger.
      (4) It is pure, therefore decreased medical complications.
      (5) No tolerance develops if used as prescribed.
      (6) Delivered in a total rehabilitation package.
      (7) Inexpensive.

   g. High success rate on long-term (7-year) follow-up.

      (1) Increased personal, family, and social responsibility.

(2) Methadone clinics have reduced crime rate up to 64%.

E. <u>Neonatal addiction</u>: Fetal drug blood level approximates that of mother. Recent data suggests about 70% of neonates born to addicted mothers will develop the general withdrawal syndrome (GWS). GWS: hyperactive CNS with resultant hyperkinesis, vomiting, sweating, sneezing, nasal discharge, dermal mottling, high pitched screaming cry, diarrhea; and, resulting dehydration that can result in febrile seizures. Addicted neonate must be medically withdrawn with a cross dependent drug.

F. <u>Toxicology:</u>

1. Following can be readily detected on routine urine toxicology.

   a. Heroin & other morphine drugs: Heroin reported as morphine.
   b. Sedative-hypnotics barbiturates
   c. Stimulants
   d. Methadone
   e. Alcohol
   f. Phencyclidine
   g. Marijuana

2. These are not readily detected:

   a. Psychedelics
   b. Volatiles

G. <u>Major medical problems</u> (besides overdose and withdrawal crises)

1. **Route of administration:** Ulceration of nasal septum and injection sites.

2. **Ingesting/injecting infectious** agents leading to e.g. bacterial endocarditis, AIDS, hepatitis, etc.

3. **Adulterants:** e.g. MPTP is neurotoxic to the nigro-striatal system, resulting in Parkinsonian like symptoms which are permanent; talc, which is not eliminated by the body and is deposited in the lungs; etc..

H. Persons treated in programs receiving federal funds have legal guarantee of <u>confidentiality</u>. Can be broken only for "life-saving" emergency or court order of records.

IV. ALCOHOLISM

   A. Definitions

   1. **Type of alcohol use** (social, problem drinker, alcoholic).

      a. Social: Drinks as much as associates. Not to excess, and only on social occasions.

      b. Problem: Problems for self and society. Can stop.

      c. Alcoholic: **Can't stop once use initiated;** problems with health, law, social life, marriage, or work.

      Uniform Alcoholism and Intoxication Treatment Act: A person who habitually: lacks self-control with regard to the use of alcoholic beverages; and, uses alcoholic beverages to the extent that health, social or economic functioning is substantially impaired.

   2. Blackouts: carries on normal appearing behavior; however, no recall later on. Not a diagnosis in and of itself.

   B. Statistics and facts of alcohol use and alcoholism in U.S.A.

   1. Overall data:

      a. Lifetime prevalence=13% of Americans
      b. Only 5% are skid-row type.
      c. Males have higher rate than females (5 to 3)
      d. BAL of 100-150 mgm% is legal intoxication in all states.
      e. Prohibition: 1920-1933.
      f. Leads all drugs in economic loss and disease related deaths.
      g. Costs billions of dollars in lost work, medical care, etc..

   2. Accidents - alcohol related:

      a. 43% of non-pedestrian fatalities.
      b. 38% of pedestrian fatalities.
      c. At least 50% of all auto deaths.

3. Arrests, aggressive acts, suicide that is alcohol related:

   a. <u>41% of all arrests.</u>
   b. 24% of violent deaths.
   c. 50-64% of all homicides (killer or victim).
   d. 41% of all assaults.
   e. 34% of all forcible rapes.
   f. 29% of all other sexual crimes.
   g. 25-36% of all suicides.

4. Morbidity and hospital care of alcoholism:

   a. 20-50% of <u>all</u> hospital admissions have a <u>primary</u> diagnosis of alcoholism.

   b. One of 7 new admissions to state mental hospitals are alcohol related.

5. Hereditary and congenital effects:

   a. Genetic predisposition for some alcoholism is strongly suggested by:

      (1) Children of at least one alcoholic biologic parent have twice the incidence of alcoholism irrespective of whether the environment be alcohol abstinence or using.

      (2) Blue-yellow color blindness is associated with alcoholism.

      (3) **Concordance rates are distributed as Monozygotic> Dizygotic> Sibs regardless of if raised together or not.**

      (4) **In adopted children, the concordance rates are higher with the biologic parent than with the adoptive parent.**

      (5) Recent data on a genetic variation on the D_2 receptor being etiologic in alcoholism is questionable at this time.

      (6) Genetic implications are certainly clear from the pattern of intolerance of some Orientals to the effects of alcohol.

b. Pathophysiological effects in neonates of alcoholic mothers.

    (1) Newborns of alcoholic mothers have a higher than normal incidence of congenital abnormalities which is dose dependent. Low dose = hyperactivity like syndromes.

    (2) The most severe, The Fetal Alcohol Syndrome (FAS) is marked by:

        (a) Pre and post natal developmental retardation.
        (b) Mid-line abnormalities.
        (c) Cranio-facial abnormalities.
        (d) Limb dislocation.
        (e) Fistulas in heart and lungs.
        (f) Mental retardation.

C. <u>Pharmacological aspects of special importance:</u>

1. NOTE: Alcohol is a CNS **<u>depressant.</u>**

2. The following are altered by alcohol:

   a. Neurophysiological functioning
   b. General metabolic and somatic functioning
   c. Psychological arousal and response
   d. Perception and cognition

3. The influencing factors are:

   a. Blood Alcohol Level (BAL): a constant blood alcohol level is the best indication that tolerance has developed.
   b. The ascending or descending limb of the alcohol curve.
   c. Sex of the person who is drinking.
   d. Personality type.

4. Metabolism rate for average size person: 100 proof alcohol at 1 oz/hr. = 90% by oxidation, 10% by lungs and kidneys.

D. <u>Teenage use:</u>

   a. Probably most abused drug; second is marijuana.

    b. Factors influencing:
        (1)   Discretionary money
        (2)   Discretionary time
        (3)   Low participation in school activities
    c. Most introduced at home - with peer's stabilizing it.
    d. Recognized by behavior dysfunction and acute GI distress.

E. Female use

    a. ETOH metabolism is tied to menstrual cycle.
    b. Reportedly progresses more rapidly than in men. Effects more profound more rapidly than in the male.
    c. Usually develops in response to specific stress.
    d. Husbands more likely to abandon than vice versa. They protect wife up to a point, then abandon.

F. Cultural factors: Cultural stance toward alcohol consumption vs. disruptive behavior is major source of alcoholism control.

    1. Portugal, France, Spain, Italy, Germany are highest.
    2. U.S. in middle
    3. U.S. Ethnicity: Presented in order of magnitude of problems

        a. Native Americans (tribe specific: i.e., not all tribes)
        b. Spanish speaking (particularly the dispossessed)
        c. Whites
        d. Blacks
        e. Orientals

    4. Lower rates in Jews, and conservative Protestants; high in liberal Protestants and Catholics.
    5. Urban>Rural
    6. Social instability increases it.
    7. Legal sanctions decreases it.
    8. Family attitudes: drinkers produce drinkers.

G. Major physical illnesses Associated with Alcoholism:

    1. Cirrhosis (14% of alcoholics die from it)
    2. Alcoholic hepatitis
    3. Pancreatitis in absence of cholelithiasis
    4. Chronic gastritis - ulcers, etc.
    5. Nutritional disorders: Pellagra, Beriberi, vitamin deficiency
    6. Cancer, particularly of upper alimentary canal and bladder
    7. Esophageal varices

H. Alcohol Induced Organic Mental Disorders:

   1. **Alcohol Intoxication:** maladaptive behavior change due to recent ingestion of alcohol.

   2. **Alcohol Withdrawal Delirium (Delirium Tremens):** tremor and visual/tactile hallucinations.

   3. **Dementia Associated with Alcoholism (Korsakoff's):** marked confabulation, disorientation, and cognitive deficits.

   4. **Alcohol Idiosyncratic Intoxication (Pathologic Intoxication):** small amount --> gross intoxicated behavior. Frequently accompanied by aggressive and violent behaviors.

   5. **Alcohol Hallucinosis (Other alcoholic hallucinosis):** vivid and persistent hallucinations that begin **after cessation or reduction** of heavy alcohol consumption.

I. Withdrawal

   1. 1st sign is gross hand tremor.

   2. Other signs: nausea and vomiting, malaise, and weakness; ANS hyperactivity (tachycardia, increased blood pressure, sweating); anxiety; depression and/or irritability; orthostatic-hypotension.

   3. Can die from withdrawal convulsions.

J. Treatment: In addition to those treatments listed above in III.

   1. **Medical management:** titration with cross dependent drug (e.g. benzodiazepines); nutritional needs; close observation; warm supportive environment.

   2. **Antabuse:** works by accumulation of acetaldehyde. If a person has a blood level of antabuse and consumes alcohol they become nauseous, vomit, have stomach cramps, tremor, and malaise.

   3. **Alcoholics Anonymous (AA):** Self help program with no charge associated. Includes abstinence, introspection, public admission of alcoholism, and meeting dependency needs. Organized "12-step" program.

   4. **Employee Assistance Programs:** high rates of success secondary to job threat.

5. **"28 day" programs.** Focus on detoxification, support of abstinence, involvement of the whole "family" system, long term outpatient follow-up, usually associated with AA in some manner.

V. AGING

A. Some statistical data:

1. 4-5% of the persons >65 years of age live in institutions. Percent increases with each decade.
2. 65%-80% of older persons live with someone else.
3. 85% of elderly have one or more chronic conditions.
4. Males over 60 who are sexually active = 70%.
5. Females over 60 who are sexually active = 20%.
6. Older persons rate selves as "happier" than do middle-aged.
7. Older workers are equally productive and reliable, and no higher rate of accidents or absenteeism. 16% in labor force.
8. By 2000 A.D., an estimated 50% of population will be over 50 years old.

B. Physiologic State

1. In the aging process, humans lose about 50,000 neurons per day.
2. Ventricles expand.
3. Cerebral oxygen consumption falls.
4. Formation of plaques increases.
5. EEG abnormalities increase.

C. Biological changes in mental functioning: organic psychoses.

1. **Senile psychoses:** studies show positive relationship between the number of plaques and intellectual decrement.

2. **Cerebral arteriosclerosis:** structural changes associated with blood supply abnormalities (thrombi, hemorrhage, narrowing arterial walls).

3. **Alzheimer's Disease**

   a. Correlated with pathology in the ACH system. Exact etiology unknown at this time.

b. The three phase manifestation:

   (1) <u>Tendency toward forgetfulness</u>: for names, places, and appointments. Show a joking anxiety about it.

   (2) <u>Confusional phase</u>: Memory for recent events severely impaired. Earlier anxiety replaced by denial.

   (3) <u>Dementia phase</u>: severe disorientation; remote memory loss is added to the recent loss; concrete; no new learning; easily confused with environmental changes; eventually become apathetic; cannot care for self.

D. <u>Important factor in predicting total state of the individual as they age is how well integrated the person was before onset of the aging process</u>. Previous patterns predict aging patterns in all areas of social behavior and performance.

E. <u>Cognitive and Performance Changes</u>

   1. Longitudinal studies show little IQ test score change.
   2. **Verbal abilities hold up best.**
   3. **Perceptual motor and speed tests decline the worst.**
   4. **Memory:** Older people take longer to register impressions, lose impressions more rapidly, and are more susceptible to interfering effects.
   5. **Learning:** New learning takes longer
   6. **Reaction time:** Consistent decrease in rapidity with which people react. Very dependent upon physiological state of brain. If slow brain speed is partialed out (e.g., dominant EEG rhythm), reaction time is constant.

F. <u>Successful Aging</u>

   1. Dependent upon culture integrating elderly into its way of life. Elderly have difficulty if are excluded.

   2. <u>The more active the older person is in maintaining activities and attitudes from middle life, the more successful the aging process. If this isn't possible then replacing or substituting other activities is an assistance to successful aging.</u>

VI. **DEATH AND DYING/GRIEF AND BEREAVEMENT**

   A. <u>Death and Dying</u>: The question for the physician is never "Shall I tell?", but rather "How do I tell?"

1. **Elizabeth Kubler-Ross** identified five stages of the dying. These are not linear; i.e., the individual will come in and go out of these stages, but will be in one more than another.

    a. <u>Denial</u>: Patient may want to get another opinion. <u>"There has to be a mistake."</u>

    b. <u>Anger</u>: The anger is not personal anger at you, although it may be directed at you or a nurse, etc. <u>"Why me?"</u>

    c. <u>Bargaining</u>: Attempt to postpone death. Contracts are made here if they can be allowed to live. <u>"Please keep me alive til my son can graduate from medical school."</u>

    d. <u>Sadness</u>: at the realization that they will lose their life. <u>"There's no use trying any more."</u>

    e. <u>Acceptance</u>: "setting their house" in order and saying goodbye to significant others. <u>"I've had a good life."</u>

2. **Common maladaptive ways** medical personnel deal with the dying patient.

    a. Place them in a room at the end of the hall.
    b. Keep the door closed.
    c. "Protect" them from being tired out by others.
    d. "Nobody wants to talk about their own death."

3. The **prescribed method** of dealing with the dying patient is to:

    a. Allow them to talk about their feelings and thoughts.
    b. Do not give false hope.
    c. Assure that you will not abandon them.
    d. Keep involved in as many normal daily activities as possible.

4. Special considerations with **dying children**.

    a. 4-5 year old children generally have <u>no concept of death</u> as permanent. This begins to develop about age 7 or 8.

    b. Instead of death, <u>children fear most</u>:

    (1) Separation from parents
    (2) Mutilation
    (3) Rejection

c. Dealing with the dying child

   (1) Answer questions honestly.
   (2) Interact with the whole family.
   (3) Decrease tension.
   (4) Continue as normal childrearing as possible, e.g. don't let dying child terrorize others.
   (5) Don't alter the child's interests.

d. In dealing with the child having surgery and procedures which may endanger their life, capitalize on the knowledge of what the child fears most. Allow the parent to be in the room with the child as much as possible. Sleep there if is feasible. Allow parents to make the child's bed feed the child and generally take care of the child's needs.

5. There is a great deal of concern at this time about **the rights of a person to die.** If a person has been seriously maimed and/or is terminal, and is being kept alive presumably against their wishes, there is question as to whether they should be allowed to leave the hospital. There have been precedence cases where the patient has won the suit against the hospital to stop treatment and be released from hospital. There are no universal laws or guidelines but it is an active controversy.

6. **Living wills,** executed while the person is of sound mind. Can direct if heroic measures taken, donation of body parts, etc.

7. **Durable power of attorney for health:** someone appointed by the person in question, while of sound mind, who has authority to make decisions for life support systems or not, etc..

8. **Do Not Resuscitate (DNR) orders:** directions given by the patient to the physician regarding no resuscitation if the patient develops a compromising condition.

B. Grief and Bereavement (Mourning).

1. This section discusses the feelings and emotions that are present in the **person who survives the deceased.**

2. **Three general stages** in this process have been identified:

   a. Acute disbelief: lasts about 2 weeks
   b. Grief work: six months to 1 year. Reformulating relationship with the dead person.

c. <u>Resolution</u>: can enter into guilt free relationship with another.

3. **Prolonged grief** (more than 1 year) can be interpreted as a form of depression, except when there is traumatic loss of a child.

4. **Anniversary reactions**: sad feelings on significant dates associated with deceased. **NORMAL**.

5. Mourning when not complete may lead to mild pathology. At different age levels, this presents differently.

   a. <u>Infant</u> might protest, deny, and detach itself away. May die if mothering figure not replaced.

   b. <u>Child</u> in the latency stage may become jocular and hypomanic.

   c. <u>Adolescent</u> might turn to antisocial acting out (alcohol, other drugs, sexual activity, delinquent behavior, etc.).

   d. <u>Middle aged</u> frequently develop hypochondriacal symptoms.

   e. <u>Older persons</u>, like infants, may withdraw and die.

6. There is a question in the mourning process whether to medicate the individual. Grief is not a state but a process. The process must be completed for the person to adequately resolve the loss. Medication may delay the process.

   Immediate medication may be reasonable to allow the person to sleep if they have been awake for a protracted period of time. The continued use of sedatives/anxiolytics can postpone the grief-mourning process and solidify it into a chronic depression.

VII. **ATTITUDES**

   A. <u>Components</u>

   1. **A belief** about something regardless of the reality: e.g., cigarette smoking is harmful.

   2. **An affect**: e.g., cigarette smoke offends the person.

   B. <u>Changing attitudes</u>

   1. **Exposure over time**: e.g., minorities on TV programs.

2. Credibility of source: e.g., an M.D. endorsing a medication.
3. Using a white upper SES professional person.
4. Argue position contrary to self-interest: e.g., physician arguing for socialized medicine.
5. Conveys disinterest in influencing opinion: e.g., patient overhears M.D.'s hallway discussion of patient's condition.
6. Sleeper effect: no immediate change. At a later time, the source and information are separated leading to a change in attitude. Usually seen when the source is disliked.
7. Attach the change desired to an already emotionally strong and accepted object, e.g., "Call your mother long distance" results in shifted attitude to increase use of long distance calls.

VIII. PREJUDICE

A. <u>Definition</u>: a belief which is characterized by the over-simplification, over-generalization, and distortion of some small element of truth; not based on overall factual knowledge.
Is a prevalent-<u>harmful</u> attitude usually toward a subgroup of people.

B. Basic prejudicial attitudes are <u>formulated at a very young age</u>. Taught at a preverbal and precognitive level before the child can conceptually grasp what it is being taught. E.g., children recognize black and white racial differences by age 3. Prejudices (because they are attitudes) are not necessarily changeable by information but need emotional alteration.

C. The <u>personality of the prejudicial person</u> is one of authoritarian and irrational beliefs (e.g., Nazis, Ku Klux Klan, etc.).

D. <u>Mechanisms of prejudice (prejudging).</u>

1. **Displacement of aggression.** Frustration of basic impulse ⟶ aggression, which can't be expressed to appropriate frustrating object due to object's authority or status; or,

2. Fear of something in the one's own self recognized in others. Therefore they displace the aggression/fear on a "scapegoat."

3. **Scapegoating:** The object:

   a. must be easily identifiable, e.g. blacks vs. whites.
   b. must be accessible.
   c. must be unable to retaliate effectively; but enough to keep conflict going.
   d. usually has been scapegoated before.

   Scapegoating operates on the basis of the defense mechanism of displacement.

4. Social conformity appears to be key to prejudice.

5. Prejudice is negatively correlated with education and has a curvilinear relationship to church attendance.

6. Person prejudiced against over time takes on the attributes of the stereotypes.

IX. SUBCULTURE PARAMETERS

A. "Minorities" used here to designate a subgroup or subculture of persons. This may refer to race, ethnicity, religion, age, etc.

B. The subgroup effects may be such to encourage or discourage the expression of a given behavior (be it action or thought).

   1. The subculture may induce persons to indulge in behaviors which other subcultures do not condone. For example, in an Irish subculture, to intoxication is encouraged. In a Jewish subculture, such behavior is not condoned. Oriental culture encourages suffering pain in a stoic, non-complaining manner; however, Italian and Jewish subcultures encourage members to be verbal and descriptive about discomfort which they are feeling.

   2. The **generation subcultures** lead to different behaviors at given times. E.g., at the present time birth rates in America have become quite stable at the point where persons are only replacing themselves. Marriage rates, however, have decreased, and divorce rates have increased markedly.

C. Socio-economic status (SES)

1. SES is determined by education and occupation, not just money.

    a. SES and mental health: There is a positive correlation between better mental health and higher SES.

    b. SES and role differentiation. As general statements:

        (1) The lower the SES of the individual, the more sharply defined the sexual expectations for males and females.

        (2) The lower the SES, the more rigidity and non-flexibility in the expectations of individuals.

    c. SES and Language

        (1) Low SES tends to decrease "richness" of the environment and consequently retards the development of acquired skills like **LANGUAGE**, etc.

        (2) Besides grammatical forms, there is also language dealing with social amenities. **NOTE:** adherence or deviation from proprietary language is one major form of class distinction. You must learn to whom you say "Yes, sir", "Yes, ma'am", etc.; when to say "fuck" and when not to say "Screw you."

        (3) Low SES language is action oriented, not verbal-conceptual. Syntax and word arrangement is different. When these people try to enter majority society, they are speaking a second language and must translate. This leads to slowness and appearance of "dullness"--"doesn't catch on quickly."

D. Community organization and mental health:

1. The more disorganized the community, the greater the mental health problems. Community disorganization is correlated with mental illness.

2. Harlow did monkey studies on community disorganization and deprivation of attention and affection. His general findings:

   a. Decreased playfulness
   b. Increased fear and aggression
   c. Rejection of sexuality
   d. Rocking movements (self consoling?)

   These could be attenuated but not eliminated later in life.

E. <u>Small group relations</u>

   1. Total group participation results in less resistance to change.

   2. **Leadership** (Good leader)

      a. Maintains group membership--doesn't dominate through restriction.

      b. Organizes and stimulates production--defines and structures own and others' work.

      c. Promotes communication between self and others, and between others.

      d. Democratic vs. Authoritarian:

         (1) **Democratic atmosphere:** high level of friendly behavior between all members. Little scapegoating. Produces some reduced output, but production is sustained.

         (2) **Authoritarian atmosphere:** highest level of discontent; scapegoating; production high while leader present, totally stops when absent.

      e. Most efficient leader is one who helps all members feel important and secure.

   3. Usually small groups (e.g. a community) become cohesive in the face of external threat (e.g. disaster).

   4. Small groups promote discussion.

   5. **Families as Small Groups**

      a. <u>Nuclear families</u> = parents and children; primary group.

b. <u>Extended families</u> = nuclear family plus families of significant others, e.g. aunts, uncles, grandparents. Also called secondary group.

c. Families can scapegoat one member or one subfamily group.

F. <u>Sick role</u>

1. **Societal expectations**

   a. Exempt from normal social-role responsibilities
   b. Not to blame for their illness
   c. Are expected to get well
   d. Are expected to seek technically competent care

2. **Performance of the sick role**

   a. <u>Economic</u>

   (1) Financially hard pressed are reluctant to seek care.
   (2) On the job injury may intensify and prolong sick role secondary to **workman's compensation** processes.
   (3) Students and persons starting careers are reluctant to assume a sick role because of interruption.

   b. <u>Personal experiences</u>: if a person sees others getting benefits from illness they may seek the role.

   c. Society's view of a particular illness may affect a person's motivation to assume the sick role if they have the illness.

3. **Psychological factors in the sick role.**

   a. <u>Personality types</u>:

   (1) **dependent and demanding:** much emotion displayed.
   (2) **orderly and controlling:** little emotion displayed.
   (3) **dramatizing:** dramatic and seductive presentation.
   (4) **long-suffering/self sacrificing:** complaining and moaning about their bad fortune.
   (5) **guarded/suspicious:** concerned about harm and being taken advantage of.
   (6) **superior/special:** look for the best care.
   (7) **aloof/seclusive:** need maximum privacy.
   (8) **impulsive:** will act out their illness aggressively.

b. <u>Personal meaning of being sick</u>

    (1)   challenge
    (2)   inherent weakness
    (3)   enemy
    (4)   punishment
    (5)   a mechanism to cope with life's demands
    (6)   reprieve from responsibilities
    (7)   overwhelming loss
    (8)   positive experience: appreciate health more

c. <u>Methods of coping with illness</u>

    (1)   cognitive: minimize or vigilant focusing
    (2)   behavioral: tackling, competitiveness, avoidance

X. PSYCHOLOGICAL ASSESSMENT

A. <u>Statistical Basis of Psychological Assessment and Prediction</u>

1. Underlying all psychological assessment and prediction is an assumption of a **normal (binomial, Gaussian) distribution** to human behavior. In psychological assessment attempt to describe behavior as deviation from a statistical norm.

2. The basics of a normal distribution are the mean (expressed by the symbol X) and the standard deviation (S.D.) from that mean.

   a. Plus and minus 1 SD equals 68.02% of the normal curve.

   b. Plus and minus 2 SD equal 95.04% of the normal distribution.

   c. Plus and minus 3 SD equals 99.06% of the normal distribution. Greater than plus and minus 3 SD equals 100%.

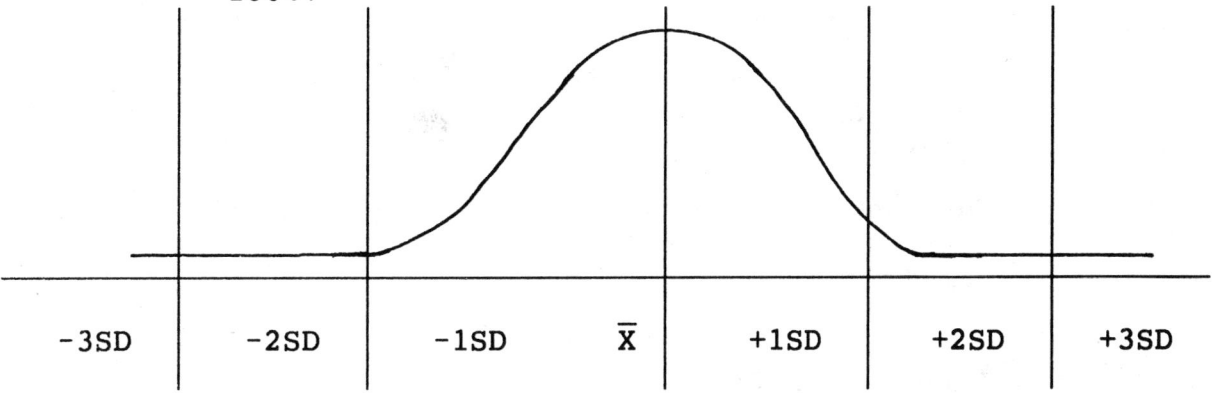

d. The <u>measures of central tendency</u> are:

    (1)   **Mean** ($\bar{X}$) = arithmetic average
    (2)   **Median** = the score which has 50% above and 50% below it
    (3)   **Mode** = most frequent score
    (4)   NOTE: For a perfectly symmetrical normal distribution, MEAN = MODE = MEDIAN
    (5)   **Range** = the highest to lowest scores

3. Graphic distributions:

   a. <u>Histogram</u>: a bar graph

   b. <u>Frequency Polygram</u>: a distribution with the number of persons getting a given score represented by an equivalent number of marks beside the given score,

       e.g. 75: XXXXXX
            74: XXXX
            73: XXXXXXXXXXXXXXXX

   c. <u>Scattergram</u>: each occurrence of an event on a two axis distribution is represented by a dot, e.g:

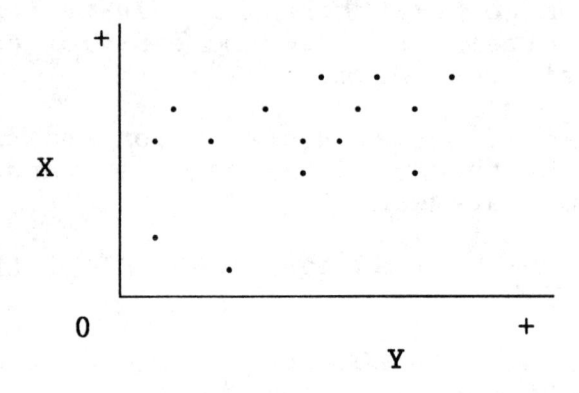

4. The statistic of prediction in <u>all</u> predictive material is the **CORRELATION** (<u>r</u>).

   a. Refers to the <u>relationship</u> between two variables. E.g., the <u>r</u> between height and weight is high. The <u>r</u> between the number of words a person produces and amount of creative ideas is low ("shallow brooks are noisy").

   b. The <u>r</u> statistic can only have values which range between -1.0 and +1.0.

c. The closer an r value to O, the less prediction there is; for example, an r of .10 (called a correlation coefficient) does not have good predictability.

d. When we speak of the r between two variables, the r is not a cause-effect statistic or statement. It can be interpreted three ways:

   (1)   A leads to B.
   (2)   B leads to A.
   (3)   A and B are both related through a third variable.

e. The sign on the r simply says whether two things are positively related or negatively related.

   (1)   **A positive sign** says as one variable increases the second variable increases.

   (2)   **A negative sign** says as one variable increases the other variable decreases.

   In review: the size of the r tells how much relationship there is between two variables, and the sign attached to the r tells the direction of the relationship.

f. r^2 represents the percent of variance explained by the relationship between two variables. E.g., if the r between two variables is +.70, then 49% of the variance between the two variables is in common.

5. **A "t" test** is a statistical procedure to determine if two samples are significantly different from each other. It uses the X and SD of each distribution to test for significance.

6. **An Analysis of Variance (ANOVA)** is similar to the "t" test but is used to determine if three or more samples are significantly different from each other. It can also test for significance of interaction between/among the three or more variables.

7. The chi-square (X^2) test is used to compare expected versus observed frequencies of an event. E.g. If the hypothesis is that the MCAT score doesn't predict medical school performance, and one looks at the number of first year medical students with an MCAT score above or below a given number (e.g. 7) who are in academic difficulty, a four-fold table is produced.

	MCAT <7	MCAT >7
No academic problems		
Academic Problems		

If MCAT scores are not predictive, one would expect an equal number of persons in the top two quadrants and an equal number in the bottom two quadrants. If one observes all academic problem students to be in the lower left quadrant and no academic problem students in the upper right quadrant, the observed versus expected is very different and therefore significant.

8. **Degrees of Freedom (df)**, is a concept that stands for the number of observations that are free to vary after certain restrictions have been placed on the data. The df for a given study are tied to the number of conditions and the number in the sample (usually N-1) for each of these.

   a. e.g., if 20 cases are to be divided between 2 categories, and you know 15 are in one category, then 5 must be in the other one. The df=1. I.e., 2-1.

   b. But if there are three categories, you must know how many are in two categories before you will know how many are in the third. The df=2. I.e., 3-1.

B. Research Design Concepts:

1. Experimental method means **use of controls**.

2. **Sample size:** There is dependence between the size of a sample and the size of the statistical test result

necessary to be significant. General rule: the larger the <u>N</u> of a sample, the smaller the size of the statistic necessary to be significant.

3. **Null hypothesis**: statement of **no difference** between conditions.

4. **Prospective studies** refer to making a hypothesis and then collecting data to test that hypothesis. Retrospective studies refer to those where the data has been collected and you then apply statistics to them to test their significance.

5. **Prevalence**: this is a term that is used to describe the <u>total</u> number of cases of a particular phenomenon.

6. **Incidence**: this term means the number of <u>new</u> cases of the particular disorder in a given time period.

7. **Double blind experiments**. Usually drug effectiveness studies where neither the subject nor the experimenter knows what the subject is getting. Used to remove experimenter bias.

8. **Random sample**: sampling where everyone in the population has an equal opportunity to be selected <u>ON EACH SAMPLING</u>.

9. **Cross sectional sample**: Different samples from different groups (e.g. age) taken at the same time.

10. **Longitudinal sample**: same sample followed over time.

11. **Concept of significance**: based on probability (gambling). States the "chance" of results occurring by chance alone. E.g., .05 level of significance means 5% probability of results appearing BY CHANCE ALONE. E.g. chance probability of drawing an Ace from a deck of 52 cards = 4/52 or 7.69%.

12. **Independent variable**: variable under experimental control (e.g. experimental drug being tried on given patients).

13. **Dependent variable**: variable influenced by the independent variable; e.g., with a given treatment (the independent variable) how many patients are cured.

14. **Diagnostic confidence:**

    a. One must consider four interpretations of a test result.

    (1) **True positive:** also called **SENSITIVITY:** the number of persons with an illness who manifest abnormal results on a test for that illness

    $$\text{Sensitivity} = \frac{\text{\# True positives}}{\text{\# all cases with the illness}} \times 100$$

    (2) **False positive:** also called Type II error. Test says it's there when it isn't.

    (3) **True negative:** also called **SPECIFICITY:** the proportion of people without an illness who do show a negative result on a test for that illness.

    $$\text{Specificity} = \frac{\text{\# True negatives}}{\text{\# all cases without the illness}}$$

    (4) **False negative:** also called Type I error. Test says it's not there but it is.

C. <u>Major Categories of Psychological Tests</u>

 1. **Intelligence tests:** The most popular and the valid for adults is the Wechsler Adult Intelligence Scale: Revised (WAIS-R); for young children, the <u>Stanford-Binet</u> is most valid; and for older children and adolescents, the Wechsler Intelligence Scale for Children-Revised (WISC-R) is the most valid. IQ scores are generally distributed in the following manner.

    a. Less than or equal to 69 = mentally defective
    b. 70 to 79 = borderline intelligence
    c. 80 to 89 = dull normal
    d. 90 to 109 = average
    e. 110 to 119 = bright normal
    f. 120 to 129 = superior
    g. Greater than or equal to 130 = very superior or genius.

NOTE: IQ test scores are highly correlated with education.

 2. **Achievement tests:** Achievement tests have been developed to assess the amount of material which an individual has accomplished. E.g., with children there

are tests that examine reading, spelling, and arithmetic skills of the child, and compare the child's scores to National norms. Another example of achievement tests are those <u>you</u> take as course examinations.

3. **Ability tests**: Ability tests presume to assess the aptitude a person has for a particular area of endeavor. For example, tests of creativity which presume to assess how creative an individual can be given a certain set of data. Ability tests also can be termed **Aptitude Tests**. E.g., the MCAT.

4. **Interest tests**: Interest tests DO NOT say anything about the person's intelligence, how much they have achieved, or their aptitude. They yield a statement of what the person is interested in. Typically these have been developed by giving a set of questions to "successful" persons in a given field e.g., medicine. Items successful persons respond to (and those they do not respond to) are used as a referent for a person trying to ascertain if their interest is in a particular area.

5. **Personality tests**: Tests which assess dimensions of an individual's personality. They are typically broken down into <u>subjective</u> versus <u>objective</u> personality tests.

   a. **Objective personality tests** are developed statistically without any regard to theory. The best example of this is the **Minnesota Multiphasic Personality Inventory (MMPI)**.

   b. **Subjective personality tests (Projective tests)**: have been developed from theories, e.g. psychoanalytic theory, and typically assume the "projective hypothesis." The <u>projective hypothesis</u>: when a person is faced with an ambiguous situation, they will project internal structure onto the external ambiguous situation. Therefore, we assume if a person is given an ambiguous stimulus, they will project their internal structure onto the ambiguous stimulus.

   c. The major personality tests are:

   (1) **Rorschach**: This test consists of very ambiguous ink-blots which presumably taps the unconscious dimensions of a person's personality functioning.

   (2) **Thematic Apperception Test (TAT)**: Consists of more structured stimulus pictures which are

ambivalent and presumably reveal more about preconscious personality.

  (3) **Sentence Completion**: Typically, the first part of a sentence is given with a blank and the person fills in the blank. There are no standard ways to score the sentence completion test.

 6. **Special Tests**: There are a series of psychological instruments constructed for very specific purposes.

  a. <u>Neuropsychological tests</u>. These are used to evaluate the integrity of the brain. <u>For this differential question the best battery of tests is the Halstead-Reitan Battery, or the Luria</u>. Another is the <u>Bender-Gestalt</u>. This is a visual sensory-motor task and indicates the level of development of motor skills.

  b. <u>Freedman and Rosenman</u>: <u>A & B Behavior Types</u>

   A Type = "running out of time"; correlated with coronary heart disease

  c. <u>Holmes & Rahe</u>: <u>The Social Readjustment Questionnaire</u> assesses the relationship between social changes (stress?) and disease.

XI. DIVORCE

A. <u>Statistics</u>: more than half of all marriages end in divorce.

 1. 1960 = 26 divorces/100 marriages
 2. 1970 = 48 divorces/100 marriages
 3. 1980 = 64 divorces/100 marriages

B. <u>Reactions of parents and children</u> to divorce are similar and in three stages:

 1. **Ego dystonic**: Shock and disbelief: denial of changed status; "everything is the same"; depression.

 2. **Ego syntonic**: Face the reality of true change, and accept the pluses and minuses of the new status.

 3. **Consolidation**: Work towards new identity.

C. <u>Etiology</u> of higher rate observed in this century apparently due to:

1. Altered basis for marriage.
2. Modern risks to marital stability.
3. Freer attitudes (legal, religious) toward divorce.

D. <u>Marital success</u> has higher success chance if:

1. Similar backgrounds and cultures (education, IQ, race).
2. Each individual can grow in the marriage.
3. The marital unit can grow and mature.

XII. **SUICIDE, HOMICIDE AND OTHER FORMS OF VIOLENCE**

A. <u>Suicide</u>

1. **Statistics:**

    a. <u>2nd (or 3rd depending on the study) leading cause of death</u> today in the 15-24 year old age range. Accidents are #1.

    b. <u>Annually</u>, 20,000-30,000 in USA (1988=30,407; 12.4/100,000). Two million in USA have tried. Overall is one of the 10 leading causes of death in America.

    c. <u>X-Cultural</u>

        (1)   High = Sweden, Germany, Japan
        (2)   Moderate = USA
        (3)   Low = Spain, Ireland, Egypt

    d. Between 25-36% are alcohol related.

    e. Increases in incidence after national crisis.

2. **Motivation**

    a. Depression: usually occurs when person is feeling better after depressive episode (about 3 months). **Best predictor is triad of hopelessness, helplessness and worthlessness.**

    b. "Revenge on others"

    c. Some think "accident proneness" is a suicidal corollary.

d. To avoid chronic painful (physical or emotional) condition.

   e. Adolescent suicide correlated with: bad love affair; family rejection of behavior e.g. grades; use chemical means, females> males, family physical and sexual abuse.

3. **Biochemistry:** 5-HIAA: Low levels have been found in the spinal fluid of depressed people and people who have killed themselves. Also low in the spinal fluid of persons who show antisocial, aggressive or impulsive personality traits.

4. **Attempters vs. Completers**

   a. <u>Attempters</u>: younger, female, impulsive and ambivalent, neurotic, personality disorders, chemically dependent, situational disorders, use medications in attempt.

   b. <u>Completers</u>: Older, male, lethal techniques, major affective disorders (NOTE: 40-70% of completers have a diagnosis of depression.), alcoholism (7-21% of alcoholics commit suicide), addicted, schizophrenic.

   Studies on completers show their circumstances were no worse than others. They had alternatives; they didn't see them.

5. **Serious persons who survived:** Poised between life and death with intense ambivalence about dying. Can't make plans (e.g., lunch date) because they expect to be dead. Felt/believed suicide was inevitable. They wanted a change in their life.

Demographic Factors in Suicide

	High Risk	Low Risk
Age	45 - Over	45 - Under

Risk steadily increases with age:

Children: Suicide is rare, but approximately 12,000 per year are hospitalized for self destructive acts.

Adolescents: Third most common cause of death (accidents and homicides are #'s 1&2). In those that try or succeed, there is a high incidence of parental abuse or neglect.

College students: Second most common cause. Accidents first.

Elderly: 10-16% of population but commit 23-25% of suicides.

1. There are major issues of illness and independence.
2. They are experiencing all types of losses.
3. They may be in abusive family situations of drugs and violence.

	High Risk	Low Risk
Sex	Male	Female

Males represent 3/4 of all suicides. Females attempt more.

	High Risk	Low Risk
Race	White	Non-White

Of males, 70% are white. Black male rate is increasing.

	High Risk	Low Risk
Religious preference	Protestant	Catholic

	High Risk	Low Risk
Marital Status	Separated, divorced, widowed	Single, married

	High Risk	Low Risk
Socio-economic Status	High and Middle	Lower

	High Risk	Low Risk
Employment	Unemployed	Employed

Unemployment undermines personal/familial stability and trigger other problems.

	High Risk	Low Risk
Living Arrangements	Alone	With Others

Person who is isolated or beginning to isolate themself.

	High Risk	Low Risk
Health	Poor	Good

	High Risk	Low Risk
Daily Routine	Changed (e.g., running, church attendance)	No Change

Most put order to their lives immediately prior to suicide.

	High Risk	Low Risk
Mental Condition	Nervous/Mental Disorder (includes alcoholism)	Normal

Almost 95% of patients who commit or attempt suicide have a diagnosed mental illness. Depression is the most common.

Alcohol: depressant drug and will exacerbate a depression.

Avoid the exacerbations of psychiatric illnesses.

Fulfill psychotic process: Voices telling to kill self.

Tends to run in families.

	High Risk	Low Risk
Disposition	Admitted to Psychiatric Center	Discharged to self or relative.

Most are undecided: gamble someone will find them.

Usually a person is only suicidal for a relatively brief period of time.

People discharged from mental hospital X34 more likely than general population. Most occur within 3 months after "improvement" of major depressive episode.

Contact with physician: Usually have been in contact with the physician in the recent past (e.g., 6 months).

	High Risk	Low Risk
Suicide note	Yes	No

If no note has been left, usually (8/10) there has been some suicide talk/warning: e.g., "You'd be better off without me."

	High Risk	Low Risk
Previous attempt	Yes	No

	High Risk	Low Risk
Method	Hanging, firearms jumping, drowning	Cutting, gas CO_2-poison

More women beginning to use guns (a more certain method) than drugs or gas. If drugs are used, usually the sedative-hypnotics, antidepressants, and anxiolytics.

	High Risk	Low Risk
Potential Consequence of method	Likely fatal	Harmless

	High Risk	Low Risk
Police description of condition of patient	Unconscious/ semi-conscious	Normal, disturbed drinking, ill

B. <u>Mechanisms of violence/aggression</u>

   1. **Neural mechanisms**

      a. Hypothalamus: Electrical stimulation leads to rage reactions in animals.

      b. Amygdala: Lesions in the medial aspects lead to increased aggressive behavior. Ablation leads to quiescence.

      c. Septum: Destruction leads to wild ferocious behavior.

   2. **Neurochemistry (Biochemistry)**

   Data from an NIMH and USN study of USN personnel who had severe acting-out problems and matched controls.

      a. Low 5-HIAA (metabolite of Serotonin, an Indolamine).

      b. High MHPG (metabolite of Norepinephrine/Epinephrine, which are Catecholamines).

      c. No change in HVA (metabolite of Dopamine, which is also a Catecholamine).

   3. **Genetics:**

      a. XYY genotypes: Tend to be tall, retarded and violent.

      b. New studies from the NIMH showing genetic linkages from twin and adoptive studies that are similar in nature to the data discussed on the genetics of alcoholism.

   4. **Modeling (Bandura):** Vicarious reinforcement. If a child sees another child rewarded for aggressive or violent behavior, an increase occurs in the amount of aggressive or violent behavior in the child which is observing.

   5. **Learning and reinforcement**

      a. Television violence only seems to lead to an increase in children's aggression/violence if behavior is rewarded.

      b. Aggression in adults is positively correlated with the use of physical punishment from their parents.

c. Aggressive children have no more frustration in their homes than non-aggressive children. Difference is in the amount of physical punishment received from their parents.

C. <u>Homicide (not premeditated)</u>:

1. Usually a **family affair**: a relative or an acquaintance.
2. Occurs at the **height of emotions** ("irresistible impulse").
3. Murdered person **often provoked** it in some way.
4. Most people who commit homicide **do it only once**.
5. Usually on **weekends** (Friday night through Sunday), close to pay day, and substance abuse (alcohol=50%) involved.
6. Usually **INTRA-racial**

   a. Black on Black= 94%
   b. White on white= 86%

7. Other data

   a. Blacks have the highest rates
   b. More in poor persons
   c. More in urban ghetto
   d. More in Catholic versus protestant

D. <u>Spouse Abuse</u>

1. Usually ETOH related
2. History of violence: same game--different players
3. Battered spouse

   a. <u>3 phases</u>: a cycle.

      (1) **Curse, throw things** (duration may be days-weeks).
      (2) **Battering**: resembles temper tantrum; nothing can stop it
      (3) **Treats battered spouse very well**

   b. <u>Batterer</u>=insecure/immature; battered spouse=emotional glue

   c. In part, is <u>culturally determined</u>.

E. <u>Rape</u>

1. Prevalence (guesstimates)

   a. 3.5% - 10% are reported

b. Typical rapist is young, disadvantaged, sexually naive, a victim of child (sexual) abuse, and in 50% of cases, is known to some degree by the victim.

c. Rape is a violent, not sexual act.

d. Once a rape has started, there is no known universal response that will stop the rapist.

XIII. SOCIAL STRESS AND PHYSICAL CONCOMITANTS

A. The <u>Life Stress Social Readjustment Rating Scale</u> was developed by Holmes and Rahe. It has 43 items.

1. The top seven life events and their values on the scale are:

    - Death of spouse   100
    - Divorce   73
    - Marital Separation   65
    - Jail Term   63
    - Death of close family member   63
    - Personal injury or illness   53
    - Marriage   50

2. Other life events of less value include:

    - Being fired   47
    - Death of close friend   37
    - Wife begin or stop work   26
    - Change in schools   20
    - Vacation   13
    - Christmas   12

B. <u>Consequences of scores</u>: scores cumulative for a year.

1. Score = or > 300 (cumulative for a year) = had serious problems like serious depression or heart attacks.

2. Score 150 - 300: had less serious problems, e.g. gastritis, ulcer

3. Score 0 - 150: had less serious problems, e.g. mononucleosis.

EXAM QUESTIONS - SECTION TWO

INSTRUCTIONS: Each of the questions or incomplete statements below is followed by five suggested answers or completions. Select the one that is BEST in each case.

1. In Freudian theory, a child who has begun to cathect a parent of the opposite sex and display some "fear" of the parent of the same sex would be in which stage of psychosexual development?

    1) Oral
    2) Anal
    3) Phallic/urethral
    4) Latency
    5) Genital

2. All of the following are considered to be functions of the ego EXCEPT:

    1) defense mechanisms
    2) delayed gratification
    3) perception
    4) personal values
    5) reality testing

3. In Erikson's theory of psychological tasks, which of the following is NOT a correct task?

    1) Integrity vs. Despair
    2) Industry vs. Inferiority
    3) Intimacy vs. Isolation
    4) Generativity vs. Stagnation
    5) Identity vs. Shame & Doubt

4. Characteristics of the General Withdrawal Syndrome in neonates include all of the following EXCEPT.

    1) Afebrile seizures
    2) Dermatologic mottling
    3) Diarrhea
    4) Hyperkinesis
    5) Vomiting

5. There are some similarities between homosexuals and transvestites. All of the following characteristics are shared EXCEPT:

    1) Occurs in both sexes
    2) Cross-dressing
    3) Value the penis
    4) Usually do not seek sex change surgery
    5) Frequently live a very satisfying life overall

6. Masturbation reportedly occurs in women at the rate of:

    1) 40%
    2) 50%
    3) 60%
    4) 70%
    5) 80%

7. The DEA (Drug Enforcement Agency) is concerned with:

    1) The safety of chemical preparations for human consumption.
    2) Planning of federal monies in the area of drug abuse.
    3) Are responsible only for security of controlled substances.
    4) Providing federal support for drug education prevention and treatment.
    5) Major responsibility for licensing methadone maintenance programs.

8. In a crisis management of persons who abuse drugs, there are certain drugs of abuse from which persons often die if they are abruptly withdrawn from the substance. Which of the following preparations constitutes a danger of death from abrupt withdrawal?

    1) Stimulants
    2) Sedative hypnotics
    3) Psychedelics
    4) Opiates
    5) Volatiles

9. By all indications, the most popular drug of abuse among young people today is:

    1) Stimulants
    2) Marijuana
    3) Alcohol
    4) Tobacco
    5) Sedative hypnotics

10. Children of at least one alcoholic biologic parent have what incidence of alcoholism compared to a control group irrespective of whether the environment be alcohol abstinence or using?

    1) One time
    2) Two times
    3) Three times
    4) Four times
    5) Five times

11. What percentage of all arrests are alcohol related?

    1) 41%
    2) 64%
    3) 29%
    4) 36%
    5) 24%

12. With regard to cognitive and performance changes as a person ages, which of the following statements is NOT correct?

    1) Intelligence tests on longitudinal studies indicate very little loss.
    2) Perceptual motor and speed tests decline the most.
    3) Older people take longer to register impressions and are most susceptible to interfering effects on memory.
    4) New learning takes longer but older people can and do improve performances.
    5) There is no decrease in the rapidity with which people react to stimuli as they age.

13. Which of the following behaviors would you judge to be an inappropriate way that medical personnel deal with a patient who is imminently terminal?

    1) Place them in a room where there is a great deal of traffic.
    2) Order complete lab work for the last day of life so the record will be complete.
    3) Allow them to have as many visitors as they wish.
    4) Making self available to talk with the dying patient about their death.
    5) If they are in pain, order sufficient medication frequently enough to control it, regardless of the addiction potential.

14. In the grieving and mourning process, we know that at different stages, the mourning can take different forms. Which of the following is an INCORRECT statement?

    1) The infant might protest, deny, and detach itself away.
    2) A child in the latency stage would probably be jocular and perhaps hypomanic.
    3) A child in the adolescent stage might turn to anti-social acting out.
    4) Middle-age persons quite frequently turn to hypochondriacal symptoms.
    5) Elderly persons typically are relieved and feel somewhat released.

15. The correlation between socio-economic status (SES) and mental health is:

    1) Positive
    2) Negative
    3) Zero
    4) Curvilinear
    5) Rectilinear

16. The correlation between the measure of community organization and mental health is:

    1) Positive
    2) Negative
    3) Neutral
    4) Curvilinear
    5) Rectilinear

17. The correlation expresses numerically something about two variables. Which of the following is an INCORRECT way to interpret the correlation statistic?

    1) Variable 1 causes Variable 2.
    2) Variable 1 is associated with Variable 2.
    3) Variable 2 is associated with Variable 1.
    4) Variable 2 and Variable 1 are both related to a third variable.
    5) Variable 1, Variable 2, and Variable 3 are related to a fourth variable.

18. The Thematic Apperception Test (TAT) is an example of what type of psychological test?

    1) Ability
    2) Achievement
    3) Intelligence
    4) Interest
    5) Personality

19. A 14-year-old male is brought into your office by his father. They have had an argument over the length of his hair. The boy reacts to you in a hostile, argumentative fashion even though you have reasonably long hair, a beard, and have not provoked the reaction from the young man. You would say that the phenomenon which is occurring is:

    1) Acting out
    2) Countertransference
    3) Regression
    4) Synthesis
    5) Transference

20. In Transactional Analysis theory, all of the following are types of transactions EXCEPT:

    1) Parallel transactions
    2) Cross transactions
    3) Complimentary transactions
    4) Ulterior transactions
    5) Intimate transactions

21. Masturbation reportedly occurs in what percentage of men?

    1) 65%
    2) 75%
    3) 85%
    4) 90%
    5) 95%

22. Which of the following statements regarding incest is NOT correct?

    1) Defined as sexual intercourse between two persons forbidden by law to marry because of close relation by blood or marriage.
    2) Incest is universally taboo.
    3) The most common form is between father and son.
    4) Mother/son incest is rare.
    5) Reportedly, the offenders are most often members of a fundamentalist religion and are lower socio-economic status (SES).

23. Which of the following is a major alcohol associated illness?

    1) Endocarditis
    2) Renal calculi
    3) Horner's syndrome
    4) Cirrhosis
    5) Meningitis

24. With regard to children who have debilitating and terminal illness, their greatest fear is:

   1) Pain
   2) Death
   3) Separation from parents
   4) What will become of their pets
   5) Being anesthetized

25. The correlation between socio-economic status (SES) and degree of role differentiation is:

   1) Positive
   2) Negative
   3) Zero
   4) Curvilinear
   5) Rectilinear

26. In the prediction statistic, the correlation, the value which would have the most predictive power would be:

   1) +.95
   2) -.35
   3)   0
   4) -1.0
   5) +.65

27. If a person scores an IQ of 120, you would classify him in what range of intelligence?

   1) Normal
   2) Average
   3) Bright-Normal
   4) Superior
   5) Very Superior

28. The terms "incidence" and "prevalence" differ in that:

   1) Incidence means the number of new cases.
   2) Incidence refers to mutually inclusive events only.
   3) Prevalence means the total number of cases minus the past year's cases
   4) Prevalence is a theoretical concept while incidence is based on data.
   5) The sampling distribution of prevalence statistics is unknown.

EXAM QUESTIONS - SECTION TWO

Answer Key

1.	3	11.	1	21.	5
2.	4	12.	5	22.	3
3.	5	13.	2	23.	4
4.	1	14.	5	24.	3
5.	1	15.	1	25.	2
6.	3	16.	1	26.	4
7.	3	17.	1	27.	4
8.	2	18.	5	28.	2
9.	3	19.	5		
10.	2	20.	5		

SECTION THREE: PSYCHOPATHOLOGY

I. ASSUMPTIONS AND RATIONALE 131

II. DEFENSE MECHANISMS 131

    A. Definition
    B. Common Ego Defense Mechanisms
    C. Normal Stress Management

III. DIFFERENTIAL DIAGNOSIS FLOW CHART 135

IV. MAJOR CATEGORIES OF PSYCHOPATHOLOGY 136

    A. Psychoses
    B. "Neuroses"
    C. Personality Disorders
    D. Psychological Factors Affecting Physical Condition
    E. Adjustment Disorders
    F. Genetics and Behaviors

V. CROSS THEORETICAL COMPARISONS 155

VI. SPECIAL PROBLEMS OF CHILDREN 158

    A. Developmental Disorders
    B. Disruptive Behavioral Disorders
    C. Anxiety Disorders of Childhood and Adolesence
    D. Physical Disorders
    E. Gender Identity Disorders
    F. General Notes on Childhood Disorders

VII. INCIDENCE/ PREVALENCE STATISTICS OF 167
     EMOTIONAL ILLNESS

    A. In Depth Studies
    B. NIMH Survey
    C. Hospitalization Data
    D. Socio-economic Status (SES) and Mental Illness

EXAMINATION QUESTIONS AND ANSWERS 169

SECTION THREE: PSYCHOPATHOLOGY

I. ASSUMPTIONS AND RATIONALE

Conflicts in living are the same for all persons. The manner in which the conflicts are handled makes the difference between whether one is "normal," psychotic, neurotic, a personality disorder, a psychophysiologic converter, an adjustment disorder, etc. I.e., humans differ regarding their mechanisms for handling conflict. That difference may be genetic, inherited, learned, cultural, etc.

A. Persons with psychotic symptoms have few effective defense mechanisms to deal with conflicts. Probably anyone can be made acutely psychotic by increasing conflict to the point that coping strategies normally used cannot handle the associated affect.

B. Persons with anxiety, dissociative, or psychosomatic symptoms handle conflicts with defense mechanisms at an unconscious level. Their symptoms are a combination of the underlying impulse and the defense mechanism. Symptoms EGO DYSTONIC; they bother the person.

C. Persons with personality disorders handle conflicts with life-long behavior pattern. Identifiable early. Their behaviors bother other persons not them. They are EGO SYNTONIC for the patient.

II. DEFENSE MECHANISMS

A. Definition: Defense mechanisms handle issues that produce conflict. They prevent awareness of the feeling or urge. Characteristics of defense mechanisms are:

1. **Unconscious:** The person is not aware of them.

2. **Not pathological:** Most defense mechanisms are used regularly by healthy people; desirable or undesirable consequences depend upon the circumstances, the manner, and the extent of use.

3. One knows a defense mechanism is being utilized when the behavioral manifestations (coming out of the defense mechanism) are "**too much.**" For instance, Shakespeare's description of Lady MacBeth's behavior, "Me thinks the lady doth protest **too much.**"

4. To identify a specific defense mechanism at work, look for the basic **underlying feeling** or urge that is operating and see what the person does with it. E.g.,

if someone continually makes the statement, "I do not get angry with my child," consider the defense mechanism of denial is in operation since parents quite normally experience anger with their children.

5. **The healthy person switches between defense mechanisms and does not use just one. The healthy person does not use defense mechanisms that grossly distort reality.**

6. Allows for partial fulfillment of the urge.

B. <u>Common ego defense mechanisms.</u>

1. **Repression** is the central defense mechanism. The <u>INVOLUNTARY</u> exclusion of a conflictual thought, impulse, or memory from awareness. Feeling component of that thought, urge, or memory <u>is still present</u> and <u>subjectively experienced as e.g. anxiety</u>.

    The remaining defense mechanisms are ways that people deal with the feeling component of the repression. One often finds there is the basic defense mechanism of repression coupled with another defense mechanism. Repression is managing the original conflicted thought, impulse, or memory. The second defense mechanism is handling the anxiety component.

2. **Suppression:** The conscious analog of repression; <u>INTENTIONAL exclusion of material from consciousness</u>; e.g., you accidentally spill a glass of red wine on the hostess's white gown. You make a conscious effort to "suppress" the entire incident.

3. **Introjection:** Assimilation of the object into one's own "ego and/or superego." E.g., in a child, the values, etc., of the parents become the child's.

4. **Identification:** Similar to introjection but is of less intensity and completeness. Unconscious modeling of oneself upon another. E.g., a resident might assume a similar mode of dress and manner that is displayed by an admired attending.

5. **Displacement:** Displacing the feelings, urges, or emotional component of one "object" to another object. E.g., a salesman is angered by a prospective customer. When he returns home he punishes one of his children overly harshly for misbehavior. He displaced anger from the customer to the child.

6. **Projection:** Place one's own feelings or impulses onto another. E.g., a person who is fears their achievements are not good enough continually attacks those of others.

7. **Reaction Formation:** Turning the impulse/feeling into its opposite. E.g., a person upset by his own sexual drives may become a censor of "X-rated" movies; and, partial fulfillment of underlying drive is attained.

8. **Sublimation:** Turning the urge into something socially acceptable. E.g., a husband is unhappy with his sex life, but won't have an extra-marital affair. He may paint his house when his wife is out of town. <u>This is the healthiest defense mechanism because it involves conscious control</u>.

9. **Compensation:** Encountering failure or frustration in one sphere of activity, one overemphasizes another. For example, a boy with residual muscle damage from poliomyelitis becomes an outstanding debater.

10. **Rationalization:** Offering a socially acceptable and logical explanation for an act or decision that was produced by an unconscious or unverbalized impulse. This is not inventing a story to fool someone else since it misleads the person who is rationalizing as well as the listener. E.g., a mother who is very angry with her child might refuse the child some candy stating she is protecting him from cavities.

11. **Isolation:** Splitting off emotional components from a thought. E.g., medical student dissecting a cadaver is not emotionally distressed bu cutting up a body.

12. **Denial:** Failure to recognize obvious implications or consequences of a thought, act or situation. E.g., a woman having an extramarital affair gives no thought to the possibilities of pregnancy even though her husband has had a vasectomy. A primitive defense mechanism that is almost always pathological in adults.

    a. The central defense mechanism in substance abuse.

    b. The central defense mechanism in not seeking treatment for an obviously pathologic condition.

    c. In some conditions (persons with a cardio-vascular accident, chronic terminal condition, etc.) some denial is healthy. E.g. the person doesn't prematurly give up and become a depressed and crippled person.

13. **Conversion:** Conflicts are represented by physical symptoms involving portions of the body <u>innervated by sensory or motor nerves</u>. **This defense mechanism is always pathological because limits full functioning.** E.g., conversion blindness.

14. **Somatization:** Conflicts are represented by physical symptoms in body systems innervated by the sympathetic and parasympathetic system. E.g., peptic ulcers.

15. **Regression:** Going back to an earlier level of maturation. E.g., during physical illness, people become demanding and generally obstreperous. In physical illness is NORMAL.

16. **Dissociation:** The splitting of a group of thoughts or activities from the main portion of consciousness. E.g., a politician works vigorously for integrity in government and simultaneously engages in businesses involving a conflict of interest. He is not consciously hypocritical and sees no connection between the two activities. This is the defense mechanism at work in Multiple Personality.

17. **Intellectualization:** Controlling feelings, affect, and/or impulses by thinking about them, not experiencing them. Characteristic of highly educated persons and adolescents.

18. **Splitting:** Separates issues/people into polar opposites, not allowing for gradations. E.g., issues are black or white, good or bad, right or wrong. Central to Borderline Personality Disorder.

C. <u>Normally, stress is handled by;</u>

1. A wide variety of non-pathologic defense mechanisms.
2. Rehearsing how to handle a situation.
3. Checking one's appearance.
4. Self reinforcement; e.g., saying to oneself, "great job!"

III. DIFFERENTIAL DIAGNOSIS FLOW CHART

When making a diagnosis, one operates from observed or reported data on a given patient, which might be a behavior, thought, feeling or emotion. The first decision is if the person is psychotic, based upon 1) whether the person can care for himself, 2) has gross personality disorganization and 3) are there grossly disturbed interpersonal relations. The relative organic status is decided from the sensorium section of the Mental Status Exam. The other components of this chart are self explanatory.

```
                    BEHAVIOR, THOUGHTS
                    FEELINGS, EMOTIONS
                            |
                  Psychotic or Nonpsychotic
          ┌─────────────┴─────────┐         ┌──────────┴──────────┐
      ORGANIC         FUNCTIONAL          ORGANIC           NONORGANIC
      BRAIN                                BRAIN
      SYNDROME     Schizophrenia           SYNDROME
                   Paranoid Disorders
      ┌───┴───┐    Bipolar Disorders       ┌───┴───┐
   Acute   Chronic Major Depressive     Acute   Chronic
                   Disorder                              ┌──────┴──────┐
                                                    Uncomfortable  Uncomfortable
                                                      To Self       To Others
                                                                        |
                                                                   Personality
                                                                    Disorders
                                    ┌───────────┴───────────┐
                              Physical Symptoms       Emotional Symptoms
                              ┌──────┴──────┐         Anxiety Disorders
                          Autonomic     Voluntary     Dissociative Disorders
                            N.S.          N.S.        Adjustment Disorders
                                                      Dysthymic Disorders
                          Psychological  Somatoform   Cyclothymic Disorders
                          Factors        Disorders
                          Affecting
                          Physical
                          Conditions
```

IV. MAJOR CATEGORIES OF PSYCHOPATHOLOGY

   A. PSYCHOSES

      1. In general:

         a. Overall incidence unknown: in all cultures and societies.

         b. Definition: Psychotic level of dysfunction. Is a statement of severity, not a diagnostic entity. Mental functioning so impaired as to:

            (1) interfere grossly with the capacity to meet ordinary demands of life; e.g., provide one's own shelter.

            (2) lead to gross personality disorganization; the person appears bizarre in their behavior.

            (3) grossly disrupt interpersonal (object) relations.

            (4) Gross disturbances in memory, perception, and language: (if these are present, probably dealing with an organically based psychosis, not a functional one).

         c. Three types: Thought Disorders, Affective Disorders and Organic Brain Disorders/Syndromes.

      2. Thought Disorders: occur in a clear Sensorium.

         a. The inability to recognize reality. The term reality testing means "can the person check out internal experience with others to find if it is 'real' or not?" Thought disorder is diagnosed in terms of a disruption in the process of thought or the content of thought in the presence of a clear level of consciousness.

            (1) Process: too much or too little of: productivity (flight of ideas; spontaneity; mutism; echolalia-echoing what is heard); continuity: circumstantiality; intrusive thinking.

                Additional forms of abnormality: over-inclusion (the person's thoughts simply will not come to any logical conclusion); neologisms (new words which have no meaning); looseness of association-words put together in sentences that are meaningless, e.g., "word salad".

(2) Content

(a) **Autistic** (has meaning only to the individual) versus logical.

(b) **Concrete** versus abstract.

(c) **Delusional**: a false fixed belief system which is not shared by the majority of peers; and not changeable by logic.

(d) **Illusionary**: a misinterpreted sensory experience

(e) **Hallucinatory**: a sensory experience for which there is not adequate sensory stimulation. Exclude dreams and "after effect".

b. There are seven subtypes of thought disorders

(1) **Schizophrenia**

(a) 1% of the population is schizophrenic. 25% of all new hospital admissions are for schizophrenia. 50% of all residents of state institutions are schizophrenics. Many homeless are schizophrenic and constitute a large health care problem.

(b) Usual onset in adolescence or late adolescence.

(c) Etiology: Schizophrenia is best regarded as a group of disorders with multiple interacting causes with expression in a final common pathway.

i) **Heredity or Genetics**: children with two schizophrenic parents have 40% chance of being schizophrenic. If one member of a monozygotic twin pair is affected, the risk is 80% for the other twin becoming schizophrenic.

REMEMBER: Monozygotic > Dizygotic > Sibs

ii) **Anatomical Sites**: dysfunctions in the septum, temporal lobes, limbic system and reticular activating system have been implicated.

iii) **Biochemistry**: Most important at this time is the Catecholamine or Dopamine Theory of schizophrenia. See Section 1 for other neurotransmitters involved. Too many D_2 receptors may be present or involved.

iv) **Familial Factors**: Core conflict= Trust/Mistrust.

    a) **Double Bind Hypothesis** (Bateson): two conflicting messages are sent to the person, each demanding a response. The victim is not allowed to comment on the bind and may not leave the field. E.g., a parent says to a child, "Don't do everything I tell you to do." While this theory has a good deal of validity, one finds these communications in other families.

    b) **Parenting**: (Jacque Schiff): dysfunctional parents transmit three statements to the child:

        1) Parents come first.
        2) You are no good.
        3) Outside world is dangerous.

v) **Socio-cultural**

    a) Apparently schizophrenia occurs in all cultures

    b) Predominance in lower SES classes and slum areas. May reflect persons who cannot adequately care for themselves or compete, drifting to slums where demands for performance are less. Low SES environments don't cause the disease; however, they do render it difficult to treat.

(d) Bleuler's Four A's of Schizophrenia.

i) **Autism**: day dreaming/self-centered fantasies; tendency to have idiosyncratic meanings to things rather than consensually validated meaning; ideas of reference (thinking emphasis on the self).

- ii) **Affective Disturbance**: mood is flat (bland) or inappropriate; or split between the mood and thought content (laughing at a parent's death).

- iii) **Associative Disturbance**: successive ideas related to each other in an unusaul manner. E.g., predicate logic: "Jesus was a man with a beard, I'm a man with a beard, I'm Jesus."

- iv) **Ambivalence**: two opposite feelings toward the same thing, usually of equal strength. E.g., simultaneously loving and hating a parent. "I love my mother that bitch!"

(e) The DSM-III-R diagnostic criteria for schizophrenia include:

- i) **delusions**: incoherence or marked **loosening of associations; catatonic** behavior; flat or grossly **inappropriate affect; bizarre delusions**: (being controlled by external forces, thought broadcasting [thoughts get out of the head and are audible to others], thought insertion [others put thoughts into the head], thought withdrawal [thoughts are plucked out of the mind]).

- ii) prominent hallucinations: running commentary, or 2 or more voices conversing with each other for extended periods of time.

- iii) Deterioration from a previous level of functioning in areas of work, social relations, self care. Of at least 6 months duration

(f) Prognosis

a) Drug treatment has reduced the length of hospitalization and the quantity of suffering, but the long term (twenty year) follow up has not changed.

b) In favor of better prognosis:

    c) Late onset
    d) Well socialized premorbid behavior
    e) No familial history of schizophrenia
    f) Affective symptoms
    g) A precipitating stress
    h) Acute onset

(g) <u>Sub-Types of Schizophrenia</u>

    i) **Schizophrenia, Disorganized Type**

    <u>Incoherence, marked loosening of associations, grossly disorganized behavior</u>

    Flat or grossly inappropriate affect (e.g. strikingly silly).

    ii) **Schizophrenia, Catatonic Type:** Major striking feature is <u>disturbed motor activity</u> (either extremely agitated or extremely stuporous to the point of no movement whatsoever.)

    Especially marked with catatonic schizophrenia is "waxy flexibility" (place their extremities in a position, and they will hold that position for a protracted period of time.) There may also be stupor or mutism, negativism, rigidity, voluntary posturing, or excitement (purposeless and not influenced by external stimuli).

    iii) **Schizophrenia, Paranoid Type:** Major feature is <u>disturbed thoughts</u>. Has delusions usually of persecution/ grandeur or jealousy. Develops later than other types and stable over time. May be aggressive, angry or fearful. May have auditory hallucinations of a single theme. <u>Best prognosis of the different subtypes.</u>

    iv) **Schizophrenia, Undifferentiated Type:** These persons may display the the signs and symptoms of schizophrenia; however, there are no one group of prominent symptoms to allow classification above.

v) **Schizophrenia, Residual Type:** History of a previous schizophrenic episode; however, at present they do not display the major symptoms. In partial remission. May have minor signs of less severe symptoms (e.g. social isolation and withdrawal; impairment in role function; peculiar behavior; impaired hygiene; odd beliefs; lack of interest/initiative; etc.).

(h) <u>Treatment</u>

i) Antipsychotic medications

ii) Environmental manipulations (milieu therapy, reward systems, total push, sheltered living).

iii) Psychotherapy

<u>Interventions will be discussed in Section Four</u>.

(2) **Brief reactive psychosis:** Acute psychotic episode of <u>up to one month duration</u> after a stress event. Symptoms: extreme turbulence and disturbance in behavior with gross deterioration of personality. Excellent prognosis if the stress is well managed.

(3) **Schizophreniform Disorder:** Differentiated from schizophrenia and brief reactive psychosis by time. Is <u>more than two weeks but less than six months</u>. Form is similar to schizophrenia except more acute onset and turbulent. Persons usually had better premorbid adjustment and mild familial history of schizophrenia.

(4) **Schizo-Affective Disorder:** Both schizophrenia and major affective disorder elements are present.

(5) **Delusional (Paranoid) Disorder (Paranoia):** Do <u>NOT</u> have flat or inappropriate affect, hallucinations, or markedly bizarre delusions. <u>DO</u> have one or more delusions of grandiosity, jealousy, persecution or somatic illness. Later in onset, often associated with immigration or emigration, or other severe stress.

(6) **Induced Psychotic Disorder (Shared Paranoid Disorder):** Delusion develops which is shared with another person. First person usually had a previous psychotic disorder diagnosis, and the second was not psychotic prior to the onset of the induced delusion. Sometimes referred to as a "folle a deux."

(7) **Psychotic Disorder Not Otherwise Specified (Atypical Psychosis):** Most common use of this classification is when there is insufficient information to make a diagnosis or the symptoms don't fit another diagnostic group.

3. Mood Disorders

   a. <u>The Depressive Syndrome</u> (major or minor proportion)

      (1) **Dysphoria (feeling bad or down) must be present.**

      (2) **AND five of the following must be present in the same two-week period:**

         (a) Sleep disturbance (too much or too little)
         (b) Appetite and weight change
         (c) Decreased enjoyment/sex (**anhedonia**).
         (d) Guilt/self reproach/worthlessness feelings
         (e) Suicidal ideas/plans/actions; recurrent thoughts of death. <u>**Suicide is serious danger in depression.**</u>
         (f) Agitation/retardation of movements
         (g) Decreased concentration
         (h) Decreased energy/easy fatigue

      (3) **In adolescents, the signs and symptoms of depression include withdrawal, decreased school performance, substance abuse, delinquency, and promiscuity.**

      (4) **Depressive Syndrome appears in physical illnesses**, sometimes as the presenting complaint: post partum, post myocardial infarction (where it leads to poor compliance), liver disease, lung cancer, pancreatitis, alcoholism, AIDS, etc..

      (5) **Simply feeling sad doesn't constitute depression;** and grief reaction should not be misdiagnosed as depression.

(6) **Depressive illness is the most overlooked mental disorder in America.**

b. <u>The Manic Syndrome</u>: There must be positive symptoms present. These include the following.

   (1) **Euphoria:** A period of abnormally and persistently elevated, expansive, or irritable mood.

   (2) Three of the following:

      (a) <u>Inflated self esteem</u> (can be delusional grandiosity)
      (b) <u>Decreased need for sleep</u>
      (c) <u>Pressure to talk</u>
      (d) <u>Racing thoughts</u> or flight of ideas
      (e) <u>Distractibility</u> (impaired attention)
      (f) <u>Increased goal-directed activity</u> (social, occupational, sexual) or physical restlessness
      (g) <u>Excessive involvement in pleasurable activities</u> that have high potential for painful consequences, e.g., buying sprees, excessive sexual behavior, foolish business investments.

c. Must have interfered with work, social life, or become dangerous to self or others.

d. **There are two psychotic level mood disorders:** Bipolar Disorder and Major Depressive Disorder.

   (1) **BIPOLAR DISORDER** (Depressed, Mixed, Manic): Note that mania, at some time severe enough to produce impaired functioning, is necessary to establish this diagnosis.

      (a) Has 1% lifetime risk;
      (b) male to female ratio is equal.
      (c) Characterized by: no obvious precipitating factor (i.e., endogenous); psychomotor changes; usually a number of episodes and <u>full recovery between attacks</u>. There is a <u>familial history</u>. There is apparently a very strong <u>genetic predisposition</u> in bipolar disorder, depressed type.
      (d) Age of onset is 30-35 years.
      (e) <u>Illness is more frequent in upper SES classes than in lower. One of the exceptions to low SES being correlated with severe mental illness.</u>

(f) Subtypes

    i) **Bipolar Disorder, Depressed Type:**

    Has had one or more manic episodes and is currently in a depressive episode.

    ii) **Bipolar Disorder, Mixed Type:**

    Currently displaying both manic and depressive episodes either intermixed or alternating every few days.

    iii) **Bipolar Disorder, Manic Type:**

    Currently in a manic episode.

(2) **MAJOR DEPRESSIVE DISORDER (Psycotic level)**

  (a) Background data:

    i) Lifetime prevalence: males=2-4%; females=5-9% (e.g., M:F=1:2).
    ii) Precipitating event found in almost 25% (50% in the elderly).
    iii) Sometimes accompanied by a thought disorder.
    iv) Onset at any age but usually in adulthood where it is spread throughout the ages.
    v) 85% have more than one episode.
    vi) Begin over 1-3 week period and, if untreated, last 3-8 months or longer.

  (b) <u>Diagnosis</u>: Presence of depressive syndrome with many of the more serious symptoms. Has never had a manic episode. Are profoundly depressed. See a profound metabolic shutdown/slowdown.

  (c) Can be assessed with the following instruments: <u>Beck Depression Inventory, the Zung, and the Hamilton Rating Scale</u>.

e. <u>There are two minor (less severe) Mood Disorders</u>:

(1) <u>Dysthymia (Depressive Neurosis)</u>: Defined as a non-psychotic disorder of lowered mood and/or anhedonia (lack of pleasure) for at least two years and never with a two-month period free of symptoms.

- (a) Feel depressed, have difficulty falling asleep, <u>feel best in the morning</u> and despondent in the afternoon, and evening. Can display any of the non-psychotic signs and symptoms of depression.

- (b) It is more common in women (3-4:1) and often develops for the first time in childhood, adolescence or early adulthood.

- (c) Exacerbated by the loss of a person, health, job, or by chronic stress such as a medical disorder.

(2) <u>Cyclothymia</u>:

- (a) Presence of mild depression <u>and</u> hypomania (less than manic level) either separately or mixed continuously or intermittently over at least a two year period. No two month period free of symptoms.

- (b) Begins in the twenties. More common in females 2:1.

- (c) Chronically disabling pattern which yields troubled interpersonal relationships, job instability, occasionally suicide attempts and short hospitalization. Marked drug and alcohol abuse.

(3) Etiology of Mood Disorders:

- (a) <u>Heredity possibilities.</u>
- (b) May represent a <u>biological rhythm</u> of some type.
- (c) In psychosocial theory, it is assumed that particularly the depressive aspects are reactions to loss, while other people feel that the depression may be a technique to "blackmail" others into "caring for the patient."
- (d) There is a catecholamine hypothesis involving norepinepherine. See Section 1.

(4) Major Treatment Modalities

- (a) <u>Anti-depressant medications</u>: See Section 4.

- (b) <u>Anti-manics</u>: The major breakthrough in treatment of bipolar illness has been lithium salts. See Section 4.

(c) Psychotherapy to work through the loss/grief mourning reaction, or the anger.

(d) Electroconvulsive therapy (ECT) is a viable alternative particularly in some mood disorder emergencies.

4. **Organic Disorders of Psychotic Proportion**

   a. <u>Dementia</u>

   (1) **Clear sensorium:** major differential factor between delirium and dementia.
   (2) **Loss of intellectual functions** severe enough to impair social or occupational functioning.
   (3) **Memory impairment** (particularly prominent in Alzheimer's Disease) is usually most prominent symptom.
   (4) **One of following four:**

   (a) Impaired abstract thinking
   (b) Impaired judgement
   (c) Impaired other higher cortical functions (e.g. aphasia).
   (d) Personality change

   (5) **Evidence of organic, physical factor** or no functional disorder.
   (6) Generally **slow and progressive** with time.
   (7) <u>Pseudodementia</u> is Major Depressive Disorder often confused with dementia in older people.

   b. <u>Delirium</u>

   (1) **Two essential features:**

   (a) Reduced ability to maintain attention to external stimuli and/or ability to shift attention to a new stimulus

   (b) Disorganized thinking: rambling, irrelevant or incoherent speech.

   (2) <u>**Reduced level of consciousness**</u>
   (3) **Disrupted sleep-wake cycle**
   (4) **Disorientation and memory impairment**
   (5) **Hallucinations/illusions**
   (6) **Acute onset** (hours to days) and **fluctuations** throughout the day
   (7) **Total duration** is usually brief
   (8) Evidence from history of a **specific organic factor**

(9) **Often emotional features** accompany delirium (exaggerated display of any emotion).

B. "NEUROSES"

The next three sections (Anxiety Disorders, Dissociative Disorders, and Somatoform Disorders) earlier were called "neuroses"; however, that term is no longer used in the classification of Mental Disorders.

Disorders characterized by underlying anxiety either directly experienced or controlled automatically by defense mechanisms (therefore experienced as uncomfortable symptoms which the patient feels are foolish and fights against (**ego dystonic**)). Usually abrupt development. No gross misinterpretation of reality or personality disorganization, i.e., they are not psychotic.

While most appear to be learned, recent research is suggesting a more biologic etiology for some.

Be familiar with two terms: primary gain and secondary gain.

> Primary gain: what the symptom does for the patient's internal psychic economy, e.g., prevents overwhelming of the ego.
>
> Secondary gain: what the symptom gets the patient, e.g., sympathy, attention, avoidance of responsibility.

1. **Group One: The Anxiety Disorders:** IMPORTANT: One must differentiate anxiety states from hypoxia, stimulant toxicity, hyperthyroidism, etc..

    a. Phobic Disorders: Intense fear of an object or situation. Usually the object or situation of which the person is fearful is not the true feared object. The object feared is being displaced upon.

    The person fears will experience humiliation or embarrassment. Encounter with the object or situation produces fear. Person avoids phobic object or situation. Recognizes the fear is excessive or unreasonable.

    b. Panic Disorder (without Agoraphobia): Has dramatic, acute symptoms lasting minutes to hours, is self limiting, and occurs in patients with or without chronic anxiety.

    (1) **The symptoms are perceived by the patient as medical and are characteristic of strong**

autonomic discharge (heart pounding, chest pain, trembling, choking, abdominal pain, sweating, dizziness, as well as disorganization, confusion, dread, and occasionally a sense of impending doom or terror).

(2) A typical panic attack can be produced by the intravenous infusion of sodium lactate in patients with panic disorder but not in normals.

(3) Run in families and occurs equally in men and women. Some had childhood episode of separation anxiety.

(4) Most also develop **Agoraphobia** (fear of being in places from which escape might be difficult). This has a higher prevalence in women. Note: Agoraphobia can occur without panic disorder.

(5) Disruption of important interpersonal relations may be a precursor of panic disorders.

c. <u>Generalized Anxiety Disorder</u>

Anxiety is subjectively experienced and accompanied by:

(1) Motor symptoms of tension, e.g. tremor, restlessness

(2) Autonomic hyperactivity; dyspnea, palpitations, sweating/cold clammy hands, dry mouth, dizziness, gastrointestinal distress, polyuria.

(3) Vigilance and scanning: "on edge," restless, exaggerated startle response, concentration problems, sleep problems, irritable.

(4) **Symptoms must last six months** during which there may be a few symptom free days.

d. <u>Obsessive-Compulsive Disorder</u>: Obsessions (thoughts: e.g., contamination, aggression, sexual, somatic, need for symetry) about; and compulsive (behaviors: e.g., checking, cleaning, counting) to do things. E.g., obsessive thoughts might be fear of killing one's child. Compulsive urges may be urges not to step on a crack. Core conflict is <u>control</u>!

More common in females than in males.

e. <u>Post-traumatic Stress Disorder</u>:

   (1) Must be the existence of a recognizable stressor that would evoke significant symptoms of stress in almost anyone (e.g. war, rape, etc.).

   (2) Re-experiencing trauma through recollection or dreams; sudden feelings as if traumatic event was reoccurring.

   (3) Numbing of responsiveness and reduced involvement with the external world.

   (4) At least two of the following symptoms that were not present before the trauma: hyper-alertness, exaggerated startle response or sleep disturbance, guilt about surviving where others have not, memory impairment/trouble concentrating, avoiding activities which arouse recollection of the traumatic event, and intensification of symptoms by exposure to events which symbolize or resemble the traumatic event.

   (5) Two subtypes: **acute**, where the symptoms occur within six months of the trauma; **chronic or delayed**, where onset of symptoms appears six months after the trauma.

   (6) NOTE: some researchers think there is a biologic predisposition with an environmental trigger.

2. Group Two: Dissociative Disorders (no known biologic eitiology)

   a. <u>Psychogenic Amnesia</u>: Sudden inability to recall important personal information. Too extensive to be explained by ordinary forgetfulness. Usually begins after severe stress.

   b. <u>Psychogenic Fugue</u>: The classic case where the man goes for a package of cigarettes and never comes back. Sudden unexpected travel away from home or one's place of work with inability to recall one's past. Frequent assumption of a new identity, either partial or complete. Usually lasts a few hours or days, but may continue for months.

   c. <u>Multiple Personality</u>: The classic "Three Faces of Eve". Existence within one body of two or more distinct personalities which are dominant at alternate times. The personality that is dominant at a particular time determines individual's behavior. Each personality is complex and integrated with its own unique pattern of social behavior.

Sometimes each has a distinct EEG pattern, eyeglass prescription, etc. When the person moves from one personality into the other, there is usually a brief altered state of consciousness when patient closes their eyes as the shift in personality is made.

Personalities usually represent poles of behavior (e.g. "a good personality vs. a bad personality"). Sometimes one will have a diagnosable mental disorder and the other will not.

d. <u>Depersonalization Disorder</u>: Ego-dystonic feelings of unreality or separation from oneself, one's body (depersonalization), or one's surroundings (derealization). May report feeling like an automaton. Differential diagnosis is drug induced states or schizophrenia. Major differential sign is that in this disorder reality testing is intact.

3. **Group Three: Somatoform Disorders**

   a. <u>Somatization Disorder</u>: history of physical symptoms of several years duration for which no pathophysiology is found, but for which the person has taken medication. There must be 13 symptoms from a total list of 35 symptoms in the DSM-III-R. Rarely diagnosed in males. These symptoms fall in the following categories:

   (1) Conversion/pseudoneurological: e.g., paralysis.
   (2) Gastrointestinal: e.g. nausea and vomiting.
   (3) Female reproductive: e.g., painful menstruation.
   (4) Psychosexual: e.g., dyspareunia.
   (5) Pain: e.g., low back pain.
   (6) Cardiopulmonary symptoms: e.g., shortness of breath.

   b. <u>Conversion Disorder</u>:

   (1) <u>Disorders of special senses or the voluntary nervous system</u>; e.g. blindness/ motor paralysis. Loss or alteration of function not intentionally produced.

(2) Often a lack of concern ("la belle indifference").

(3) Rule out malingering, psychophysiologic reactions.

(4) Usually the symptom is symbolic of the conflict. For example, if a person does not like their job, they may develop a symptom that does not allow them to work. Note that in psychophysiologic reactions, there is no symbolic expression (conversion defense mechanism).

c. Somatoform Pain Disorder: Preoccupation with pain for at least 6 months in the absence of adequate findings to explain the pain or intensity. The pain is inconsistent with anatomic distribution of the nervous system. When there is related organic pathology, the complaint is in excess of what is expected from physical findings.

One can usually establish a temporal relationship between environmental events and exacerbation or initiation of the pain. It allows the individual to avoid some activity; and, it lets the individual get environmental support.

d. Hypochondriasis: Preoccupation with one's body and misinterpretation of physical signs as evidence of presumed disease not supported by physical evaluation.

4. Treatment:

a. The major treatment for all three groups is psychotherapy.

b. Sometimes anxiolytics are prescribed. However, addiction is a great risk, the symptoms may become fixed. The medications do not solve the underlying problem.

c. For some disorders (e.g. Panic Disorder) specific medication regimens have been helpful.

C. Personality Disorders

1. Personality refers to a person's relatively stable way of behaving and relating. When these become so intense, rigid, or maladaptive as to cause difficulty between a

person and his environment, a personality disorder is said to exist.

2. Personality Disorders are characterized by:

   a. Life long process (from adolescence or before), but should not be diagnosed before age 18.

   b. <u>Maladaptive behavior</u> in: 1) relationships, 2) adjustments to society, 3) pursuit of instinctual goals. <u>It is maladaptive behavior, not symptoms</u>.

   c. Usually anxiety is absent except when there is external stress. Often tolerate stress poorly so minor problems of living lead to anxiety. Premorbid history of seriously ill psychiatric patients often reveals pre-exising personality disorder.

3. Etiology:

   a. Some research suggests <u>constitutional predispositions</u>.
   b. Developmental factors:

      (1) Adults rewarded maladaptive behavior.
      (2) Parents of the same sex modeled the behavior.
      (3) Circumstances prevented developing normal behavior.

4. Characterized by rigid and inappropriate use of one or a few defense mechanisms.

5. Most are probably learned. Taught through frustration, models, and experience.

6. As opposed to the "neurotic" disorders the personality disorder <u>usually does not feel anxiety</u> nor is the person aware their behavior is maladaptive. <u>Others</u> experience difficulties with the behaviors--not the patient. The maladaptive behaviors are **ego syntonic** to the patient.

7. Specific Personality Disorders:

   a. <u>Paranoid Personality Disorder</u>: Interprets others' behaviors as deliberately demeaning or threatening. Hypersensitive, suspicious; jealous and envious; blaming others. Quick counterattack, holds grudges.

   b. <u>Schizoid Personality Disorder</u>: Indifferent to social relations. Shy, reclusive, avoids close relationships; daydreaming but no loss of reality testing; difficulty in expressing ordinary aggressivity. No close friends, indifferent to social rewards, chooses solitary activity.

c. <u>Schizotypal Personality Disorder</u>: Have features of schizoid **and** they are peculiar. Relate strange mental experiences, reason in odd ways, and are difficult to get to know. None is of psychotic proportion. Manifest anxiety in social situations, have eccentric behavior, may be suspicious.

Increased frequency of schizophrenia in first degree family members of persons who are schizotypal.

d. <u>Histrionic Personality Disorder</u>: Emotional instability (flighty); over-reactivity and dramatization; attention-seeking. (Sexualize everything; except bed). Self-centered and vain; superficial; dependent.

e. <u>Narcissistic Personality Disorder</u>: Usually symptom free and function well. Chronically unsatisfied due to constant needs for admiration. Believe selves to be "special persons" who are <u>"entitled"</u>; ideas of omnipotence; usually exploitative in interpersonal relationships. Grandiose, lacking in empathy and hypersensitive to evaluation by others.

f. <u>Antisocial Personality Disorder</u>: Incapable of sufficient loyalty, so can't sustain a monogamous relationship for more than one year; no guilt; lies; slow to learn from experience or punishment; low frustration tolerance; can't delay gratification; reckless; rationalization/blame others for difficulties; grossly impaired parenting ability; can't hold a job; <u>frequent difficulty with the law. Very high familial distribution of this disorder and is more common in males</u>.

g. <u>Borderline Personality Disorder</u>: show clear symptoms of schizophrenia but no history of a psychotic episode in these individuals. Have difficulties forming relationships, although frequently report the desire for such. Display vagueness, pan-anxiety and pan-sexuality. Lives marked by instability in identity, mood and relationships. Often self-mutilation. Emotional lability and dyscontrol.

Have been known to have "micro-psychotic" episodes in which they deteriorate very rapidly into a blatantly psychotic condition with hallucinations, delusions, etc., for a period of one to two minutes.

Reconstitute without assistance. Micro-psychotic episodes are precipitated by stress.

    h. <u>Avoidant Personality Disorder</u>: Very shy and hypersensitive with low self-esteem. Have social discomfort, timid, and fear negative evaluation and embarassment. Would rather avoid personal contacts than face any potential social disapproval, even though they want personal involvement. Often have anxiety and depression as accompaniments.

    i. <u>Dependent Personality Disorder</u>: Passive, unsure of self. Tend to be loners who entirely depend on one or more people, and consequently can't be alone. If relationship becomes threatened, deteriorate into anxiety and depression; so, go to great lengths to preserve relations in order to avoid feelings of abandonment. Hurt by negative feedback.

    j. <u>Obsessive-Compulsive Personality Disorder</u>: NOTE: This is different from the Obcessive Compulsive Disorder. In this disorder, behaviors don't tend to bother the person them, but they **bother others**. Excessive conformity and adherence to standards of conscience; overinhibited; overdutiful; unable to relax. "Always right". Have trouble making decisions and therefore being productive. No generosity. Pattern of perfectionism and inflexibility. Poor (absent) interpersonal relations. Always aware of their relative place on a dominance hierarchy. More common in males.

    k. <u>Passive-Aggressive Personality Disorder</u>: Inappropriate expression of one or more of the following: hostility, aggression, independence/ dependence, dominance/ submission. Procrastinators who rebel by doing nothing. Display passive resistance for adequate social and occupational performance. Won't do appropriate share of work. Scorns authority.

D. <u>Psychological Factors Affecting Physical Condition</u>

  1. Definition: **Physical symptoms and changes in the physical structure of the body caused by emotional factors.** Can be an exacerbation of a physical condition, e.g. angina pain.

  Differentiate from Conversion Disorders on the following:

  a. These controlled by the autonomic nervous system, while the Conversion Disorders involve portions of the body innervated by the voluntary nervous system or the special sense organs.

   b. Don't symbolize the conflict like Conversion Disorders do.

   c. Might be GI tract ulcers, migraine headaches, etc.. These can produce tissue damage; Conversion Disorders do not.

E. Adjustment Disorders

   1. **Definition:** Acute maladaptive reaction to an identifiable overwhelming psychosocial stress that occurs within three months of the stressor. Extant for no more than six months. If stressor continues, reaction can continue.

   2. **Symptoms:** may vary dramatically between individuals and within an individual from time to time. Impair social and occupational function; are "too much" reaction to the stressor.

   Disorder can depressed, anxious or mixed reactions; behavioral problems; or mixed emotional and behavioral problems.

F. Genetics and Behavioral Variants

   1. Much research has been done on inheritability of behaviors.

   2. The following have a suggestion of genetic involvment.

      a. Schizophrenia
      b. Mood Disorders: Bipolar and Major Depressive Disorder
      c. Antisocial and Borderline Personality Disorders
      d. Alzheimer's Disease; Huntington's Chorea; Tourette's
      e. Alcoholis and some other forms of chemical dependence
      f. Obcessive Compulsive Disorder; and, some Anxiety Disorders (e.g., Panic Disorder)
      g. Enuresis and some Learning Dysabilities
      h. Homosexuality

V. **CROSS THEORETICAL COMPARISONS**

   On the following page is a diagram comparing psychoanalytic, Eriksonian, and developmental theories. It includes defense mechanism emanating from each stage as well as some crude formulations of "where psychopathology comes from" when speaking of stages of development.

AGE	NORMAL	ERIKSON	PSYCHOSEXUAL DEVELOPMENT	DIAGNOSTIC CLASS	DEFENSE MECHANISM
0-18 Mo.	Touching, stuffing oneself, visual and tactile incorporation, self-incorporation, optimism, self-assurance, dependency, independency needs. Essentially a basic feeling of being well cared for and loved.	Trust – Mistrust Normal organ mode is incorporative.	Oral. Trust and dependence	Analytic depression	Denial, projection
18 Mo. to 3 Years	Dominant submissive issues of clean-dirty, autonomous, angry rebellion, passive-aggressive, compulsive messiness issues, stubborness, and doubtfulness.	Autonomy vs. Shame and Doubt. Normal organ mode is retentive.	Anal: Holding in vs. letting out	Obsessive-compulsive Depressive	Isolation undoing
3 to 6 Years	Competitive (peeing contests) "Let me show you how great I am," machismo, self-assured recklessness.	Initiative vs. Guilt. Normal organ mode is intrusive.	Phallic – Urethral Oedipal-electra complex is here. Attention to the penis or anything that goes up.	Homosexuality, hysterical personalities, phobic neuroses	Repression conversion
6 to 13 Years	School entrance; peer relationships, danger-sense of inadequacy especially away from home and with equals.	Industry vs. Interiority	Latency		Displacement
13 to 18 Years	Rapid changes, ambiguous period. The task is to maintain one's identity and incorporate changes into the self.	Sense of identify vs. Role confusion	Adolescence		Acting out rationalization, reaction formation

AGE	NORMAL	ERIKSON	PSYCHOSEXUAL DEVELOPMENT	DIAGNOSTIC CLASS	DEFENSE MECHANISM
18 to 25 Years	Person knows who he is; must develop affiliation with others and some intimacy with them.	Intimacy vs. Isolation	Young adulthood		
25 to 50 Years	Guiding the next generation, acquiring personal meaning in life, making a contribution.	Generativity vs. Stagnation	Maturity		
50 to ? Years	Maintain dignity of personal life	Integrity vs. Despair	Senescence		

VI. **SPECIAL PROBLEMS OF CHILDREN**

Most of the disorders of adults can occur in children (e.g., schizophrenia, affective disorders, etc.). However there are disorders of childhood that are differentiated from those of adults. Children show problems of adjustment as they mature, but typically they develop out of these. Some become disorders.

These special disorders are grouped into 5 categories.

A. <u>Category 1: Developmental Disorders</u>

1. **Mental Retardation**

    a. Composed of at least 3 variables

    (1) **Organic:** structural/physiologic problems. E.g., microencephaly; phenylketonuria; Down's Syndrome (Trisomy 21); mercury, lead encephalopathy; cretinism, Leach-Nyhan Syndrome (metabolic enzyme deficiency leading to self mutilation e.g., chewing lips and fingers; and is mentally retarded), thalidomide, irradiation, and possible psychoactive drug exposure or ingestion during pregnancy.

    Infections: bacterial meningitis, congenital syphilis, viral encephalitis, tuberculosis meningitis, cytomegalovirus, rubella mycoplasma, toxoplasmosis etc., during the first trimester of pregnancy.

    (2) **Functional:** "disability" arises from individual's psychological reaction to limitation imposed on function by organic impairment or by psychological and/or social forces.

    (3) **Social:** special roles assigned to the retarded individual within the family, peer groups, schools, society, etc. The way primary impairment and functional disability alter socially expected performance determines the degree of "mental handicap." **Families tend to socialize less if there is a retarded child in the home.**

    b. Poverty and lower SES class decrease access to medical care during and after pregnancy, resulting in increased prematurity, poor nutrition, more infections, and deprivation; all contribute to an increase of incidence of mental retardation (particularly mild retardation).

   c. More diagnosed in males. Diagnosis for both males and females usually at school entry.

   d. IQ Scores and Classification (DSM-III-R):

   (1)   Mild: 50-55 to about 70. Educable
   (2)   Moderate: 35-40 to 50-55. Trainable.
   (3)   Severe: 20-25 to 35-40. Custodial.
   (4)   Profound: below 20-25. Custodial.

   e. Onset before age 18. If occurs after 18, considered to be dementia.

2. **Autistic Disorder** (Pervasive Developmental Disorder)

   a. First distinction. Kanner (1943): inability to relate self in the ordinary manner to people and situations **from the beginning of life**." Don't withdraw from previous existing participation with others (as in the schizophrenias).

   b. Second distinction: failure to use language for communication. Often thought to be deaf since do not respond to communications. Can be differentiated from deafness by auditory evoked potential.

   c. Third distinction: an anxiously obsessive desire for sameness. They display fear of new patterns.

   d. Fourth distinction: fascination for objects while having poor or absent relationships to people.

   e. Most have a co-existing diagnosis of mental retardation.

   f. Very marked restriction in repertoire of activities and interests. Sometimes display bizarre behaviors e.g., head banging and rocking. Don't play normally with other kids.

   g. Do not respond to mother's affection or tenderness.

   h. Treatment modalities for these children include behavior mod techniques (food and smiling rewards for behaviors desired to appear). More traditional psychodynamic therapy also used. Important prognostic milestone is if the child has useful language by the age of 5.

i. Long-term follow-up: even if have become somewhat socialized in a "normal" way, as adult tend to be loners and seek solitary occupations.

j. The etiology of this disorder is not known. The incidence is approximately 1 per 2,500 children. Have found correlates of neurologic dysfunction.

3. **Specific Developmental Disorders**

   a. <u>Academic Skills Disorders</u>

      (1) Reading. <u>Dyslexia</u>: defined as a perceptual problem which can occur in any sensory modality (usually in the visual and auditory senses) and which interferes with learning.
      Characterization:

      (a) Above average intelligence, vocabulary and social development. Male to female is 10:1. Usually left handed.

      (b) Visual perceptual defect

         i) Position in space difficulties; inability to differentiate mirror letters, e.g. "b" and "d".

         ii) Foreground/background reversals: If looking at chalkboard with writing on it, alternately keys visual perception on the white lines and then the spaces formed by the letters.

         iii) Form constancy: Inability to equate two items that differ in minor characteristics but are basically the same. E.g., "dog" is not recognized as the same as "DOG"

         iv) Visual motor coordination: problems for males in athletics since cannot catch a ball when thrown to him.

      (c) Auditory perceptual defect: similar phenomenon here to the visual counterpart.

      (d) Etiology: believed to be brain dysfunction, maturational lag in brain development, and/or heredity.

(2) Arithmetic
(3) Expressive/receptive language
(4) Articulation
(5) Writing
(6) Coordination

B. **Category 2: Disruptive Behavior Disorders**

1. **Attention-Deficit Hyperactivity Disorder**

    a. Definition: characterized by overactivity, restlessness, short attention span, & distractibility. It is almost unceasing and is not outgrown (if at all) until late in development. Data suggest 5-10% of the school population suffers from the disorder.

    b. Course of the disturbance:

    (1) Infant often unusually active, develops rapidly, sleeps little, and cries frequently.

    (2) Problem heightened when reaches the age for socialization and formal education. Literally cannot sit still enough to learn.

    (3) Oversensitivity to stimulation makes it impossible to attend to more than one stimulus at a time, but is also unable to reject the stimulus.

    (4) Usually quite bright; rarely retarded. This in turn leads disapproval from adults who do not understand their behavior.

    c. Diagnosis is made primarily from the patient's history, but transient neurological signs, EEG changes, and lowered seizure thresholds have occasionally been found. **Differentiate these children from those who are mentally retarded, hearing impaired, or emotionally disturbed.**

    d. Treatment usually consists of daily doses of CNS stimulants which have a "paradoxical" effect on hyperkinetic children.

    e. It has been said that the disorder is outgrown between 12 and 18 and the medication is discontinued. This finding is questioned today. Emotional problems which may have developed secondarily to hyperkinesis

must be dealt with therapeutically from a
psychological standpoint.

2. **Conduct Disorder**

   a. Repetitive and persistent pattern of conduct (lasting at least 6 months) in which the basic rights of others and social norms are violated. Can be solitary aggressive, group, or undifferentiated type. Physical aggression (e.g. rape) and stealing are common. Often from homes where adults dx'ed as Antisocial Personality Disorder.

   b. <u>Juvenile Delinquency</u>: (May be a conduct disorder, <u>but is a legal label not a psychiatric diagnosis</u>. Usually includes a background of:

   (1) Parent separation or severe neglect/abuse/incest.
   (2) Psychological disabilities, e.g. dyslexia.
   (3) Feelings of (physical) inferiority.
   (4) Some reports of EEG abnormality (positive spiking).
   (5) Includes a complex of aggressive/destructive behaviors that are externally directed. May be a "rejection of rejectors."
   (6) "**Runaways**" are frequently classified as Juvenile Delinquents and sometimes as Conduct Disorders. They often have a history of incest, family violence, and/or restrictive parents.

   Over time, runaways tend to become involved in violence, drugs, promiscuity, and venereal disease, particularly if not returned to their home <u>and/or</u> the home conditions have not changed.

3. **Oppositional Defiant Disorder**

   a. Negativistic, hostile and defiant (blames others, swears, vindictive, deliberately annoys others, etc.).

   b. Generally do not violate the rights of others.

C. <u>Category 3: Anxiety Disorders of Childhood or Adolescence</u>

   1. **Separation Anxiety Disorder**

      a. Excessive anxiety concerning separation from attachment figure. Includes unrealistic worry, school refusal, repeated nightmares about separation, and excessive signs of distress on separation. May get to the point of panic.

    b. School Phobia is a special type of Separation Anxiety Disorder.

        (1) Considered an emergency equivalent to childhood suicide.

        (2) Etiology usually lies in the mother/child relationship where the child fears that the mother will not be home when he returns. Sometimes has onset after mother has been ill.

        (3) Other causes are peer abuse, fear of teachers and authority, fear of failure.

        (4) Distinguish from truancy: parents don't know child is missing school.

2. **Avoidant Disorder**

    a. Painful shyness and withdrawal from unfamiliar people, leading to interference in social functioning with peers.

    b. Must last for at least 6 months, and the child must be at least 2 1/2 years old.

3. **Overanxious Disorder**

    a. Persistent anxiety or worry, not related to separation from significant others (e.g. unrealistic worry about future or past events, etc.).

    b. Must last at least 6 months.

D. <u>Category 4: Physical Disorders</u>

1. **Eating Disorders**

    a. <u>Anorexia nervosa</u>: refuse maintaining body weight, fear of gaining weight.

        (1) No organic cause for the weight loss
        (2) Weight loss of at least 25% of body weight
        (3) Usually adolescent female, accompanied by amenorrhea. Can be male.
        (4) Disturbed body image where **believes** is overweight. Frequently, sexual identity issues where the young person doesn't "want to grow

up". Maintenance of thinness gives prepubertal image.

  (5) About 1/3 had a minor weight problem and significant others reinforced weight loss.

 b. <u>Bulimia Nervosa</u>

  (1) A "gorge and purge" syndrome

  (2) Gorging done in a discrete time period, and person feels have no control. May be planned and usually high calorie foods are eaten.

  (3) Purging usually done through induced vomiting and sometimes with laxatives. May take on aspects of relieving guilt for gorging.

  NOTE: The constant vomiting results in erosion of teeth due to acidity in the mouth.

  (4) Underlying characteristics are similar to anorexia nervosa.

 c. <u>Pica</u>: eating non-nutritive substances (e.g. paint, plaster, hair, dirt, sand, pebbles, etc.) for at least one month; **not during pregnancy**.

 d. <u>Rumination disorder of infancy</u>

  (1) Partially digested food is brought into the mouth, rechewed, and swallowed or reswallowed.

  (2) Usually appears between 3 and 12 months of age.

2. **Tic Disorders**

 a. <u>Tourette's Disorder</u>: multiple motor and one or more vocal tics (e.g. coprolalia, nonverbal sounds, grunts); occur multiple times during the day; lifelong; possibly genetic.

 b. <u>Chronic Motor or Vocal Tic Disorder</u>: Motor or vocal tics; present > one year.

 c. <u>Transient Tic Disorder</u>: Tics present <12 months.

3. **Elimination Disorders**

 a. <u>Enuresis</u>: In non-retarded, non-brain dysfunctional children, after age 3, especially if diurnal as well as nocturnal wetting. Males> females. Can be intentional.

(1) Forms

    (a) <u>Primary</u>: child has never achieved bladder control. Usually same sex parent was bed wetter. Probably due to deep Stage 4 sleep where full bladder cues can't awaken the child. First 1/3 of the night.

    (b) <u>Secondary</u>: child achieved bladder control, begins wetting again usually after identifiable psychic trauma: e.g., birth of sibling, a move, etc..

(2) Rarely occurs as only symptom; often associated with fire setting, impulsiveness, delinquency, etc.

(3) Rule out physical cause first; found in < 5-10%.

(4) Treatment: Behavior Modification with bell and pad; awaken child in the first 1/3 of the night to void; medications to lighten Stage 4 sleep.

b. <u>Encopresis</u>

(1) Child repeatedly has bowel movements in places that are age inappropriate.

(2) May be purposeful.

(3) Once per month for at least 6 months, and child's mental and chronological age is at least 4 years.

E. <u>Category 5: Gender Identity Disorders</u>

1. **Gender Identity Disorder of Childhood**

    a. Persistent and intense distress in a child about assigned sex and desire to be; or insistence that is the other sex. Won't accept anatomic body or function of the biologic sex.

    b. Females do not like female clothing.

    c. Males want to dress like a female and involve self in activities that are clearly feminine.

2. Transsexualism

   a. After puberty, the child has wanted for at least two years to be rid of own sex characteristics and get those of opposite gender. Uncomfortable with assigned sex.

   b. Variant: person is uncomfortable with assigned sex; cross-dresses not for sexual excitement; and has no wish to be rid of primary or secondary sex characteristics.

F. General Notes on Childhood Disorders

1. Neurologic dysfunction assessed through developmental delay.

2. Uually measured through perceptual deficits and behavioral deviance.

3. "Emotional disturbance" can be the cause or the effect of behavioral concomitants, e.g. short attention span.

4. TREATMENT

   a. Behavior mod have been invaluable in addressing many basic childhood disorders, e.g. bed wetting, encopresis, etc.

   b. Learning disabilities: special educational techniques have been developed to address the specific dysfunctions.

5. PREVENTION: Programs e.g., "Headstart", implemented to attempt prevention in "disadvantaged" areas. Also, preschools have attempted to prevent serious dysfunction. Results show:

   1) If preschool focus is on early academic training (drill), the child appears to be advanced for the first two grades. by grades three and four, there is no significant gain.

   2) If focus is on training attention or concentration skills--there is long term advantage.

VII. INCIDENCE/PREVALENCE STATISTICS OF EMOTIONAL ILLNESS

A. In-depth studies involving both <u>urban and rural</u> samples:

1. 25% of the general population is crippled by emotional illness, and will require treatment.

2. 55% are mildly to moderately crippled.

3. 20% are free of significant psychopathology.

B. 1984 National Institute of Mental Health <u>(NIMH) survey</u> of Baltimore, New Haven, and St. Louis.

1. #1 problem: <u>alcohol abuse</u> or dependency. 13.6% of persons surveyed were positive at some time in their life.

2. #2 problem: <u>phobias</u>. 11.3% had experienced phobias. **If you combine all the anxiety disorders, they are the #1 problem.**

3. #3 problem: <u>depression</u>. 5.7% experienced **major** depression.

4. #4 problem: <u>drug abuse</u> and dependency (excludes ETOH) - 5.6%.

5. The three <u>LEAST</u> common disorders were:

   a. Schizophreniform
   b. Somatization
   c. Anorexia Nervosa

6. Other pertinent facts:

   a. Men have higher rates of psychiatric disorders than women.
   b. Men have higher incidence of alcoholism and antisocial personality disorder than women.
   c. Women have higher rates of depression.
   d. Women have higher rates of phobias.
   e. The 25-44 age group has the highest rate of psychiatric disorders.
   f. There is virtually no difference in rates between blacks and whites regarding mental disorders.

C. <u>Hospitalization Data</u>: data <u>exclude</u> psychosomatic disorders.)

1. 1/10 of persons in America will be hospitalized for psychiatric reasons during some period of their life.

2. The trend for the last 15 years is a decrease in the number of persons who occupy hospital beds for emotional illness.

3. NOTE: <u>Admission rate has not changed--the length of stay has</u>. This is secondary to appropriate medications being developed.

D. <u>Socio-economic Status</u> (SES) and Mental Illness

1. High positive correlation between SES and Bipolar Disease as well as "neuroses."

2. From the inner city to the suburbs, there is a positive correlation with mental HEALTH (<u>Hollingshead and Redlich</u>).

EXAM QUESTIONS - SECTION THREE

INSTRUCTIONS: Each of the questions or incomplete statements below is followed by five suggested answers or completions. Select the one that is BEST in each case.

1. All the following appear to have significant promise for research into the etiology of schizophrenia EXCEPT:

    1) CNS lesions/dysfunction
    2) Dopamine
    3) Double bind communication processes
    4) Heredity
    5) Increased level of etiocholanolone

2. A 35-year-old salesman presents in your office with a sudden fear of cars. He cannot ride in a car, drive a car, or be in the vicinity of one. He is diagnosed as a phobic reaction. Which of the following defense mechanisms is most likely at work?

    1) Aim inhibition
    2) Displacement
    3) Projection
    4) Reaction Formation
    5) Suppression

3. Which of the following defense mechanisms is always pathological?

    1) Conversion
    2) Denial
    3) Dissociation
    4) Isolation
    5) Rationalization

4. All of the following statements about psychotic disorders are true EXCEPT:

    1) Can be life threatening.
    2) Characterized by non-existent or primitive defense mechanisms.
    3) Found mainly in "civilized" societies.
    4) Include GROSS distortion in the capacity to recognize reality.
    5) Interfere with the capacity to meet ordinary demands of life.

5. A mother brings her 17-year-old daughter to you with the complaint that the daughter has become incapacitated in her general functioning. By history, you obtained the fact that the mother and daughter were having an argument and the daughter raised her arm to make a gesture toward the mother and froze in that position with the arm upraised for 45 minutes. As the mother describes the positioning of the arm to you, the mother is not clear whether the daughter was going to strike her or reach out in affection. This is an example of which of the following?

   1) Affective disturbance
   2) Alienated disturbance
   3) Ambivalent disturbance
   4) Associative disturbance
   5) Autistic disturbance

6. You are on your third year clerkship in the Department of Psychiatry and are assigned to the general psychiatric unit at V.A. While accompanying the psychiatric OD one evening, you are called to the Emergency Room at the V.A. to evaluate a man for admission to the psychiatric unit. You review his historical chart and find that he has previously had a recorded schizophrenic episode, but on evaluation at the present time, you are not able to establish the presence of the four A's or any secondary symptoms. What is the most appropriate diagnosis for this man at this time?

   1) Catatonic schizophrenia
   2) Chronic undifferentiated schizophrenia
   3) Disorganized schizophrenia
   4) Residual schizophrenia
   5) Schizoaffective disorder

7. All of the following is are descriptive of persons with a schizophrenic diagnosis **EXCEPT**?

   1) Are found in all cultures
   2) Are found predominantly in the lower classes
   3) Are not assisted by chemotherapy
   4) Have a better prognosis if associated with affective symptoms
   5) One-third get better, one-third stay the same, one-third get worse

8. In paranoid conditions, which of the following defense mechanisms is primary in determining presenting symptoms?

   1) Denial
   2) Identification
   3) Projection
   4) Repression
   5) Sublimation

9. A patient presents in the Emergency Room stating that he has just invented the perpetual motion engine and others are attempting to steal his invention from him. The patient's relatives are in accompaniment and upon questioning them, you find that the patient has been gainfully employed as a dishwasher for the last fifteen years. He has no mechanical ability, no background in theoretical and applied mechanics, and the patient's report would appear to be inaccurate. You would say the patient is experiencing:

   1) Ambivalence
   2) Delusion
   3) Depersonalization
   4) Hallucination
   5) Illusion

10. A patient presents in the Emergency Room with complaints that as he was climbing the stairs to his second floor apartment, he reached the landing of the second floor and saw a jeep parked in the middle of the hallway. He walked through the jeep and realized there was no jeep there, yet his perception was truly that he saw a jeep on the landing. This is an example of:

    1) Confabulation
    2) Delusion
    3) Derealization
    4) Hallucination
    5) Illusion

11. All of the following statements are characteristic of Bipolar Disorder, depressed type **EXCEPT**?

    1) Motor retardation
    2) No obvious precipitating factor
    3) Onset usually between 30 and 35 years of age
    4) Usually a number of episodes and full recovery between attacks
    5) Usually no family history

12. Of the following treatment modalities, which is the **LEAST** indicated modality of treatment for Major Depressive Disorder?

    1) Electroconvulsive therapy
    2) Hospitalization for suicidal behavior
    3) Lithium carbonate
    4) Psychologically working through a reaction to loss
    5) Tricyclic medication

13. A 35-year-old male comes into your office complaining of feelings of unreality and a detachment away from himself as well as his family and general environmental state. He is notably anxious about this, he denies any significant drug misuse, and fears that he is going "insane." He is able to work and has retained his job for 10 years. Which of the following is most appropriate diagnosis for this complex of symptoms?

    1) Catatonic schizophrenia
    2) Chronic undifferentiated schizophrenia
    3) Depersonalization disorder
    4) Disorganized schizophrenia
    5) Bipolar Disorder

14. A 29-year-old public accountant has been somewhat lax in keeping his clients' books in order. Auditors are coming to examine the books in two months. The accountant awakens one morning with a total paralysis of his right arm; however, there is no organic basis for this paralysis. This paralysis obviously prevents him from completing the work that is necessary on his clients' books. This is an example of:

    1) Autism
    2) Automatism
    3) Loose association
    4) Primary gain
    5) Secondary gain

15. As a physician in a rural area you are called by the local court as an expert witness with regard to an 18-year-old male who has been beating up 12-year-old children and taking their lunch money away from them with no apparent feeling of inappropriate behavior. He has been punished several times for this in the past. During the trial, he continually interrupts the judge and asks, "When will this whole fucking mess be over?". The most appropriate diagnostic category for this person is:

    1) Anti-social personality
    2) Hysterical personality
    3) Inadequate personality
    4) Paranoid personality
    5) Passive aggressive personality

16. A 25-year-old public relations man presents to his physician's office with a complaint, "Doctor, I have a pain in my stomach and I'm worried about it." Upon thorough examination, a peptic ulcer is diagnosed. This is an example of:

    1) Asthenic personality
    2) Conversion reaction
    3) Obsessive-compulsive personality
    4) Psychophysiologic reaction
    5) Residual schizophrenia

17. The defense mechanism of reaction formation typically appears in which stage of Erikson's task system?

    1) Autonomy vs. Shame & Doubt
    2) Identity vs. Role Confusion
    3) Industry vs. Inferiority
    4) Initiative vs. Guilt
    5) Trust vs. Mistrust

18. A 32-year-old housewife from an upper middle class background is married to an affluent junior executive who must travel a great deal. She does not work, but pours herself into volunteer organizations, bridge club, working at the local orphanage, and visiting sick people in hospitals. In a social gathering, she rather pointedly occupies the center of attention and generally gives the impression of "anything you can do, I can do better." She is also deathly afraid of riding on elevators. At which stage of Erikson's tasks of development is this woman fixated?

    1) Generativity vs. Stagnation
    2) Identity vs. Role Confusion
    3) Industry vs. Inferiority
    4) Initiative vs. Guilt
    5) Intimacy vs. Isolation

19. With a hyperkinetic child, all of the following statements are correct EXCEPT:

    1) Hyperkinetic children are usually quite intelligent.
    2) It occurs in 25% of the school population.
    3) The hyperkinetic infant is unusually active, develops rapidly, sleeps little, and cries frequently.
    4) There is an exacerbation of the problem when the child goes to school.
    5) Treatment usually consists of central nervous system stimulants.

20. The child who is diagnosed as a childhood schizophrenic differs from an adult schizophrenic in that:

    1) Does not display all of the four A's of schizophrenia.
    2) Hallucinations are more frequently present.
    3) There is usually spontaneous remission at puberty.
    4) Usually displays a clouding of consciousness.
    5) None of the above

21. The prevalence rate of admission to hospitals for psychiatric reasons in America is:

    1) 20%
    2) 15%
    3) 10%
    4) 5%
    5) Less than 5%

22. Which of the following defense mechanisms would you naturally expect to occur as a psychological concomitant of physical illness, where the person is placed in a hospital?

    1) Compensation
    2) Iitrojection
    3) Isolation
    4) Regression
    5) Symbolization

23. With regard to Bipolar Disorder, circular type, there is a tendency for it to occur more frequently in:

    1) Persons of Irish decent
    2) Middle socio-economic classes
    3) The early fifties
    4) The early twenties
    5) Upper socio-economic classes

24. Which of the following statements is most characteristic of neurotic disturbances as opposed to other classifications of emotional disorders?

    1) Consist of unwanted symptoms.
    2) Predominantly based in organic dysfunction.
    3) Represent ineffectual defense mechanisms.
    4) They are life-long.
    5) They involve the total personality.

25. During the counterculture demonstrations for peace, it was "quite the thing to do" to stuff daisies in the barrels of rifles of National Guardsmen who were attempting to maintain order in the demonstrations. This is an example of:

    1) Anti-social behavior
    2) Asthenic behavior
    3) Hysterical behavior
    4) Paranoid behavior
    5) Passive-aggressive behavior

26. A patient typically demonstrates the defense mechanisms of denial and projection to the exclusion of utilization of all other defense mechanisms or all other ways of interacting with the world. All of the following would be true statements EXCEPT:

    1) Most likely psychiatric diagnosis would be a paranoid psychosis.
    2) The person was disrupted in the oral stage of psychosexual development.
    3) Would be overly including all aspects of the environment into their personality.
    4) Would be preoccupied with issues of cleanliness vs. uncleanliness.
    5) Would be struggling with trust-mistrust issues.

27. Which of the following is NOT a correct statement with regard to incidence statistics of emotional illness?

    1) 25% of the general population is crippled by emotional illness.
    2) The trend for the last 15 years is an increase in the number of persons who occupy hospital beds for emotional illness.
    3) 20% of the general American population is free of significant psychopathology.
    4) 10% of persons in America will be hospitalized for psychiatric reasons during some period of their life.
    5) 55% of the general American population are moderately to mildly crippled with emotional illness.

EXAM QUESTIONS - SECTION THREE

Answer Key

1. 5	11. 5	21. 3
2. 2	12. 3	22. 4
3. 1	13. 3	23. 5
4. 3	14. 5	24. 1
5. 3	15. 1	25. 5
6. 4	16. 4	26. 4
7. 3	17. 2	27. 2
8. 3	18. 4	
9. 2	19. 2	
10. 4	20. 5	

SECTION FOUR: DIAGNOSIS AND INTERVENTION

I. **MENTAL STATUS EXAMINATION, INTERVIEWING AND COMPLIANCE** 179

    A. Mental Status Exam
    B. Interviewing
    C. Compliance

II. **MAJOR TREATMENT MODALITIES** 182

    A. Behavior Modification
    B. Psychotherapy
    C. Psychopharmacology
    D. Somatic Therapies

III. **GROUP METHODS** 197

    A. Group Treatment
    B. Group Process

IV. **ENVIRONMENTAL MANIPULATIONS** 198

    A. Milieu Treatment Facilities
    B. Therapeutic Community
    C. Community Mental Health Centers
    D. Family Therapy

V. **MEDICAL LEGAL ISSUES** 200

    A. Competency to Stand Trial
    B. Informed Consent: Adult
    C. Informed Consent: Parent for Child
    D. Informed Consent When the Patient Cannot Provide It.
    E. Committed Mentally Ill
    F. Patient Refusing Treatment
    G. Privileged Communication
    H. Abortion
    I. Good Samaritan

EXAMINATION QUESTIONS AND ANSWERS 203

SECTION FOUR: DIAGNOSIS AND INTERVENTION

I. MENTAL STATUS EXAMINATION AND INTERVIEWING

A. <u>Mental Status Exam</u>: way of organizing and documenting observations.

1. Appearance and Behavior

    a. General Description
    b. Psychomotor Activity: Posture and speech
    c. Expressive Mannerisms
    d. Attitude: Cooperativeness; Contact and Rapport

2. Sensorium: Dysfunction here suggests an organic condition.

    a. Consciousness: Level and fluctuations
    b. Orientation: Person, Place, Time and Situation
    c. Memory:

       (1) Remote: verifiable data (e.g. Pearl Harbor Day)
       (2) Recent: Current news events (2 weeks)
       (3) Immediate: recall three things in the interview

    d. Attention and concentration--attend to interview: Serial 7's

3. Thought process

    a. Production of thought: pressured, blocked, retarded
    b. Continuity of thought: loose, tangential, circumstantial

4. Thought Content and Intellect

    a. Relationship to reality: autistic, delusional, etc..
    b. Concept formation: abstract or concrete--interpret proverbs
    c. Topics and Issues: focus of patients talk
    d. Morbid preoccupations: phobia, obsession, suicide, homicide
    e. Values and Ideals: what kind of person do you want to be?
    f. General Intellect: general information, vocabulary
    g. Insight and Judgment: cause of illness; social judgement.

5. Perceptual disturbances: hallucinations, illusions

6. Emotional Regulation

    a. Subjective: what patient reports
    b. Objective: what you see
    c. Appropriateness: does affect fit the topic?
    d. Ambivalence: towards significant others
    e. Depersonalization/derealization

7. Volition: energy/spontaneity, will, goal directedness

8. Somatic Functioning: sleep, appetite, weight, libido, ROS.

B. <u>Interviewing</u>

1. General stance in interviewing: non-critical, data gathering.

2. Interview styles

    a. <u>Associative</u>: Interviewer says (verbally and non-verbally) the least to allow the patient to get on with their agenda. Interviewer associates next question to what the patient brings up. Generally, the best way to open an interview is a nod, or "What brings you to see me?" Generally leads to highest compliance rate from patients in their treatment.

    b. <u>Laundry list</u>: Interviewer structures interview with preset questions to get specific data. Rarely helpful in dealing with the practice of psychological medicine. Misses a great deal of the patient's agenda and gives the impression of "I know what's important, you don't".

3. Concepts

    a. <u>Support</u>: A response that shows interest in, concern for, or understanding of the patient.

    b. <u>Reassurance</u>: A response that tends to establish the sense of merit, well-being, or self-reliance in the patient.

    c. <u>Empathy</u>: A response that recognizes or names the patient's feeling and does not criticize it. Accepts patient's feeling even though interviewer may believe the feeling to be wrong.

d. <u>Confrontation</u>: A response by the interviewer that points out to the patient his feeling, behavior, or previous statement.

e. <u>Reflection</u>: A response that repeats, mirrors, or echoes a portion of what the patient just said.

f. <u>Interpretation</u>: A confrontation that is based upon an inference rather than upon an observation.

g. <u>Silence</u>: A communication, a response. A silent response can show interest, withdrawal, lack of interest, support, or it can show that the doctor is not listening. Most useful are the supportive silence and the interested silence.

h. <u>Summation</u>: A response that reviews patient's information

4. Can make the patient defensive by:

   a. Not listening
   b. Judging (critical parent)
   c. Being a "Know-it-all"
   d. Assuming or implying something is true
   e. Lecturing
   f. Talking <u>to</u> or <u>at</u>, not <u>with</u>

5. Can assist the flow by:

   a. Least leading question possible
   b. Focus on the feelings
   c. Clarify
   d. Get congruence

6. Good M.D.-Patient relation produces good compliance. Poor relation produces: M.D. shopping, going to non-M.D., increased malpractice actions, increases in depression in the patients.

C. <u>Compliance</u> (also called adherence): approximately 30-35% of patients fail to comply.

1. **At Risk Persons**

   a. Chronic illness: Big 3 are CV, Mental Disorders and Arthritis/rheumatoid
   b. Long term maintenance
   c. Preventive medications
   d. If D/C, only gives subtle or remote effects
   e. Children, elderly, and disadvantaged
   f. Hostile

g. Risk takers
h. Hypochondriacs

2. **M.D.'s who get good compliance**

   a. Talks <u>with</u> patient about how patient <u>feels</u> about treatment.
   b. M.D.'s attitudes toward drugs as well as patient
   c. Gives close supervision
   d. Patient likes the doctor and satisfied with management.

3. **Variables affecting**

   a. Easy to learn
   b. Easy to carry out
   c. Takes little time
   d. Doesn't lead to social isolation
   e. Decrease fear
   f. Patient believes is ill

4. **Medications**

   a. Correlate with daily activities, e.g. meals
   b. As few as possible; less than or equal to 3
   c. As infrequent as possible; less than or equal to 4
   d. Few side effects
   e. NOT PRN
   f. Meaning of drugs: e.g. more drugs = sick

II. **MAJOR TREATMENT MODALITIES**

   In regard to the overall treatment of the mentally ill:

   60% cared for by primary care physicians.
   20% cared for by trained mental health professional.
   20% get no treatment at all.

   A. <u>Behavior Modification</u>

   1. Behavior modification therapies are based on psychological principles which have been covered in Sections I and II above.

      a. <u>Reinforcement</u>: Identification of the appropriate reinforcer is the central issue in behavior modification.

      b. <u>Learning</u> is the basis of all Behavior Modification therapies. Know the concept of <u>shaping behavior</u> by positive reinforcement.

c. <u>Anxiety gradient</u>: understand the relationship between the nearness to a feared object and the height of the anxiety.

d. IMPORTANT NOTE: attempting only to <u>change symptoms</u>. Success rate for target symptoms: generally the upper 90%.

2. Different Behavior Modification Therapies

   a. <u>Operant Conditioning</u> (Skinner)

   (1) Basic principle is to reward an appropriate behavior and, over time, that behavior will repeat. Or remove something the person likes (e.g., attention) and the behavior will disappear.

   (2) In the treatment of autism, the child is food deprived and each time he makes a sound he is given something to eat. At first, any sound will do; later on, the child only gets fed for producing words. This is the principle for <u>shaping behavior</u>.

   (3) <u>Token economy systems</u>: focus is on social behavior. Can earn tokens towards something they desire (weekend pass) if they produce certain types of behaviors. At first, any behavior will do, but later, the behavior must be more socialized to get the token.

   (4) Pain control as an example.

      (a) Pain is influenced by: <u>ethnicity</u>; <u>symbolic meaning</u>, e.g. "I'm not a man"; and <u>learning</u>: therefore, chronic pain can persist after organic reasons are gone.

      (b) Can attenuate by: <u>no reinforcement</u> (remove attention); <u>relaxation</u>; <u>biofeedback</u>; <u>hypnosis</u>

   b. <u>Aversive Therapy</u>

   (1) Applications:

      (a) Alcoholics who take antabuse

      (b) "Junk food addict": person views picture of favorite "junk" food and is shocked while looking. Shock is stopped when the person presses a button that replaces the original picture with a more wholesome food.

- (c) Enuresis: the patient is not routinely shocked; but rather, wetting the bed completes a circuit which turns on a light or bell. Consequently, the child in sleep learns to recognize the pressure of urine building up in the bladder and awakens.

c. Desensitization: The person is encouraged to interact with the frightening objects or ideas until they are successful or until that particular idea or object no longer provokes anxiety, e.g. stage fright; the person is placed in a similar situation and forced to speak to an audience.

d. Systematic desensitization variant of the desensitization procedure. (WOLPE)

  (1) First a hierarchy of parts of the feared situation is established. Then, the person is taught to relax.

  (2) After he has relaxed, the person visualizes the lowest item on the hierarchical list. If no anxiety appears, proceeds to the next step in the hierarchy. If anxiety appears, imagery is stopped and person re-relaxes.

  (3) Person is relaxed and uses visual imagery only. Anxiety is not allowed to appear.

  (4) The hypothesis is that relaxation and anxiety cannot occur simultaneously. If you keep the person relaxed during the imagery, they cannot attach anxiety to the mental representation.

3. Flooding therapies: Same as desensitization but uses imagery not the real feared object.

4. Biofeedback

a. Biofeedback: a biological or physiologic process of which the persons are not normally aware is fed back to them (e.g., turning on a light) and they are requested to continue keeping that physiological or biological process going by maintaining the feedback signal.

b. Alpha waves and theta waves of the EEG; and the EMG of the frontalis muscle have been used.

c. Typically, what is fed back to the person is a biological or physiological process that is incompatible with a particular symptom. E.g., being in the EEG Alpha state is incompatible with anxiety. Also, the frontalis and occipital muscles being relaxed are incompatible with tension headaches.

d. Biofeedback has been utilized to teach epileptic patients to abort seizures; to teach people to raise the temperature of their skin by vasodilation which can attenuate migraine headaches. Other applications have been to decrease blood pressure, reduced stomach acidity, etc..

B. Psychotherapy

1. In traditional psychotherapy are treating the psychodynamics psychological processes within the individual and how these interact with the family, his small group, and the community.

2. In psychological therapies, the relationship between the therapist and the patient is emphasized. The therapist is doing something with the patient, not to him (in contrast to the Behavior Modification therapies, which imply doing something to the patient against their will).

3. Three important elements to all psychotherapies: talking freely to someone who is relatively non-critical; catharsis or "blowing off steam"; desensitization - simply by going over something, it is less disturbing. Additionally,

    a. Clarification: as one hears oneself talk about a problem, it may be understood differently.

    b. Abreaction: as a person talks about something, he often releases "repressed" feelings which may vent in the session.

4. Important elements about the therapy: patient may feel he is **not alone**; that he **can be understood**; and he is **not hopeless**.

    a. Corrective emotional experience: the patient may go through some difficulties with the therapist that caused trouble before, but that he now understands differently.

    b. Termination: the therapist must terminate the therapy in such a way that there is a final clear, healthy termination of the relationship between the patient and the therapist.

5. Specific therapeutic undertakings by the therapist:

   a. <u>Interpretation</u>: helping the patient make sense out of what is going on so that the patient can assume some control.

   b. <u>Therapist attitudes</u>: the therapist must become congruent with himself and expect people to get well. The therapist who is nurturant is a much more curative factor than the types of therapeutic methods (TA, Gestalt, etc.) used by the therapist. Apparently, <u>over time</u>, therapists who come from different philosophical or theoretical schools look more alike in what they do than they look different.

6. **Classical psychoanalysis**: requires many years for completion (approximately 3-10). <u>It works best with persons who are not psychotic and are distressed by their symptoms</u>.

   a. Aim is to make unconscious material conscious. Focuses on dream interpretation, transference issues, and insight. Strengthens the Ego. "Where Id is there shall Ego be."

   b. The assumption is that if the pathogenic unconscious becomes conscious, the patient can understand and control symptoms.

   c. Resistance is the same as defense mechanisms. As resistance is overcome (defenses are broken down), the patient develops a "transference neurosis" to the therapist which is "worked through."

   d. <u>Free Association</u> (saying the first thing that comes into awareness without any censoring) and analysis of dreams are the principle methods of psychoanalysis in getting to unconscious material that "needs to be made conscious."

   e. <u>Transference Neurosis</u>: The patient projects on the analyst (re-experiences distorted feelings, etc.,) from the past as if they are happening again, leading to an exacerbation of the conflict within the hour. Skillful interpretation by the analyst allows working through of the transference.

f. Psychoanalysis has been adapted to treating psychotic individuals, but this treatment is extremely time consuming and therefore expensive.

7. Psychoanalytically oriented psychotherapy:

   a. Aimed towards restructuring the basic psychodynamics and personality of the individual person.

   b. They go from a common assumption that unless a child is born brain damaged or autistic, the child develops disorders as a reaction to the environment and parents. Probably somewhere around the ages of 7-9 years old, this reaction can become internalized; therefore, changing the environment or the parents will not matter a great deal.

   c. Rogerian therapy's basic orientation is that the therapist assumes an unconditional positive regard for the patient in the context of a warm, accepting, and understanding environment; coupled with mainly reflecting the patient's statement in a non-evaluative way to the patient, the patient will have a corrective emotional experience and be less debilitated.

   d. Transactional Analysis as a therapy <u>focuses on understanding</u> the transactions among one's own Ego States; and between one's and other's Ego States which reinforce pathologic life scripts. Useful to help people think before they act.

   e. Gestalt therapy, on the other hand, is grounded in Gestalt psychology theory. In Gestalt therapy the focus is on the figure ground reversals in the person's perceptions and closure of uncompleted Gestalts. <u>Gestalt focuses on internal feelings--not words</u>. Useful to help people feel.

      (1) In Gestalt it is assumed that patients "scare themselves" by:

         (a) What they do with their breathing: usually they hold their breath.

         (b) The strength of inhalation: they either hyperventilate or hypoventilate.

         (c) They get out of the here and now and begin to imagine future catastrophes (catastrophic expectations).

8. Crisis intervention = <u>CARE</u> <u>CO</u> <u>LTD</u>

    a. CA = Catharsis
    b. RE = Reassurance
    c. CO = Counseling or advice giving
    d. LTD = Limited use of medication

9. Supportive Psychotherapy: This is sometimes called brief psychotherapy. The techniques that are especially valuable in brief psychotherapy are:

    a. Active interpretation of reality
    b. Ventilation, catharsis, or abreaction in a supportive atmosphere
    c. Suggestion, persuasion, or direction
    d. Re-education
    e. Installation of a sense of hope and optimism

C. <u>Psychopharmacology</u>:

The goal of therapy is usually reduction of symptoms. Frequently, psychopharmacological agents are used adjunctively. Prognosis is best when the patient has a strong ego, a stable environment, adequate intelligence, and has temporarily decompensated under overwhelming stress.

Psychopharmacology has dramatically decreased the length of hospitalization for the major psychiatric disorders. It has decreased the degree of suffering from both psychotic and non-psychotic disorders.

There are four major classes of psychotropics: Antipsychotics; Anti-depressants; Anti-manics; and the Anxiolytics.

1. Antipsychotics: (neuroleptics; "major tranquilizers")

    a. See the summary Table on page 192 for comparison of different neuroleptics.

    b. Primary indications: <u>Schizophrenia</u>; Delusional disorder; psychotic depressions; mania; agitation in elderly; Tourette's Syndrome; organic brain syndromes including delirium and dementia, and some personality disorders (ex: borderline) for agitation and behavioral dyscontrol. These are poorly tolerated in the mentally retarded with psychosis (use low doses).

c. General Statements

   (1) Phenothiazines--reduced inpatient census of psychotic hospitals by one-half since 1955. Reduced length of hospitalization for schizophrenics from years to weeks. Changed psychiatry from custodial to medical intervention specialty.

   (2) No singular superiority of one antipsychotic over another; certain patients are more responsive to one versus another. Side effects and potency are important in choosing which drug to use.

   (3) In small doses, antipsychotics have been used to control anxiety states; but, the risk of developing tardive dyskinesia precludes this practice at present.

   (4) Antipsychotics modify behavior, affect, and thinking, not just generalized sedation. They effect primary symptoms of schizophrenia. They provide acute symptomatic relief and prophylaxis for thought disorders.

   (5) Persons with acute psychosis usually reintegrate with IM meds within 72 hours. Full effect is not seen till 2-3 weeks; chronic schizophrenics take longer to reconstitute. Poor prognosis schizophrenics (disorganized, undifferentiated) are less responsive to antipsychotics.

   (6) Antipsychotics have been used with patients with psychogenic pain (e.g., cancer). Note: it masks pain (e.g. abdominal) and seems to potentiate analgesic properties of narcotics.

d. Mode of Action

   (1) Antagonizes DA transmission in mesolimbic and mesocortical projection as well as nigro-striatal and tuberoinfundibular projections.

   (2) **Where they act:** In animals, the chemicals are found in synaptic cleft, not in neurons themselves. Sometimes are found around the cell body but not within the cell itself.

(3) Antipsychotic properties are related to post-synaptic blockade of the D_2 dopamine receptor.

e. <u>Side Effects</u>

(1) **Extrapyramidal due to basal ganglia D_2 receptor blockade:** 30-40% of patients on antipsychotics have these three types: akathisia (restless legs); Parkinson's syndrome; acute dystonia.

These are not toxic effects but side effects. Usually benign and treatable with anti-Parkinsonian medications (Artane, Cogentin, Benadryl, Symmetrel). Sometimes beta-blockers and benzodiazepines helpful.

(2) **Autonomic Nervous System:** (mainly anti-cholinergic due to muscarinic cholinergic receptor blockade) dry mouth, increased respiration, urine retention, increased heart rate, blurred vision, mental confusion.

(3) **Orthostatic Hypotension:** (due to $alpha_1$-adrenergic receptor blockade) can be dangerous in cardiac patients. Tachycardia often develops. <u>Do not treat with Epinephrine</u>. Use levophed or alpha stimulator.

(4) **Endocrine Effects:** Amenorrhea and galactorrhea secondary to stimulation or disinhibition of prolactin by blocking D_2 receptors in the tuberoinfundibular system. Males are sometimes impotent or unable to ejaculate.

(5) Serious effects are:

(a) <u>Agranulocytosis</u>: most commonly seen with clozapine (1-3%); very rare with others.

(b) <u>Tardive Dyskinesia</u> consists of perioral movements, protrusion of the tongue, grimacing, choreoathetoid movements. This condition usually appears when the drug is discontinued or decreased after prolonged use. Most patients don't develop this, but it may be permanent.

Does not respond to anti-Parkinsonian agents. Is an effect of chronic medication - <u>not</u> an acute effect. Usually occurs in older persons and in females more than males.

(c) <u>Cholestatic Jaundice</u>: probably due to hypersensitivity reactions in predisposed individuals. Not very common.

(d) <u>Ocular pigmentation</u>: over 800 mg. of Mellaril can cause retinitis pigmentosa.

(e) <u>Neuroleptic Malignant Syndrome</u> (NMS): a very serious idiosyncratic reaction to neuroleptics. Rigidity, fever, autonomic instability, encephalopathy. Mortality rate about 20%. Treatment consists of supportive care and removal of neuroleptics and agonist drugs. Specific treatments with Dantrolene (a direct acting muscle relaxant) and bromocriptine (a DA agonist) have proven useful.

ANTIPSYCHOTICS

DRUG	CLASS	COMMENT
Thorazine (chlorpromazine)	Phenothiazine (aliphatic)	Commonly used; high sedative side effects; low problems with EPS; high BP S.E.
Mellaril (thioridazine)	Phenothiazine (piperidine)	High sedative effect; low EPS; high BP S.E.
Trilafon (perphenazine)	Phenothiazine (piperazine)	Moderate EPS; low sedation; low BP S.E.
Prolixin (fluphenazine)	Phenothiazine (piperazine)	High EPS; moderate sedation; low BP S.E. Available in long acting form. Given I.M. every two weeks.
Stelazine (trifluoperazine)	Phenothiazine (piperazine)	High EPS; low sedation; low effect on BP S.E.
Serentil (mesoridazine)	Phenothiazine (piperazine)	Very similar to Mellaril.
Haldol (haloperidol)	Butyrophenone	Useful in mania; high EPS; low sedation; low BP S.E. Also available in long-acting form.
Navane (thiothixene)	Thioxanthene	High EPS; low sedation; low BP S.E.
Loxitane (loxapine)	Dibenzoxazepine	High EPS; low sedation; low BP S.E.
Clozaril (clozapine)	Dibenzoxazepine	Low EPS; high sedation; high BP S.E.; monitor WBC weekly; used for refractory schizophrenia.
Moban (molindone)	Dihydroindolone	High EPS; low sedation; low BP S.E.

EPS = Extra Peripheral Side Effects
BP S.E. = Blood Pressure Side Effects

2. Anti-depressants

   a. Major preparations: Tofranil (imipramine), Elavil (amitriptyline), Vivactil (protriptyline), Norpramin (desipramine), Pamelor (nortriptyline), Ludiomil (maprotiline), Sinequan (doxepin), Asendin (amoxapine), Desyrel (trazodone), Wellbutrin (bupropion), Prozac (fluoxetine).

   b. Indications:

       (1) Bipolar Disorder - depressed or mixed type
       (2) Dysthymic Disorder (depression without psychoses)
       (3) Major Depression with or without psychotic features/melancholia (<u>associated</u> with loss)
       (4) Panic Disorders/Phobic Disorders/Obsessive Compulsive disorders/PTSD
       (5) Enuresis/school refusal/separation anxiety/ADHD
       (6) Bulimia
       (7) Organic affective disorders
       (8) Chronic pain syndromes
       (9) **MAO inhibitors** (Nardil, Parnate) are used in selected depressions (atypical).

   c. Mechanisms of action and general considerations

       (1) Probably work by decreasing monoamine pre-synaptic reuptake and by down-regulation of post-synaptic $beta_1$-adrenergic receptors as well as serotonin $5HT_2$ receptors.

       (2) Takes days-weeks to get an effective blood level.

       (3) Can be lethal in overdose.

   d. Side effects

       (1) Majority of the side effects are the same as the antipsychotics (anticholinergic, orthostatic hypotension, sedation).

       (2) There are <u>SELDOM</u> extrapyramidal effects.

       (3) <u>Cardiac</u> side effects are most important.

       (4) Sexual dysfunction can be seen in males and females.

(5) Patients on MAO inhibitors can't eat tyramine containing foods e.g. aged wine and cheese. Possible hypertensive crisis may result.

3. Anti-manics

   a. <u>Lithium carbonate</u>: Useful in the <u>MANIC</u> phase of Bipolar Disorder (manic depressive illness). Provides relief of acute manic phase and prophylaxis for mania and depression in Bipolar Disorder, mixed type. May be useful in other cyclic disorders (cluster headaches, binge drinking, episodic dyscontrol) as well as the affective lability and emotional instability of borderline personality disorder.

   Also effective in some unipolar depressions.

   Not usually effective in most schizophrenias.

   (1) Dose level - one needs a blood level of .6 to 1.2 mEq/l. Less than .6 is insufficient, <u>greater than 1.5 is toxic</u> and perhaps can be fatal. Early signs of Lithium toxicity are GI, (nausea, diarrhea, vomiting), CNS (slurred speech, ataxia), cardiac (arrhythmias); may be combined with an antipsychotic for initial 5 to 6 days to control acute manic episode.

   (2) Contraindications:

   (a) Renal disease with impaired creatinine clearance
   (b) Sodium exchange diuretics
   (c) Cardiac disease (relative)
   (d) Brain damage
   (e) Pregnancy (relative)

   b. <u>Anticonvulsants</u> - Carbamazepine (Tegretol), Valproic (Depakote) - effective in acute mania, Bipolar prophylaxis, possibly some depressions and episodic dyscontrol syndromes.

   (1) Works in the limbic system; stabilize neuronal membranes and prevents kindling.

   (2) Hematologic monitoring necessary for Tegretol, liver function monitoring for Depakote; blood levels necessary (8-12 μg/ml, 40-150 μs/ml for Depakote).

(3) Most useful in patients unresponsive to lithium.

4. Anxiolytics (minor tranquilizers)

   a. Agents: Benzodiazepines (Serax, Tranxene, Librium, Valium, Ativan, Xanax, Halcion); β-adrenergic blockers (Inderal, Tenormin, Lopressor); Buspirone (BuSpar).

   b. Indications:

   (1) Generalized anxiety disorder, some phobias, panic disorder, insomnia, ETOH withdrawal, adjust with antipsychotics for agitated psychosis, some seizure disorders.

   (2) Time limited (not over 2-3 months, e.g. situational adjustment reactions). Long term use sometimes indicated in panic disorder.

   (3) Use warranted by the clinical circumstances (e.g., free floating anxiety). Xanax coupled with antidepressants useful for panic symptoms. Beta-blockers more useful with some performance anxiety and social anxiety.

   (4) Best used in conjunction with brief supportive therapy.

   (5) Best not used in patients with history of ETOH or other drug use/abuse.

   (6) Useful in alcohol withdrawal and various seizure disorders (benzodiazepine only).

   (7) Differ with respect to half-life and rate of onset.

   c. CAUTIONS: While the original thinking regarding the benzodiazepines was that they were not physically addicting, data are clear: <u>they can cause physical dependence and can be psychologically habit-forming</u>.

   (1) No tolerance to antianxiety effect only to sedation. Many patients do well even with long-term therapy but physical dependence and subsequent withdrawal syndromes do occur (especially with high potency drugs) and need to be taken seriously).

(2) Confusion common in elderly.

d. Mechanisms of action.

(1) Benzodiazepines work through the BZD/GABA receptor complex.

(2) Benzodiazepines are best absorbed orally (Ativan can be given I.M. also)

(3) BuSpar (buspirone) is a non-benzodiazepine anxiolytic. Doesn't appear to interact with GABA; may be anti-dopaminergic. Not cross tolerant with benzodiazepines. Is a partial agonist at $5-HT_{1a}$ receptors which decreases serotonin turnover. Requires 4-6 weeks to reach maximal effectiveness. Does not produce dependence or withdrawal symptoms.

D. <u>Somatic Therapies</u>

1. Electro-convulsive therapy (ECT)

   a. Indications:

   (1) Treatment of choice for major depression with melancholia.

   (2) Quite effective in other psychotic depressions.

   (3) Also effective for acute schizophrenic symptoms, especially catatonic,

   (4) NOT effective with character disorders or "neurotics."

   b. General data

   (1) ECT is painless.

   (2) There is no consistent documented data that suggest that repeated ECT administration leaves residual CNS dysfunction.

   c. Mechanism of action.

   (1) ECT produces a seizure which results in a usually **transient** (hours) organic brain syndrome with confusion, memory dysfunction, and disorientation.

(2) ECT is effective because of seizure not electricity.

d. Complications

(1) Major complications result from the general anesthesia, NOT the ECT.

(2) Only true contraindications are increased intracranial pressure and recent MI.

2. **Psychosurgeries**

a. Frontal lobotomies and lobectomies were done by separating the frontal supraorbital cortex from the subcortical bodies, mainly the thalamic nuclei. Were done to decrease the active and aggressive symptoms of schizophrenia.

b. Temporal lobectomies are done to control temporal lobe epilepsy (psychomotor).

c. Commissurotomies: severs the corpus callosum in humans to attenuate intractable seizures. This surgery may make the brain more responsive to anti-convulsant medication. Initial complication is that literally, the left hand does not know what the right hand is doing.

d. Stereotactic procedures have been attempted to attenuate violent behavior in human beings.

III. **GROUP METHODS**

A. Group Treatment: In group treatment, there is one therapist with many patients. The therapist is clearly defined and his role can be to direct and clarify the therapeutic interactions among and between the various patients. Group treatment can be of any specific theory orientations; that is, TA, Gestalt, Psychoanalytic, etc.. Group treatment offers the advantages of therapy in the context of group support and confrontation.

B. Group Process: Here there is no designated leader and the process between the persons in the group is examined. It is the role of group facilitators to point out the interactions in the group, but they are by no means therapists. This is not treatment.

IV. **ENVIRONMENTAL MANIPULATIONS**

   A. <u>Milieu Therapy</u>: The assumption is that "if a person can be driven crazy, they can be driven sane". The <u>structure</u> of the environment is used to set boundaries, limitations, and to define the world as safe for the patient. Most therapeutic endeavors with persons who have psychotic level disturbance are milieu therapy oriented.

   1. Short term inpatient hospitalization

      a. Brief stay: 1-2 weeks
      b. Person has had an acute onset of severe problems
      c. Focus on relief from stressors (protection)
      d. Diagnostic workup
      e. Medication stabilization
      f. Other somatic stabilization

   2. Day hospital

      a. Continuum of care from short term inpatient hospitalization.
      b. Indications: person who has had acute short term inpatient hospitalization; or a patient who doesn't need total inpatient care.
      c. Is really outpatient care; however patient is present in the facility from 1/2 to full day; 3-5 days per week.
      d. Does not sleep over in the facility.
      e. Patient usually attends for a few months.
      f. Often a transition to outpatient, once/week, psychotherapy.

   3. Day treatment

      a. Non-residential expanded care; usually for chronically mentally ill persons.
      b. Spends major portion of their day in this facility.
      c. Does not sleep over in the facility.
      d. May have a sheltered workshop associated where patients can earn money.
      e. Patients usually stay with these facilities for years.

   B. <u>Therapeutic Communities</u>: In therapeutic communities, there is an agreement between patients and staff that patients have a significant voice in the management of the unit, as well as the management of other patients. For instance, the patient group as a whole may recommend that a particular patient's medication be increased or decreased.

1. Usually these are facilities that are addressing a self destructive life style, e.g., chemical dependence. Usually not dealing with psychotically disturbed individuals.

2. Highly structured with a strong work ethic to progressively earn more freedom of action and status in the community.

3. NOTE: In Milieu Therapy as well as Therapeutic Community facilities, if one finds patients acting out (fighting, having sexual relations on the unit, running away from the institution, committing suicide), entertain two possibilities:

    a. Patient behavior is reflecting staff behavior (members of the staff are fighting or they are having affairs (either "fighting or fucking").

    b. A new patient has been admitted who is serving as a role model for the behavior. That is, contagion phenomenon that one patient has seen another patient do the act and imitates.

C. Community Mental Health Centers (CMHCS): Have been part of the Public Mental Health System. Traditionally supported in part by federal monies to state mental health departments and a sliding scale patient fee system.

1. There are 12 services which CMHCS offer. These are: inpatient services, outpatient services, partial hospitalization, 24-hour emergency psychiatric service, consultation, education to the community, court screening, transitional living facility, special services for children, special services for elderly, programs for alcoholics, and programs for drug dependent persons.

2. Major focus is a continuity of care so a given person can enter at an Inpatient Unit, be released to a transitional living facility or a more outpatient program (and vice-versa); yet still be within the same health care delivery system.

3. Usually requires a Board of Directors with which representatives of the community and the consumer populations are involved.

4. Operate in a given catchment area so treatment can be effected close to the home of the patient.

D. <u>Family Therapy</u>: Because of the assumption that the family is frequently the etiology of a person's disturbance, treatment has begun to focus on the family as a whole.

1. **Indicated patient**: in a disturbed family situation, there is one person is, by common agreement of the family, the "indicated patient." That person manifests psychopathological traits on behalf of the family.

2. **Role stability**: In "sick families" there may be very stable roles in the family, e.g. blamer, placator, irrelevant, intellectualizer; but the person who fills each role may switch. (<u>Virginia Satir</u>).

3. If the indicated patient is treated outside the family and "gets well," someone else in the family may fill the patient role.

4. Usually, when a family comes to a therapist requesting a change, what they mean is that they want the family to go back to what it was before the children began to have sexual urges, rebellious aggressive urges, etc.

5. **A family is a system**: All systems have three common characteristics.

   a. <u>External boundaries</u>: We can fight like hell among ourselves but no one else (physician) can say anything bad about us.

   b. <u>Internal maintenance</u>: Types of feelings allowed to go on within the family system. E.g., it is OK to fight and hate one another, but it is not OK to love.

   c. <u>Roles</u>: Can be either verbal or non-verbal. Define e.g., the roles of big people vs. the roles of little people.

V. MEDICAL LEGAL ISSUES

A. <u>Competency to Stand Trial</u>. Is the patient able to:

1. Understand nature of the charges.
2. Understand the possible penalties.
3. Understand the legal issues and procedures.
4. Work with the attorney.
5. Participate rationally in his own defense.

B. <u>Informed Consent</u>-**Adult**. Does the patient understand:

1. Reason for treatment.
2. What is being prescribed.

3. What probable outcomes are.
4. What side effects are known to occur (e.g., Tardive Dyskinesia).
5. Alternate treatments.

C. Informed Consent-**Parents** giving informed consent for their children.

1. The parents must be told everything.
2. The parents must give permission.
3. If they won't give permission and the child's life is threatened, the courts can overrule the parents.
4. Birth control information and devices; and, treatment for venereal disease without parental consent vary by State.

D. Informed consent when the patient cannot provide it.

1. A court appointed conservator or an attorney-in-fact can be designated with a "Durable Power of Attorney for Health Care."

2. Immediate family members or close friends can be surrogate decision makers.

3. If surrogate decision makers disagree; physician should continue to treat until a decision is reached or a conservator is appointed by the courts.

4. If known, the patient's wishes take priority over other's.

5. Physician should always act in best interest of the patient.

E. Committed Mentally Ill:

1. Must have treatment available.
2. Can refuse treatment.
3. Can require a jury trial to determine "sanity."
4. Retains competence for conducting business transactions, marriage, divorce, voting, driving, etc.
5. Sanity and competence are legal terms, not psychiatric diagnosis.
6. Restrictions on patient:
   a. Civil liberty to come and go.
   b. Emergency detention can be effected by M.D. or law enforcement for 48 hours pending a hearing.
   c. M.D. can detain; a judge can commit.

d. **With children, M.D. cannot detain;** only parents or juvenile courts.
   (1) only for imminent danger to self or others;
   (2) can't care for self;
   (3) parents have no control over dangerous behavior (fire-setting).

F. <u>If a patient refuses treatment</u>:

1. If life threatening can treat to save the life.
2. If not life threatening one must determine if they have the ability to make decisions; e.g., do they have a psychotic level disorder (e.g., delirium, Brief Reactive Psychosis, etc.).
3. Physician can detain against the patient's will if they are a danger to self or others. Can't treat against the patient's will unless they are a danger to self or others.
4. If can't detain and the patient wants to leave, try to get they to sign a document that they are leaving Against Medical Advice (AMA). If they won't sign, carefully document all actions in the patient's records.

G. <u>Privileged Communication</u>: Generally the following hold.

1. If the person is a threat to self or others you can break confidentiality and notify the victim, police. Helps legally if you have told the patient in advance of these potentials.

2. Police can't do anything until the patient does, unless it is the President, a Senator, the Pope, etc. Otherwise need a release of information.

3. Real controversy today regarding legal issues and suicide/homicide and breaking confidentiality

H. <u>Abortion</u>: The issues.

1. Public financing for abortion.
2. Wife obtaining an abortion without husband's permission.
3. Ethics of abortion: Is it ever ethical?
4. Is the physical and mental health of mother O.K.?

I. <u>Good Samaritan</u>:

1. Under no obligation to stop (you're a free citizen).

2. If you do stop to stabilize - - you are protected as long as you do what you are competent to do.

EXAM QUESTIONS - SECTION FOUR

INSTRUCTIONS: Each of the questions or incomplete statements below is followed by five suggested answers or completions. Select the one that is BEST in each case.

1. In the Mental Status Examination, we speak of orientation in four spheres. All the following are included EXCEPT:

    1) Cultural Background
    2) Person
    3) Place
    4) Present situation
    5) Time

2. On the Mental Status Examination, attention and concentration is usually judged by having the patient:

    1) Do serial subtraction.
    2) Interpret proverbs.
    3) Multiply 3 times 4.
    4) Recite 3 non-related words given previously at a later time.
    5) Recite the alphabet.

3. On the Mental Status Examination, under the subsection of Characteristics of Talk, all of the following are descriptions which are normally used under the characteristics of talk EXCEPT:

    1) Autistic verbalization
    2) Blocking
    3) Circumstantiality
    4) Pressure of speech
    5) Quality of voice

4. On the Mental Status Examination, under Contact and Intellect is the category of Insight and Judgement. A person is judged to have insight if he:

    1) can do serial sevens.
    2) can identify similarities and differences.
    3) can interpret proverbs.
    4) is oriented in four spheres.
    5) understands problems are emotional in origin.

5. There is a treatment modality in which persons establish a hierarchy of frightening steps toward an object of which they are phobic. The person is then taught to relax and, using visual imagery, the hierarchy of objects is worked through in a relaxed state, starting with the lowest anxiety provoking object and moving to the next highest. This type of therapeutic intervention is called:

   1) Aversive therapy
   2) Biofeedback
   3) Desensitization
   4) Operant conditioning
   5) Systematic desensitization

6. Underlying most of the psychoanalytically based psychotherapies is the assumption that:

   1) Abreaction is really "poor form" on the patient's part.
   2) If the unconscious material becomes conscious, the patient will be able to rid himself of his symptoms.
   3) If the person gains insight, they are cured.
   4) Resistance is a normal part of human life and should not necessarily be overcome in therapy.
   5) The primary focus should be the psychological processes within the individual and his small group.

7. The long-acting form of Prolixin is particularly useful for patients who:

   1) Are mentally retarded with agitation and psychosis.
   2) Are not reliable in taking medication.
   3) Have more neurotic than psychotic symptomatology.
   4) Need less sedative effect.
   5) Show an anaphylactic reaction to Thorazine.

8. Consider these symptoms:

    - Parkinsonian symptoms
    - Oculogyric crisis
    - Tardive dyskinesia
    - Akathisia
    - Convulsions

    Choose one answer that is applicable to all the above.

    1) Are likely to appear with lithium use.
    2) Are most likely to appear with phenothiazine derivatives.
    3) Frequently appear with chronic use of anti-anxiety medications.
    4) May appear regardless of what neuroleptic is being used.
    5) May occur as a side effect of chronic alcohol consumption.

9. Lithium carbonate has been found to be a powerful drug in the field of psychiatry. Its indicated use is:

    1) Bipolar Disorder, manic phase
    2) In psychotic persons who have cardiac or renal disease.
    3) Major Depression
    4) Paranoid states
    5) Schizophrenia

10. Which of the following statements regarding minor tranquilizers is correct?

    1) Are being well regulated in their prescriptions.
    2) Can be used for unlimited time span.
    3) Can give extrapyramidal side effects.
    4) They have no addictive potential.
    5) Use should be warranted by clinical circumstances and not administered prophylactically.

11. All of the following are services of a Community Mental Health Center EXCEPT:

    1) 24-hour emergency psychiatric service
    2) Community education
    3) Community consultation
    4) Partial hospitalization
    5) Psychiatric research

12. In psychotherapeutic intervention, token economy systems are an example of:

    1) Aversive therapy
    2) Classical conditioning
    3) Milieu therapy
    4) Operant conditioning
    5) Desensitization

13. Alcoholics are sometimes treated with Antabuse. This substance, when in the body, produces a strong physiologic reaction including nausea and vomiting. This type of behavior modification therapy is called:

    1) Aversive therapy
    2) Biofeedback
    3) Classical conditioning
    4) Desensitization
    5) Systematic desensitization

14. In Biofeedback therapy, a biological process of which the person is not normally aware is fed back to them in that they are requested to keep that biologic process going. This particular behavior modification technique has been useful in all of the following conditions EXCEPT:

    1) Hypertension
    2) Migraine headache
    3) Personality disorders
    4) Seizures
    5) Tension headache

15. With regard to the attributes of a therapist, all of the following statements are true EXCEPT that therapists:

    1) coming from Psychoanalytic, Rogerian, Transactional Analysis and Gestalt schools represent similar theoretical orientations.
    2) expectations of people getting well is an important factor.
    3) from different philosophical and theoretical schools do different things in their therapeutic endeavors.
    4) who is nurturant is a more curative factor than the types of therapeutic methods used by the same therapist.

16. Antipsychotics may be useful in all of the following diagnostic classifications EXCEPT:

    1) Dysthymic Disorder
    2) Mania
    3) Organic Brain Syndromes
    4) Paranoia
    5) Schizophrenia

17. With regard to the broad classification of neuroleptics, all of the following statements are true EXCEPT:

    1) Some patients are more receptive to one versus another of the neuroleptics.
    2) These medications have some effect on the pattern of thinking.
    3) These medications have their main effect in the synaptic cleft.
    4) These medications sometimes help control subjective pain which is not equivalent to physical cause.
    5) These medications usually take a minimum of 7 days to have their effect.

18. With regard to anti-depressants (Elavil, Vivactil, Tofranil, Pertofrane), in which of the following disorders is it NOT recommended?

    1) Bipolar Disorder, depressive phase
    2) Bipolar Disorder, manic phase
    3) Dysthymic Disorder
    4) Major Depression with melancholia
    5) Panic Disorder

19. Which of the following statements regarding electroconvulsive therapy is NOT correct?

    1) Immediately after ECT, memory dysfunction and disorientation is to be expected.
    2) It is the treatment of choice in Major Depression with Melancholia.
    3) It is the treatment of choice for schizophrenia.
    4) The effectiveness of the treatment is due to the seizure.
    5) There is no consistent data suggesting repeated ECT administration leaves residual CNS dysfunction.

20. All of the following statements are true of supportive psychotherapy EXCEPT:

    1) Encourages the indicated patient to express feelings.
    2) Is more effective when the person is immersed in a stable environment.
    3) Is more oriented towards symptom relief than personality reformation.
    4) Little utilization of psychopharmacological agents.
    5) Makes active use of re-education.

21. In looking at the family as a system, which of the following is NOT characteristic of the dysfunctional system?

    1) Children, regardless of age, are consistently treated as if they don't count.
    2) It's O.K. to hate, but it's not O.K. to love.
    3) Non-family members cannot comment on the system.
    4) One family member may be scapegoated as the indicated patient.
    5) Successfully treating the one patient lets other family members focus on themselves in a healthy manner.

22. In Gestalt theory and treatment, it is assumed that patients "scare themselves" by all of the following EXCEPT:

    1) getting involved in "games".
    2) getting out of the here and now.
    3) holding their breath.
    4) reversing the figure and ground of the situation.
    5) the strength of the inhalation of breath.

23. There appear to be some important common elements to all psychotherapies. These are all of the following EXCEPT:

    1) Catharsis or "blowing off steam".
    2) Checking the results of the treatment.
    3) Desensitization.
    4) Focus of the therapist on helping in the general sense.
    5) Talking freely to someone who is relatively non-critical.

24. Which of the following is NOT considered to be group therapy?

    1) Family Therapy
    2) Group process
    3) Group treatment
    4) Milieu therapy
    5) Therapeutic communities

25. Which of the following statements is/are associated with patient who is LEAST likely to follow medical directions in a therapeutic regimen? The patient who:

   1) is chronically ill.
   2) likes their physician.
   3) perceives their illness as serious.
   4) take medications for acute illnesses.
   5) trusts the doctor's judgement.

26. Virginia Satir has labeled various pathological roles in dysfunctional families. These include all of the following EXCEPT:

   1) Blamer
   2) Intellectualizer
   3) Irrelevant
   4) Placator
   5) Scapegoater

27. Criteria for competency to stand trial include:

   1) ability to handle money
   2) can endure possible incarceration
   3) cooperative in planned psychiatric care
   4) freedom from psychosis
   5) understanding of the charges

28. Who can give informed consent for the treatment of a child below the age of majority?

   1) A grandparent.
   2) An adult sibling.
   3) The child if its an emergency.
   4) The courts.
   5) The physician if its an emergency.

29. If a patient is too ill to make a decision about discontinuing care, who can make that decision if the patient's wishes are not known?

   1) A business partner.
   2) A close friend.
   3) A divorced, but friendly ex-spouse.
   4) A durable power of attorney for health.
   5) The long term family physician.

EXAM QUESTIONS - SECTION FOUR

Answer Key

1.	1	11.	5	21.	5
2.	1	12.	4	22.	1
3.	5	13.	1	23.	4
4.	5	14.	3	24.	2
5.	5	15.	3	25.	1
6.	2	16.	1	26.	5
7.	2	17.	5	27.	5
8.	4	18.	2	28.	4
9.	1	19.	3	29.	4
10.	5	20.	4		

SECTION FIVE: INTRODUCTION TO HEALTH CARE SYSTEMS

I. **INTRODUCTION** 215

    A.   Purpose
    B.   Structural Change
    C.   Corporate Change
    D.   Public Policy
    E.   Economic Pressure
    F.   Challenges

II. **THE HEALTH OF THE NATION** 216

    A.   Definition of Health
    B.   The Health Characteristics of a Population
        1.   The aging population
        2.   The uninsured and under-insured
        3.   Human immunodeficiency virus infections

    C.   Health Statistics
        1.   Sources of data
        2.   Mortality data
        3.   Morbidity data
        4.   Fertility and natality

    D.   Utilization of Health Care Services
        1.   Ambulatory care services
        2.   Hospital services

    E.   Conclusion

III. **HEALTH MANPOWER** 239

    A.   Historical Notes
    B.   GMENAC Report
        1.   Purpose
        2.   Conclusions
        3.   Recommendations
        4.   After GMENAC

    C.   Practice Classification
        1.   Active physicians
        2.   Specialty distribution

IV. **AMBULATORY CARE: TRADITIONAL MODELS** 244

    A.   Introduction
    B.   Traditional Practice Models
        1.   Solo practice
        2.   Partnerships
        3.   Group practice
        4.   Conclusions

V. AMBULATORY CARE: ALTERNATIVE MODELS 249

    A. Historical Background
    B. Health Maintenance Organizations
        1. The Federal HMO Act of 1973
        2. Federal amendments
        3. Comprehensive health services
        4. Enrollment
        5. Cost containment and quality of care

    C. Preferred Provider Organizations
    D. Other Private Ambulatory Care Services
        1. Hospitals
        2. Urgent care centers

    E. Federal Government
        1. Uniformed Services and Veterans Administration
        2. Indian Health Service
        3. Federally funded programs

    F. State and Local Government
        1. Public health departments
        2. State and community neighborhood centers
        3. Municipal and county hospitals

    G. Conclusions

VI. INSTITUTIONS FOR HEALTH CARE 257

    A. Hospitals
        1. Historical notes
        2. Classification schemes
        3. Structure and organization

    B. Nursing Homes
        1. Definition
        2. Classification
        3. Summary

    C. Mental Health Services
        1. Historical perspective
        2. Organization

VII. FINANCING PATIENT CARE 266

    A. Introduction
    B. Reimbursement and Financing Mechanisms
        1. Direct or out-of-pocket payment by the patient
        2. Indirect patient payments
        3. Non-patient dollars

    C. Private Health Insurance
        1. Historical notes
        2. Scope

3. Common terms and concepts

D. Government Programs-Medicare and Medicaid
1. Historical notes
2. Medicare
3. Medicaid

E. Medicare Prospective Payment and Diagnosis Related Groups
1. TEFRA legislation
2. Purpose
3. Peer Review Organizations
4. Hospitals affected
5. DRG assignment
6. Assignment of reimbursements
7. Effects on hospitals
8. Summary

F. Resource-Based Relative-Value Scale
1. Background
2. Development of fee schedule
3. Projections

G. Capitation or Prepaid Health Plans
1. Historical notes
2. Definition of capitation
3. Premium distribution
4. Outcomes

H. Flow of Health Care Dollars
I. Trends for the Future
1. Physicians
2. Ambulatory care
3. Hospitals
4. Commercial insurance carriers
5. Federal programs
6. National or universal health insurance

VIII. **REGULATION AND QUALITY ASSURANCE** 295

A. Introduction
B. Licensure
1. Historical notes
2. General characteristics
3. Implementation of licensure laws
4. Continuing medical education
5. Summary

C. Institutional Licensure
D. Self Regulation
1. Code of ethics
2. Impaired physician programs
3. Grievance committees

E. Certification
1. Definition
2. Board Certification
3. Professional specialty organizations

F. Accreditation
1. Definition
2. Accrediting organizations

G. Audit Systems
1. Introduction

H. Health Care Planning
1. Introduction
2. Health Systems Agencies and Certificate of Need

I. Summary

IX. COMPARATIVE MODELS OF HEALTH CARE SYSTEMS 306

A. Key Elements

B. Health Care System Models
1. Mutual aid model
2. State model
3. Professional model
4. Corporatist model

C. The British System
1. Democratic state model
2. Development
3. Administration
4. Physicians' services
5. Private insurance

D. The Canadian Model
1. Corporatist model
2. Development
3. Administration
4. Physicians' services
5. Private insurance

E. Comparative Studies

IX. FINAL COMMENTS 312

X. SELECTED BIBLIOGRAPHY 313

STUDY QUESTIONS 316

ANSWERS 324

SECTION FIVE: INTRODUCTION TO HEALTH CARE SYSTEMS

I. **INTRODUCTION**

   A. <u>Purpose</u>: This section introduces the organizational structure and economic basis of the American health care system. Students of medicine are part of the continuous evolution of the American health care system and will need a working knowledge of the organization, economics, and dynamics of the American health care system In order to respond to:

   1. advances in knowledge and technology,

   2. increased demands for high quality cost effective care,

   3. pressures of increased competition, and

   4. factors shaping health care needs in the future.

   B. <u>Structural change</u>: The health care system of the United States has evolved from a simple system, characterized by the solo practitioner in a horse and buggy of centuries past, to a complex one, characterized by a multitude of components interacting with one another, forming the health care system as it is known today. Today's system is often described as pluralistic and operates through numerous collaborative activities or partnerships that link the many and diverse components together.

   C. <u>Corporate change</u>: As health care costs skyrocket and large corporations enter into the health care industry, history, for the first time, is seeing a greater emphasis on the business of health care delivery, wherein a profit motive may dominate, as opposed to the traditional service motive, characteristic of the community-based health care delivery systems of the past.

   D. <u>Public policy</u>: The major objectives of public policy in the development of the health care system have been to:

   1. insure access to equal medical care for all people,

   2. develop new health care technology, and to transfer that technology into practice (for example, the National Institute of Health spends more than 4.5 billion dollars annually to fund basic biomedical and clinical research to develop new methodologies

which can benefit the health care of the American people), and

    3. promote quality assurance in health care to insure that the health care system delivers the highest quality care possible.

E. <u>Economic pressure</u>: More recently, escalating health care costs have become a major concern to the American public, government, and industry. For example, health care benefits now constitute a significant portion of employee benefits provided by large companies. Representatives of several large corporations agree that the rising cost of health care is one of the major problems facing U.S. industry today. The health care costs problem began to escalate with the enactment of the Medicare and Medicaid legislation in the mid-1960s. In order to entice physicians and health care facilities to meet the needs of the elderly and the indigent, the system was based on an open-ended cost reimbursement basis. That is to say, whatever it cost to provide a service, Medicare and Medicaid would reimburse for it. Inflationary increases in Medicare costs led to more regulations. Regulatory changes, in an attempt to control hospital costs, resulted in implementation of the Medicare Prospective Payment System based on diagnostic related groupings (DRGs). More recently, in an attempt to control ambulatory costs, a physician fee schedule based on the resource-based relative-value scale (RBRVS) was developed and implemented.

F. <u>Challenges</u>: Today, the issue in health care is a tradeoff between the objectives of equal access for all, progressive technological developments, and quality assurance versus cost. No longer can the U.S. government afford to spend so much money on health care. Public objectives and cost containment are grossly out of balance. The challenge for the future is to continue to provide the highest quality medical care available to as many people as possible, but at the same time to keep costs within acceptable limits.

II. THE HEALTH OF THE NATION

It is a foregone conclusion that the purpose of a health care system is to promote the health of the population it serves. Ironically, the health care system in the United States, as well as other countries in the world, tends to deal with diagnosis and treatment of disease and not health promotion. It is apparent, at least in this country, that this paradox is beginning to be addressed. Not only are better diagnostic and treatment related services being developed, but there is also a national movement towards health promotion and preventive medicine. This is witnessed by the development of fitness centers, smoking cessation programs, formal health risk assessment programs, and numerous approaches towards developing more healthy life styles. In short, the consumers, health care providers, and government leaders are broadening the focus of health care to include not only illness and treatment of disease but also disease prevention and health promotion.

A. Definition of health

   1. The <u>World Health Organization</u> defines health as a "state of complete physical, mental, and social well-being and not merely the absence of disease or infirmity."

   2. A more realistic definition, offered by Terris, states that "health is a state of physical, mental and social well-being and ability to function and not merely the absence of illness or infirmity". The emphasis is on the ability to function not on the state of perfectness implied by the first definition. Disease and illness indicate some sort of a disruptive influence on health.

B. The <u>health characteristics of a population</u> in terms of its health, disease, and illness are important to a health care system as it attempts to meet the needs and demands of its population. The demands and needs of a population can be understood by looking at three types of data - population data, health care statistics and utilization data.

   <u>Population Data</u> describe the population demographically and are useful in health planning activities. The present population of the United States is estimated at 250 million people. The most extensive mechanism for gathering population data is the census. It is required by the United States Constitution and is taken every ten years. These data are helpful in predicting trends in the population based on age, sex, birth rates, and socioeconomic factors. Significant issues include:

   1. <u>The aging population</u>: One of the most significant changes in the population which will effect health care in the future is the gradual shift toward an older population. The increased number of geriatric patients will force the health care system to develop cost effective methods to meet the demand for additional health care services and new and different health care services. Health planning activities are beginning to focus on the

development of health services for the elderly, including a renewed emphasis on home care services as well as nursing home services.

2. <u>The uninsured and under-insured</u>: A second major challenge due to changes in the population centers on the uninsured and under insured. The increasing number of people in this group has led to increased interest in universal health insurance.

   a. In 1986 it was estimated that less than half of the poor and near poor were eligible for the short-term care benefits provided by Medicaid.

   b. An estimated 35 million Americans have no financial protection from the expenses of medical care - no insurance or other coverage, public or private. As many as 80 million persons are not covered by major medical policies.

   c. Insured, working-age adults have less access to medical care than the elderly and poor, black, and Hispanic persons in this group are at risk for even greater problems with access to care.

3. <u>Human immunodeficiency virus infections</u>: Confirmed world cases of AIDS as of October 1991 were 418,403. Estimates of AIDS cases are as high as 1,500,000. In the U.S.A. there have been 202,843 cases confirmed and 130,687 deaths due to AIDS as of November 1991.

   a. From 1982 through 1989, $5.5 billion were spent on HIV-related illness by the federal government.

   b. It is estimated that federal spending in 1992 will reach $4.3 billion and combined public and private spending will account for 1.6 percent of all health related costs in the United States.

   c. Federal spending for HIV research and prevention is similar to funding for other major diseases that now have a greater impact on mortality.

C. <u>Health Statistics</u> describe the health status of a population primarily in terms of mortality and morbidity data. Mortality and morbidity data are utilized in health planning and for allocation and reallocation of health resources. The health status of a population influences the supply, demand, and need for health care services. The prevalence of conditions and disorders dictates the health care services, professionals, and types of facilities needed to provide care.

1. Sources of data: In traditional public health terms, vital statistics include documenting births, deaths, marriages, and divorces. In the United States, the primary responsibility for collecting these data rests with the states, but not all states collect all categories of data.

   a. The National Death Index was established by the National Center for Health Statistics requiring a computerized record of deaths to be kept beginning with the year 1979.

   b. The National Center for Health Statistics is primarily responsible for compiling and publishing the mortality and morbidity data for of the United States.

2. Mortality Data, expressed as the number of deaths per 100,000 population, refer to various causes of death within various age groups. The crude death rate in the United States has ranged between 8 and 10 deaths per 1000 population per year since 1955. In recent years there has been a slight downward trend. There are certain inherent problems in collecting mortality data such as the cause of death. For example, a patient who has coronary artery disease and dies of a heart attack, but who also has hypertension and diabetes as co-existing or aggravating conditions may be listed as a death due to atherosclerotic heart disease and not be counted as a death related to hypertension or diabetes. The tables and graphs which appear at the end of this subsection present selected mortality data for the United States.

3. Morbidity Data identify the prevalence of conditions within a population and the degree of disability created by the conditions. It is difficult to obtain accurate information regarding the morbidity of a population because a large portion of illnesses, and some diseases, are treated outside of the formal health care system. Morbidity data are even more difficult to compile than mortality data since the endpoint or outcome is often more poorly defined. Mechanisms developed to determine disease and illness prevalence in the

United States include patient completed surveys, abstracts of physicians' office records, and hospital discharge data.

There are inherent problems in compiling morbidity data. Patients may report symptoms, while a physician's or hospital's record may report specific diagnostic categories, creating considerable overlap or significant discrepancies when comparing one source of data to the other. Since many illnesses go unrecognized by both health professionals and patients themselves, it is an impossible task to get a complete and accurate assessment of the actual health status of any population.

a. <u>Sources of morbidity data</u>: In addition to the <u>Center for Disease Control</u> (CDC) the <u>National Center for Health Statistics</u> is the other regular source of morbidity data in the United States. The results of various surveys are published periodically in "Vital and Health Statistics" and monthly in "Vital Statistic Reports". Combined, these activities constitute the <u>National Health Survey</u>.

(1) The <u>Hospital Discharge Survey</u> reports mortality and morbidity data generated from hospital sources. These reports indicate that approximately 70% of hospital discharges are accounted for by six diagnostic groups listed in Table 1 below.

(2) The <u>National Ambulatory Medical Care Survey</u> is a continuing national probability sample of ambulatory medical encounters. The scope of the survey covers physician-patient encounters in offices of non-federally employed physicians classified as "office-based, patient care" physicians. and will eventually cover all loci of ambulatory care. It provides information on the frequency of diagnoses from the physician's perspective. There are obvious differences between general internal medicine profiles and profiles from family medicine practices. A representative sample of common diagnoses is provided in Table 2 below.

Table 1: Major Hospital Discharge Diagnostic Groups

Diagnostic Groups	Percent of Total
1. Diseases of the Circulatory System	13%
2. Diseases of the Digestive System	12%
3. Complications of pregnancy, childbirth and the puerperium	12%
4. Accidents, poisonings, and violence	10%
5. Diseases of the Genitourinary System	10%
6. Diseases of the Respiratory System	10%

Table 2: Major Diagnostic Categories in Ambulatory Care Practices

General Internal Medicine		Family Medicine	
1. Essential benign hypertension	9.3%	1. Medical or special examination	6.3%
2. Chronic ischemic heart disease	7.9%	2. Essential benign hypertension	5.9%
3. Diabetes mellitus	4.5%	3. Acute upper respiratory infection	3.6%
4. Medical or special examination	4.1%	4. Diabetes mellitus	2.5%
5. Acute upper respiratory infection	2.6%	5. Medical and surgical aftercare	2.4%
6. Neuroses	2.3%	6. Acute pharyngitis	2.2%
7. Osteoarthritis and allied conditions	2.3%	7. Chronic ischemic heart disease	2.2%
8. Symptomatic heart disease	2.0%	8. Other eczema and dermatitis	2.2%
9. Medical and surgical aftercare	1.8%	9. Influenza, unqualified	2.1%
10. Rheumatoid arthritis and allied conditions	1.6%	10. Obesity	2.1%

b. Reportable Diseases

The law requires that all deaths must be reported, but it is much less specific about the categories for sickness and illness. The only diseases or illnesses which are required to be reported are communicable or infectious diseases. These data are often times reported to state and local public health departments, which in turn furnish reports to the Center for Disease Control (CDC).

The CDC combines these data and reports them in a publication called the "Morbidity and Mortality Weekly Report." Significant conditions which must be reported in the United States include:

(1) Chicken pox
(2) Gonorrhea
(3) Hepatitis-A, B, and unspecified
(4) Measles, Mumps, Rubella
(5) Salmonella and Shigella infections
(6) Tuberculosis
(7) Syphilis
(8) AIDS

c. Disability data

(1) <u>Limitation of activity caused by chronic conditions</u> is one measure of disability. Tables 3 and 4 provides selected statistics from the <u>National Health Interview Survey</u> for 1988.

(2) The National Health Interview Survey also estimates the <u>disability days due to acute conditions</u>. Table 4 presents data for the incidence of acute conditions and the associated disability days for 1988.

d. Another estimate of morbidity comes from <u>self-assessment of health</u>. Selected data from the National Health Interview Survey for the year 1988 are presented in Table 5. For the total population 40.2% reported excellent health, 27.7% reported very good health, 22.7% reported good health, and 9.4% reported fair or poor health.

Table 3: Disability and Limitation Due to Chronic Conditions

Characteristic	Limited but not in major activity	Limited in amount or kind of major activity	Unable to carry on major activity	Total with limitation of activity
Age Groups				
Under 15 years	1.2%	3.4%	0.4%	5.0%
15-44 years	2.7%	3.5%	2.2%	8.4%
45-64 years	5.5%	8.4%	8.6%	22.4%
Over 65 years	14.4%	12.1%	10.5%	37.0%
Sex[1]				
Male	3.7%	5.2%	4.3%	13.2%
Female	4.3%	5.3%	3.4%	12.9%
Race[1]				
White	4.0%	5.3%	3.5%	12.8%
Black	3.8%	5.9%	6.6%	16.3%

[1] Age adjusted

Table 4: Incidence of Acute Conditions and Associated Disability

Age Group	Incidence of Acute Conditions[1] (No. per 100 people)	Restricted-activity Days (No. per person)	Bed-disability Days[2] (No. per person)
All ages[3]	184.8	7.1	3.1
Under 15 years	296.5	8.1	3.9
15-44 years	162.6	6.7	2.8
45-64 years	107.9	5.8	2.4
Over 65 years	108.9	8.2	3.4

[1] Excludes conditions involving neither medical attention nor activity restriction
[2] A subset of restricted-activity days
[3] Age-adjusted

Table 5: Self Assessment of Health Status by Age, Sex, and Race

Characteristic	Excellent	Very Good	Good	Fair or Poor
Age Groups[1]				
Under 15 years	53.3%	26.6%	17.4%	2.7%
15-44 years	42.6%	30.5%	21.4%	5.5%
45-64 years	28.2%	26.5%	28.2%	17.1%
Over 65 years	16.3%	21.5%	32.8%	29.4%
Sex[1]				
Male	42.2%	27.5%	21.4%	8.9%
Female	38.3%	27.8%	24.0%	9.9%
Race[1]				
White	41.8%	28.4%	21.4%	8.5%
Black	30.1%	23.3%	30.2%	16.4%

[1] Age-adjusted

4. <u>Fertility and Natality</u>: Fertility rates and birth statistics have been traditional indicators of the health of a given population. Significant information for the United States include:

    a. In 1987 there were 3.8 million live births and 2.1 million deaths. The <u>natural increase</u> in population of 1.7 million per year is fairly stable.

    b. The fertility rate in 1987 was 65.7 live births per 1,000 women age 15-44 and has remained essentially unchanged since 1975.

        (1) During this period, birth rates in women 30-39 years of age have increased by one-third.

        (2) During the 1980s, the proportion of births to teenage mothers has decreased for all racial groups.

(3) The proportion of births to unwed mothers has risen steadily since 1970 in all racial and ethnic groups. Percent of live births to unwed mothers for 1987 were:

White	16.7%
Black	62.2%
Asian and Pacific Islander	11.5%
Native American	44.9%

c. Approximately 75% of women receive prenatal care in the first trimester. There are large racial differences in early prenatal care.

d. Approximately 7% of all live births weigh less than 2500 grams. This figure has remained relatively constant since 1980.

D. <u>Utilization of Health Care Services</u> data serves a descriptive purpose and are important in planning health care services. As in other measures concerning the measurement of health and health care utilization, quantifying the utilization of health services can be sampled from either the patient's or the provider's perspective. The discrepancies which arise are important because both sets of data are used for health care planning strategies.

1. <u>Ambulatory Care Services</u>: The National Health Interview Survey (NHIS), a patient perspective survey, indicated that patients perceive their use of hospital resources to be less than hospitals perceive the use of their resources. The NHIS also indicated that patients believe they used doctor's offices to a greater extent than the National Ambulatory Medical Care Survey indicated, which is a physician or provider-based survey. According to the NHIS in 1988, there were approximately 5.3 physician contacts per person, including telephone contacts. This represents an increase from 4.8 contacts per person in 1978 and 5.1 contacts per person in 1983. Approximately 75% of the population made at least one visit to a physician's office. In general, females utilized ambulatory services (6.0 contacts per person) more often than males (4.6 contacts per person). As expected, the visit rate for both men and women increased with age. Table 6 compares the place of contact and percent distribution for 1983 and 1988.

Table 6:   Distribution of Physician Contact in Selected Ambulatory Settings

Place of Contact	1983	1988
Doctor's Office	56.1%	59.3%
Hospital Outpatient Departments[1]	14.9%	12.8%
Telephone	15.5%	13.7%
Home	1.5%	1.4%
Other	12.0%	12.7%

[1] Includes outpatient clinics and emergency rooms

2. Hospital Services

    a. <u>Utilization</u>: Table 7 summarizes data from the National Health Interview Survey (NHIS) on hospital utilization for selected years for short-stay hospitals in the United States.

    The <u>National Hospital Discharge Survey</u>, which is a provider-based survey, indicated some minor discrepancies in the data for 1988.

        (1) The reported discharge rate per 1000 population was 117.8, compared to 93.4 from the NHIS.

        (2) The reported number of days of care per 1,000 population was 754.8 compared to 622.7 from the NHIS.

        (3) The average length of stay was 6.4 days compared to 6.7 from the NHIS.

    b. The most common first-listed discharge diagnoses and surgical procedures non-federal short stay hospitals along with the percent distribution for 1988 are shown in Table 8 below.

    c. The <u>Annual Hospital Statistics Report</u> is the other major source of hospital utilization data and comes from the American Hospital Association.

    d. <u>Summary</u>: Current trends, influenced by prevailing economic pressures, indicate that hospital utilization is decreasing and that

the average length of stay may also be
decreasing slightly. In addition to economic
pressures, alternative delivery systems
undoubtedly account for part of these downward
trends in utilization and length of stay.
These systems include managed health care
plans, home health services, ambulatory
surgery programs, and increased emphasis on
outpatient diagnostic procedures.

Table 7: Short Stay Hospital Utilization for Selected Years 1964 - 1988

Indicator	1964	1984	1988
Discharges (Per 1,000 population)	109.1	114.7	93.4
Days of Care (Per 1,000 population)	970.9	871.9	622.7
Average Length of Stay (No. of days)	8.9	7.6	6.7

E. Conclusion

It is important to describe, qualify, and quantify the
health status of the population of the United States and
the utilization of health care services. These data
provide an important basis to plan health manpower
programs, institutional programs, research and
technological development, and financial planning and
developing payment strategies.

There appears to be a trend toward expanding the
emphasis of health to include health promotion and
preventive medicine while retaining the diagnosis and
treatment approach. Population shifts, with respect to
age distribution, and disease and illness prevalence can
also provide the stimulus for reallocating health care
resources and developing alternative methods to meet the
health needs and demands of the United States
population.

Table 8: Percent Distribution of Discharge Diagnosis and Procedures for Short Stay Hospitalizations for Males and Females

First-Listed Diagnoses (All Ages)	Percent Distribution	Operations for Inpatients (All Ages)	Percent Distribution
Both Sexes			
Females with delivery	11.3%		
Diseases of the heart	11.2%		
Malignant neoplasms	5.3%		
Fracture, all sites	3.2%		
Pneumonia, all forms	3.1%		
Males		**Males**	
Diseases of the heart	15.5%	Cardiac catheterization	6.6%
Malignant neoplasms	6.0%	Prostatectomy	3.9%
Fracture, all sites	3.9%	Reduction of fracture	3.7%
Pneumonia, all forms	3.9%	Repair, inguinal hernia	2.9%
Cerebrovascular disease	2.6%	Coronary artery bypass	3.0%
Inguinal hernia	1.9%	Tonsillectomy with or without adenoidectomy	1.0%
Females		**Females**	
Delivery	20.4%	Procedures to assist delivery	18.9%
Diseases of the heart	8.1%	Cesarean section	5.6%
Malignant neoplasms	4.8%	Repair, current obstetrical laceration	4.2%
Fracture, all sites	2.5%	Hysterectomy	3.1%
Pneumonia, all forms	2.5%	Salpingo-oopherectomy	2.7%
Pregnancy with abortive outcome	1.5%	Bilateral destruction, fallopian tubes	2.5%

FIGURE I

Life Expectancy at Birth By Sex
Selected Years 1900-1987

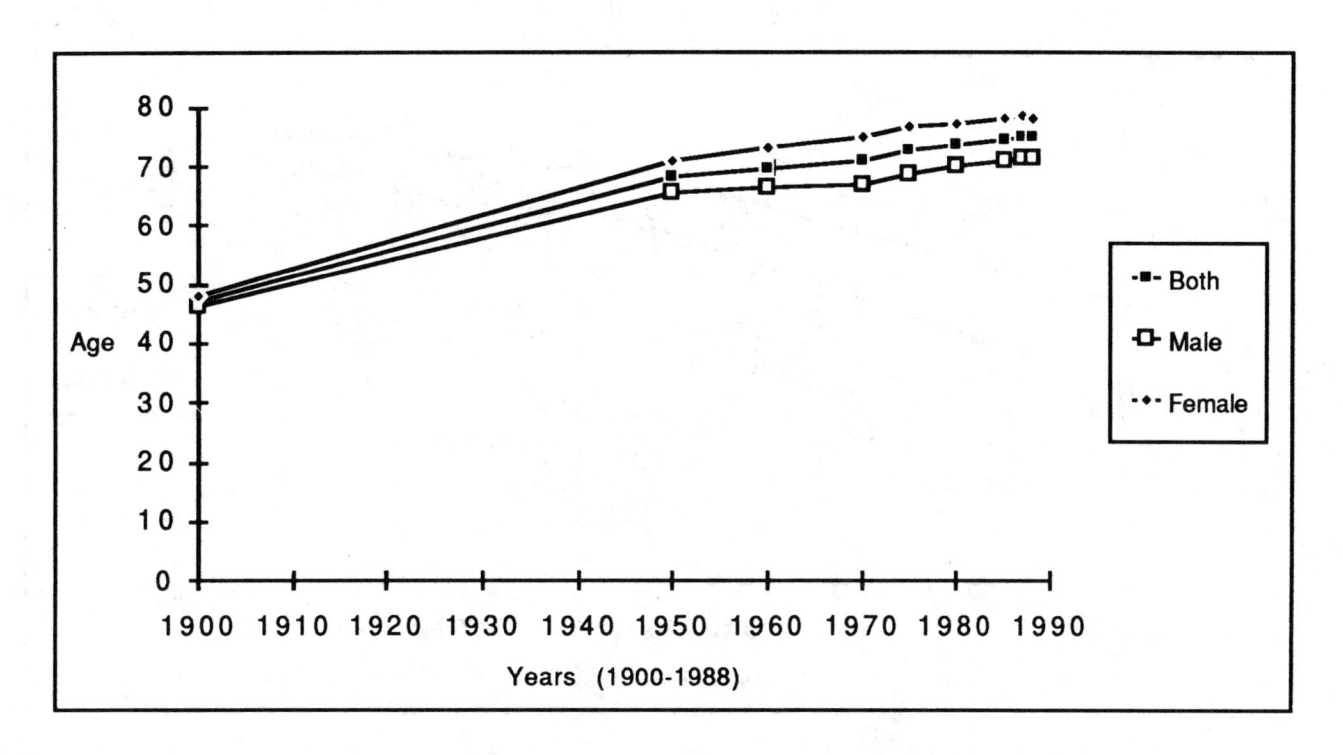

Life expectancy at birth of persons of both sexes in the United States has gradually increased since 1900. The most dramatic increase occurred between 1900 to 1950. This can be attributed in part to public health measures, immunizations, antibiotics, and advances in medical technology. In general females live longer than males.

FIGURE II

Life Expectancy at Birth By Race
Selected Years 1900-1987

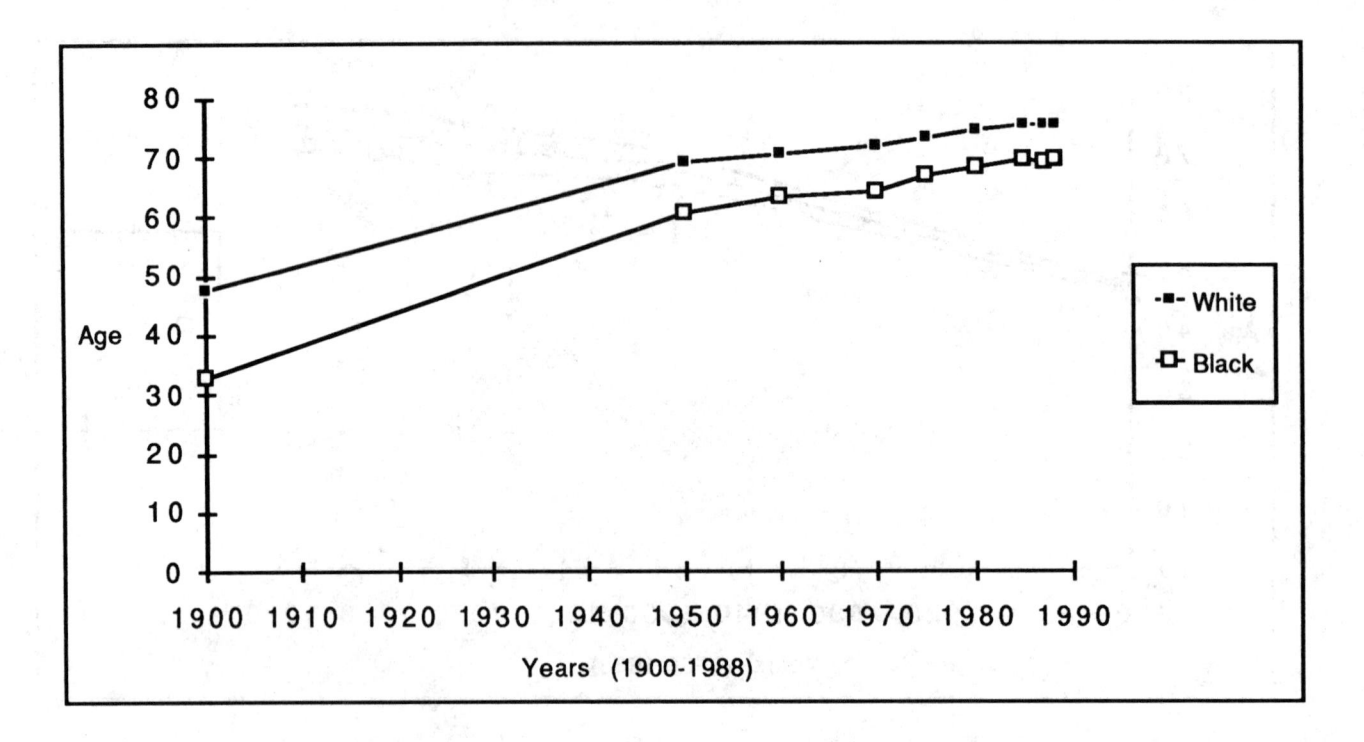

Life expectancy at birth for whites and blacks of both sexes has steadily increased. The differences in life expectancies between males and females and whites and blacks is more obvious at birth than it is at age 65 (See Figure III). However, white females consistently live the longest, and black males consistently have shorter life expectancies.

FIGURE III

Life Expectancy at Age 65 By Race
Selected Years 1900-1987

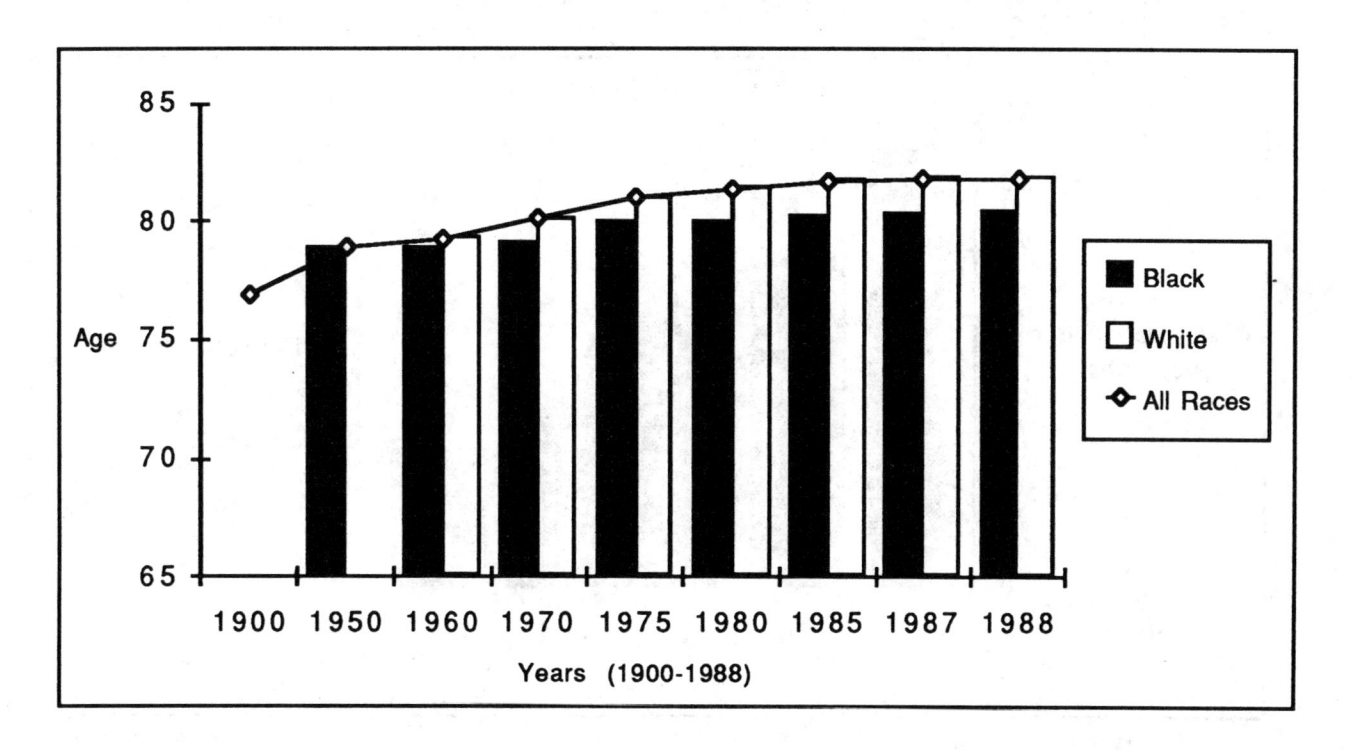

Life expectancy at age 65 has increased by only 5 years since 1900 and by only 0.5 years in the last decade. Racial differences continue to exist with whites living approximately 1.5 years longer than blacks. In 1988 white females at age 65 could expect to live an additional 18.7 years, black females an additional 17.1 years, white males an additional 14.9 years, and black males an additional 13.6 years. Even though human longevity has not increased to a great extent since 1900, more people are living to an older age.

FIGURE IV

Perinatal and Infant Mortality Rates
Selected Years 1960-1987

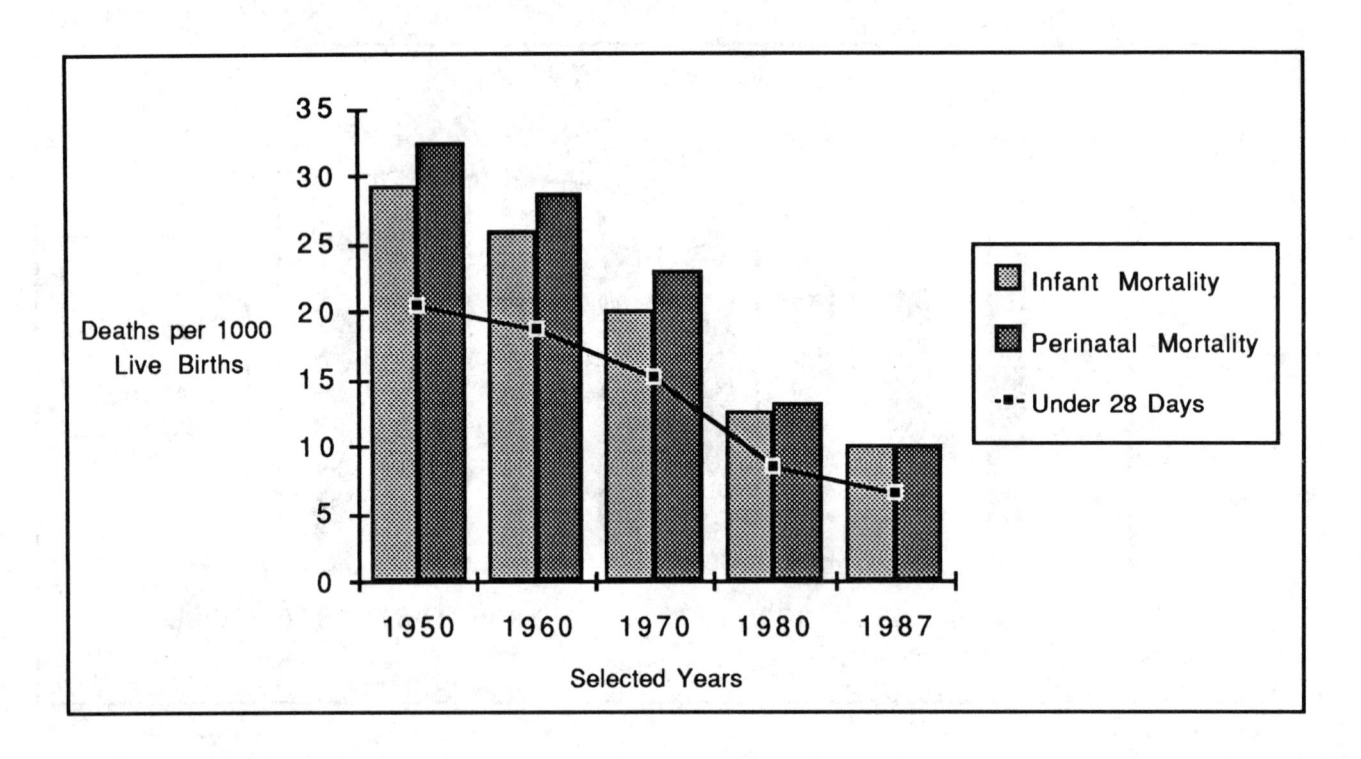

The infant mortality rate is defined as the number of deaths of infants under one year of age per 1000 live births. The neonatal death rate, indicated by the line overlay, occur within 28 days of birth and accounts for approximately two-thirds of all infant deaths. The perinatal mortality rate is the combination of late fetal deaths (number of fetal deaths of 28 weeks or more gestation) plus the infant deaths within 7 days of birth per 1000 live births. The United States ranked 22nd in the world in infant mortality in 1986 (10.4 deaths/1000 live births). Infant mortality among blacks is approximately twice that of whites. Japan had the lowest infant mortality rate at 5.2 deaths/1000 live births followed by Finland, Sweden, Switzerland and Hong Kong. Canada ranked seventh and Great Britain ranked eighteenth.

FIGURE V

Death Rates for All Causes
Selected Years 1950-1987

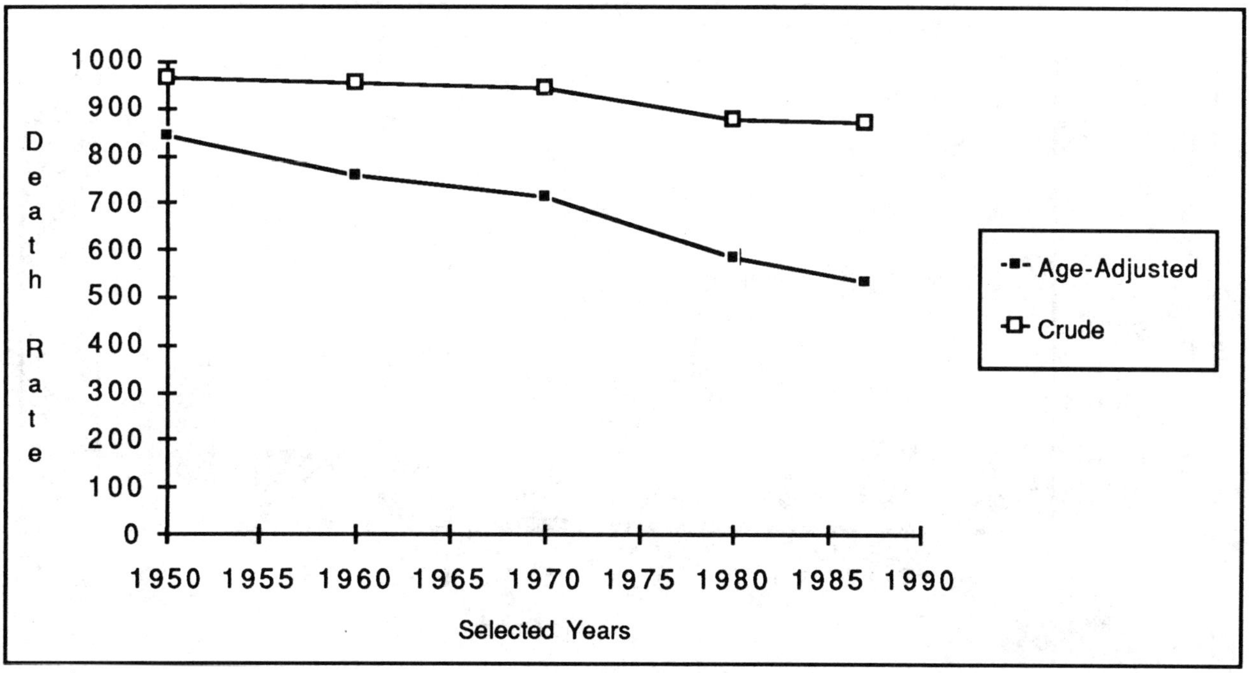

The Death Rate is the number of deaths per 100,000 resident population

The age-adjusted and crude death rate for all ages, races and sex have gradually declined over the last several decades. This seems largely due to decreases in deaths due heart disease and cerebrovascular diseases.

FIGURE VI

Age-Adjusted Death Rates By Age
1987

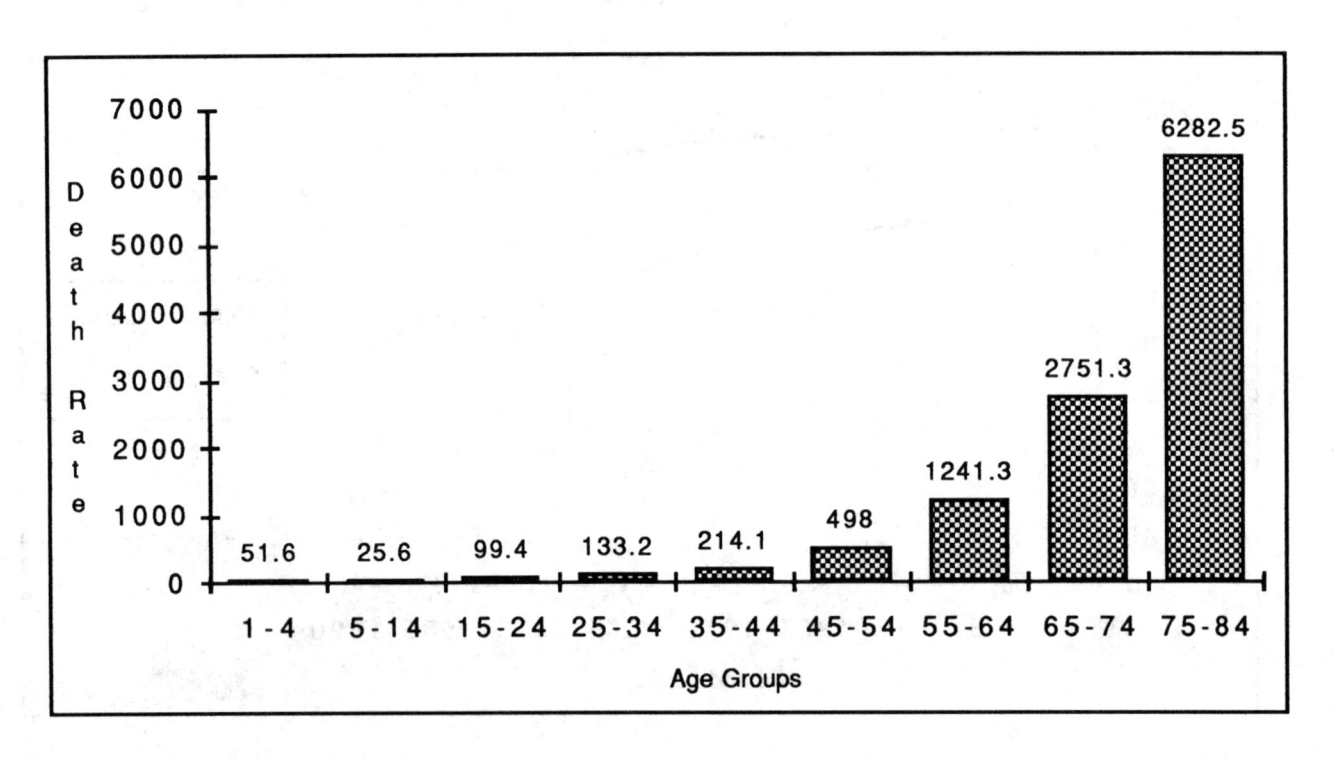

[Bar chart showing Death Rate on y-axis (0-7000) versus Age Groups on x-axis:
- 1-4: 51.6
- 5-14: 25.6
- 15-24: 99.4
- 25-34: 133.2
- 35-44: 214.1
- 45-54: 498
- 55-64: 1241.3
- 65-74: 2751.3
- 75-84: 6282.5]

The Death Rate is the number of deaths per 100,000 resident population

The age-adjusted death rates for 1987 for various age groups are shown in Figure VI. The values above the columns represent the actual death rate. Not shown are the death rates for infants less than one year of age (1018.5 deaths per 100,000 resident population) and for persons over 85 years of age (15,320.8 deaths per 100,000 resident population). In general death rates for whites are lower than the death rates for blacks in the corresponding age group. This is also true for sex differences where the death rates for females is lower than males.

FIGURE VII

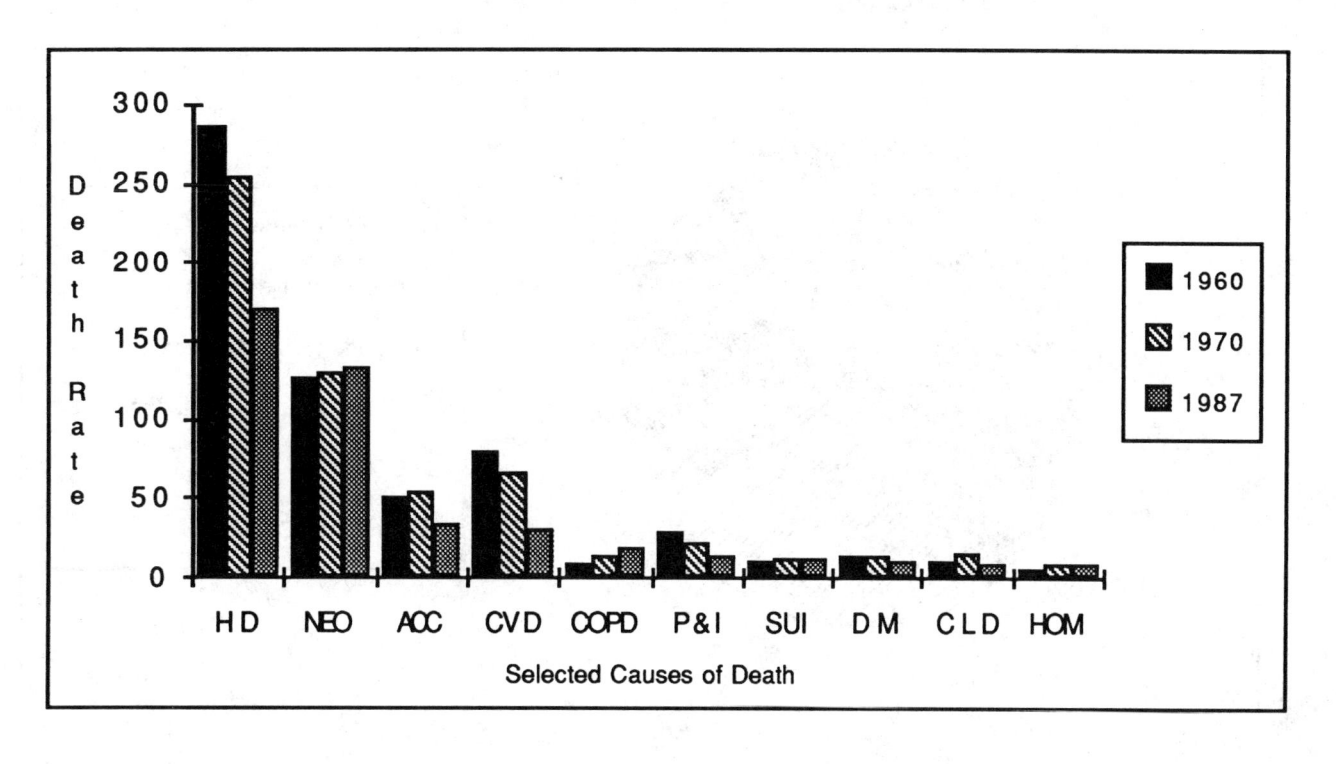

Age-Adjusted Death Rates For Selected Causes of Death
Selected Years 1960 - 1987

Key:
- H D = Diseases of the heart
- NEO = Malignant neoplasms
- ACC = Accidents
- CV D = Cerebrovascular disease
- COPD = Chronic obstructive pulmonary disease
- P&I = Pneumonia and influenza
- SUI = Suicide
- DM = Diabetes mellitus
- C L D = Chronic liver disease/cirrhosis
- HOM = Homicide and legal interventions

The age-adjusted death rates for the selected causes of death depicted in Figure VII is for all age groups, races, and sexes. Note the gradual increase in deaths due to malignant neoplasms and COPD. Ischemic heart disease accounted for 67% of the deaths due to heart disease which is down from 74% in 1980. Approximately 55% of the deaths due to accidents are caused by motor vehicle accidents. Alcohol is frequently involved. The causes of death are arranged in rank order according to 1987 figures except for homicide which ranks twelfth. AIDS was the fifteenth leading cause of death in 1987.

FIGURE VIII

Leading Causes of Death For 1987 For All Ages
Percent Distribution of Total Deaths

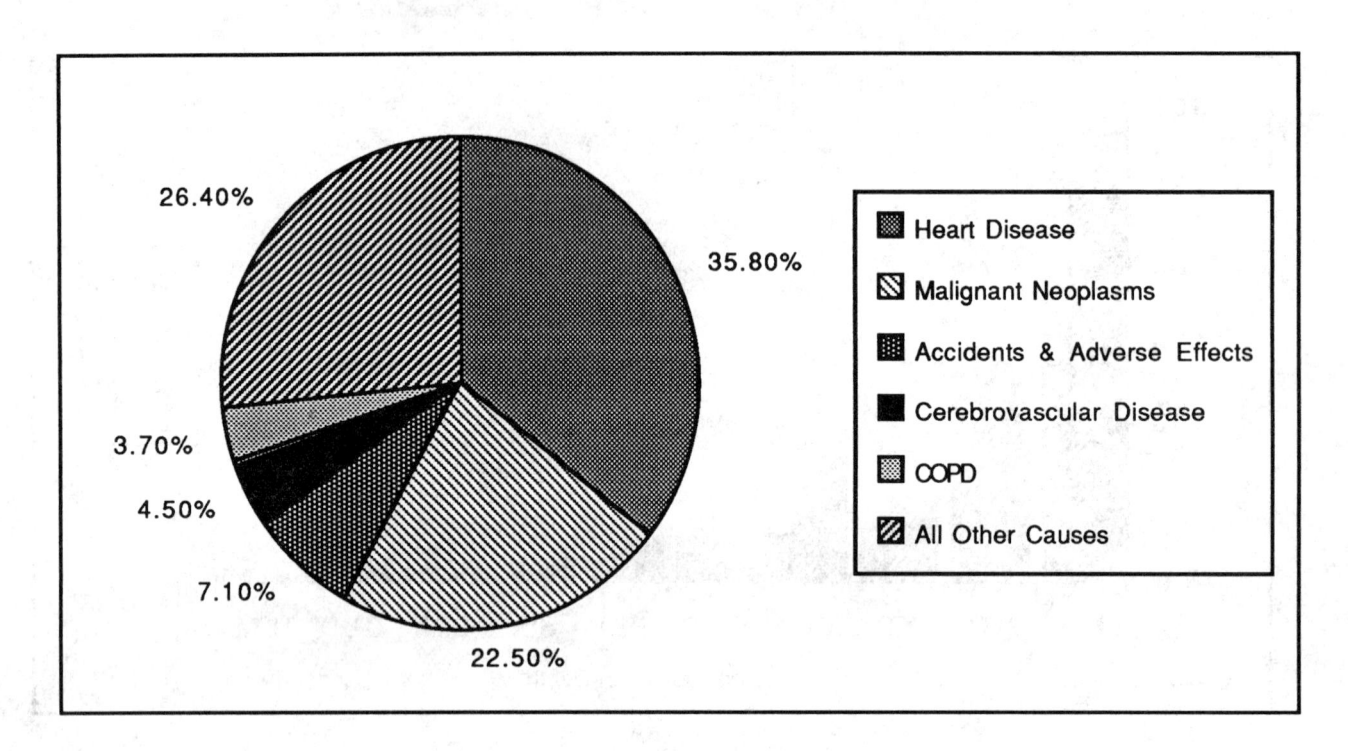

- Heart Disease — 35.80%
- Malignant Neoplasms — 22.50%
- Accidents & Adverse Effects — 7.10%
- Cerebrovascular Disease — 4.50%
- COPD — 3.70%
- All Other Causes — 26.40%

The chart demonstrates the distribution of the five leading causes of death in the United States for all men and women of all ages. Heart disease continues to be the leading cause of death with ischemic heart disease the single most common disease process accounting for deaths. Malignant neoplasms are second with cancer of the lung, colon, prostate, and breast accounting for 69% of all cancer related deaths. The next five leading cause of death in order include pneumonia and influenza (3.3%), diabetes mellitus (1.8%), suicide (1.5%), cirrhosis of the liver (1.2%), and diseases of arteries (1.1%).

TABLE 1

Leading Causes of Death - 1987
Percent of Total Deaths for Selected Age Groups

Leading Causes of Death Ages 1-14	Leading Causes of Death Ages 15-34	Leading Causes of Death Ages 35-54	Leading Causes of Death Ages 55-74	Leading Causes of Death Ages Over 75
1. Accidents and Adverse Effects 43.9% (2:1)	1. Accidents and Adverse Effects 36.9% (3.5:1)	1. Malignant Neoplasia 29.1% (1:1)	1. Heart Disease 35.3% (1.8:1)	1. Heart Disease 43.1% (1:1.5)
2. Malignant Neoplasia 10.4% (1.4:1)	2. Homicide 12.4% (3.5:1)	2. Heart Disease 23.7% (3:1)	2. Malignant Neoplasia 32.6% (1.3:1)	2. Malignant Neoplasia 16.3% (1:1)
3. Congenital Anomalies 8.5% (1.2:1)	3. Suicide 12.1% (4.5:1)	3. Accidents and Adverse Effects 9.4% (3.1:1)	3. Cerebrovascular Disease 5.2% (1.1:1)	3. Cerebrovascular Disease 10.0% (1:2)
4. Homicide 4.6% (1.2:1)	4. Malignant Neoplasia 7.6% (1.1:1)	4. Suicide 4.7% (2.9:1)	4. COPD 4.8% (1.5:1)	4. Pneumonia & Influenza 4.9% (1:1.3)
5. Heart Disease 4.0% (1.1:1)	5. HIV Infection 5.8% (7.5:1)	5. Chronic Liver Disease 4.2% (2.5:1)	5. Diabetes Mellitus 2.2% (1.1:1)	5. COPD 3.8% (1.5:1)

Table 1 presents data for the five leading causes of death for five different age groups. The numbers following each cause of death represents the percent of total deaths for that age group due to a particular cause of death. The ratio in parentheses under the percentage figures represent the approximate ratio of male to female deaths in that age range. In addition to the obvious sex differences there are significant racial difference also. Particularly in young black males, deaths due to violence is much more common than in the comparable white population.

FIGURE IX

Leading Causes of Cancer Deaths - 1987
Percent Distribution of Deaths Due to Cancer

Site	Percent
Lung	27.2%
Colon/Rectum	11.7%
Female Breast	8.6%
Prostate	5.8%
Pancreas	4.8%
Ovary	2.5%
Stomach	0.9%
Bladder	0.7%
CNS	0.5%
Uterus	0.5%

Percent of All Cancer Deaths

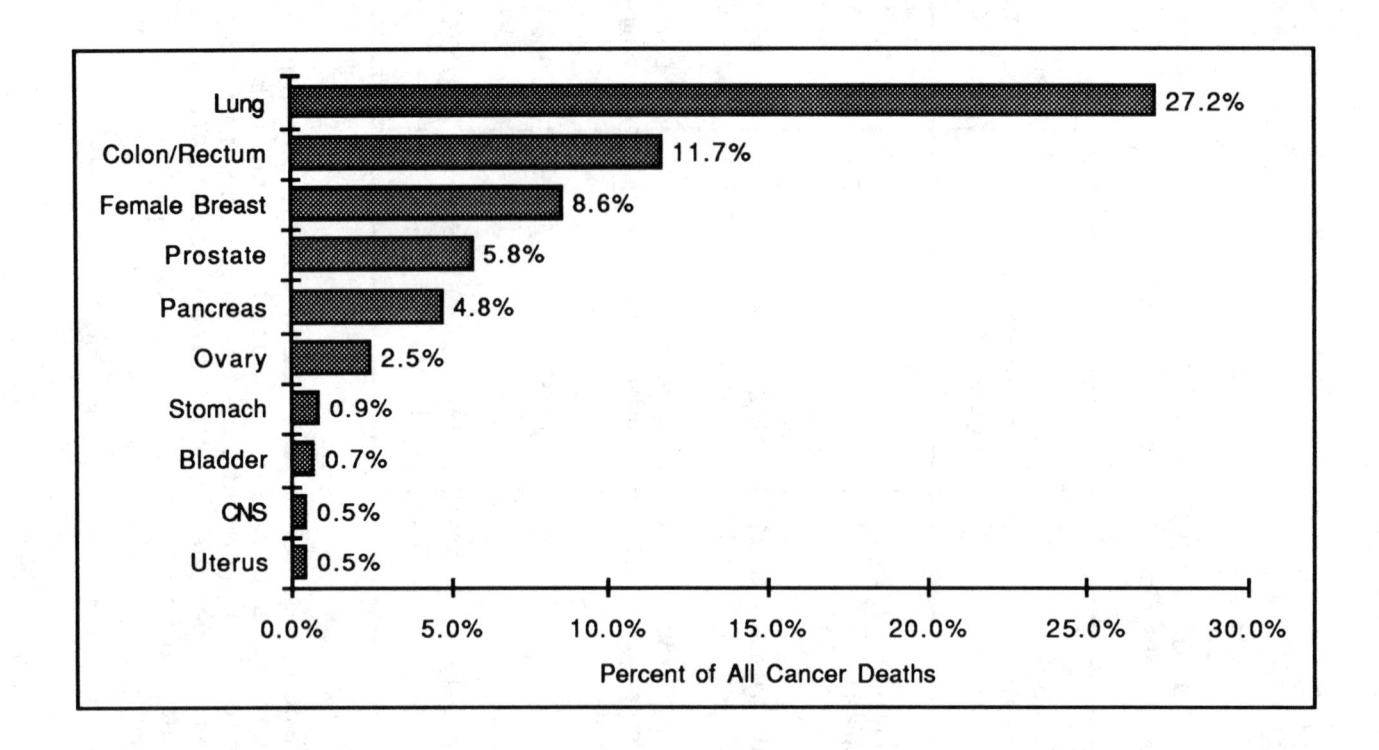

This graph depicts the distribution of cancer deaths in the United States in 1987 for the ten leading causes of cancer for all ages. Nearly 500,000 people died of cancer in 1987 with a slight male predominance. The following table, Table 2, lists the five leading causes of cancer deaths for 1987 by age group for males and females. Note that lung cancer is now the leading cause of death from cancer for both men and women.

TABLE 10

Leading Causes of Cancer Deaths - 1987
By Sex and Age Groups

Rank	Ages Under 15	Ages 15-34	Ages 35-54	Ages 55-75	Ages Over 75	All Ages
MALES						
1	Leukemia	Leukemia	Lung	Lung	Lung	Lung
2	Brain & CNS	Brain & CNS	Colon & Rectum	Colon & Rectum	Prostate	Colon & Rectum
3	Non-Hodgkin's Lymphomas	Non-Hodgkin's Lymphomas	Brain & CNS	Prostate	Colon & Rectum	Prostate
4	Connective Tissue	Hodgkin's Disease	Non-Hodgkin's Lymphomas	Pancreas	Pancreas	Pancreas
5	Bone	Skin	Pancreas	Stomach	Bladder	Leukemia
FEMALES						
1	Leukemia	Breast	Breast	Lung	Colon & Rectum	Lung
2	Brain & CNS	Leukemia	Lung	Breast	Breast	Breast
3	Connective Tissue	Uterus	Colon & Rectum	Colon & Rectum	Lung	Colon & Rectum
4	Bone	Brain & CNS	Uterus	Ovary	Pancreas	Pancreas
5	Kidney	Non-Hodgkin's Lymphomas	Ovary	Pancreas	Ovary	Ovary

III. **HEALTH MANPOWER**

   A. <u>Historical Notes</u>: Prior to 1900, the training of physicians varied greatly across the United States. Some training, such as Harvard and Johns Hopkins, was rigorous and produced physicians who were highly skilled and well-educated. Other, free standing schools, had virtually no consistent curriculum or quality assurance. Indeed, some physicians may have obtained their degrees through mail order catalogs. In 1910, Abraham Flexner undertook an extensive study of the medical education system in the United States and concluded that the system was disorganized and lacked accountability. He recommended that medical schools become associated with universities, where the biological sciences, based upon well-founded research, could be taught by university faculty. He further stated that clinical training should occur in the context of university faculty and lend itself to accountability, consistency, and quality. By 1925 many of Flexner's recommendations had been implemented, ushering in a new era of medical education in the United States.

Many of the for-profit medical schools were forced to close, as a consequence of the Flexner recommendations, eventually creating a physician shortage. This shortage continued through World war II and into the early 1960s. Government legislation was directed at alleviating the shortage by providing financial incentives to medical schools to train more doctors. The legislation has been very effective, perhaps too effective, because today the nation faces a potential physician surplus.

In 1978, there was an estimated deficit of 45,000 physicians to meet the health care needs of the United States. The Graduate Medical Education National Advisory Committee (GMENAC) predicted there would be 536,000 physicians by 1990, a surplus of 70,000 physicians, and by the year 2000, a surplus of as many as 145,000 physician.

B. GMENAC Report

   1. **Purpose**: In 1977, GMENAC was charged with studying the problem of physician manpower. The committee was directed to determine the:

       a. number of physicians required to meet the health care needs of the nation's people,

       b. appropriate physician specialty distribution,

       c. most favorable geographical distribution of physicians,

       d. appropriate way to finance graduate medical education, and to make

       e. recommendations based on an analysis of data.

   2. **Conclusions**: GMENAC studied the problem from 1977 through 1980, and after spending 4.5 million dollars, the Committee drew the following conclusions.

       a. There would be a surplus of physicians by the year 1990.

       b. Despite the surplus, some specialties would continue to have shortages. Table 11 lists the specialties which were predicted to be in surplus, in balance, and in deficit.

c. Increases in non-M.D. health care providers would aggravate the surplus.

d. An uneven geographical distribution of physicians would continue to exist.

e. A medical school's influence on a student's choice of a specialty was unclear, because students usually made their choice either during pre-med years or during residency.

f. The cost of graduate medical education was unknown because funds come from many different sources thereby making it impossible to separate the cost of training a resident from the cost of providing basic medical services.

g. The financial influence on specialty choices was uncertain.

3. Recommendations: Although numerous recommendations were made, the major GMENAC recommendations included the following:

a. Allopathic and osteopathic medical schools should reduce their entering class size, in aggregate, by a minimum of ten percent by 1984 relative to the 1978 size (not implemented).

b. Graduates of foreign medical schools entering the U.S. should be severely restricted (implemented).

c. Training non-physician health care providers should be stabilized and studied in view of the projected oversupply of physicians (not implemented).

d. Voluntary cutbacks should be made in residency training positions (partially implemented).

e. Planning should focus on geographical as well as specialty requirements.

f. Ambulatory care training should be emphasized

g. Reimbursement methods should be developed to help achieve health policy objectives.

TABLE 11: GMENAC Predictions for Specialty Distribution

Specialties in Surplus Percent of Predicted Need		Specialties in Balance Percent of Predicted Need		Specialties in Shortage Percent of Predicted Need	
Pulmonary Medicine	195%	Urology	120%	Hematology & Oncology	90%
Cardiology	190%	Gen'l Pediatrics & Subspecialties	115%	General Psychiatry	80%
Endocrinology	190%	Otolaryngology	105%	Preventive Medicine	75%
Neurosurgery	190%	General Internal Medicine	105%	Emergency Medicine	70%
Nephrology	175%	Family Medicine	105%	Child Psychiatry	45%
Rheumatology	175%	Osteopathic Gen'l Practice	105%		
Adult Allergy & Immunology	150%				
General Surgery	150%				
Infectious Disease	145%				
Obstetrics & Gynecology	145%				
Plastic Surgery	145%				
Ophthalmology	140%				
Thoracic Surgery	140%				
Orthopedics	135%				

4. <u>After GMENAC</u>: In 1987 there were 560,300 active physicians (536,200 M.D. and 24,100 D.O.) which exceeded GMENAC predictions.

   a. 1990 Projections: 601,100 active physicians or about 65,000 more than GMENAC predicted.

   b. Geographic maldistribution continues to exist as depicted in Table 12.

   c. It is likely that increasing numbers of physicians will seek salaried positions to avoid uncertainty in the increasingly competitive private sector.

   d. The number of hours a physician works may decline and thereby offset some of the surplus.

e. The real income of physicians may decline slightly.

f. Physician will have to increase services and promote better physician-patient relationships.

Table 12: Geographic Distribution of Physicians - 1987

Geographic Region	Primary Care	Patient Care	Total Physicians
	Number per 10,000 civilian population		
New England	6.2	24.2	27.2
Middle Atlantic	6.0	23.6	27.3
East North Central	5.1	17.1	19.9
West North Central	5.3	16.4	19.1
South Atlantic	5.4	18.6	20.8
East South Central	4.7	14.9	15.9
West South Central	4.5	15.2	17.1
Mountain	5.2	16.3	18.5
Pacific	6.5	20.9	22.9
United States	5.5	18.9	21.4

C. <u>Practice Classification</u>: Most medical education and clinical training is hospital-based, providing a narrow perspective of the organization of medical care services. On the contrary, most practicing physicians are office-based and spend a significant portion of their time in ambulatory care. The AMA has traditionally classified doctors engaged in patient care by locus of practice, organization of practice, and type of service or specialty. Table 13 show the distribution of physicians in the United States.

1. Of all <u>active physicians</u> in 1987, 90.1% were involved in patient care with 64.9% office-based and 25.2% hospital-based. Approximately 10% (9.9%) were involved in medical teaching, administration, research, clinical fellowships or other activities. About 15% of physicians were women, up from 7% in 1967.

2. <u>Specialty distribution</u>: In 1987, 39.7% of non federal office-based physicians were in primary care specialties including general and family practice (16.3%), internal medicine (16.4%), and

pediatrics (6.9%). Seven percent were general surgeons, 7.2% were in obstetrics and gynecology, 5.5% were in psychiatry, 2.2% were in emergency medicine, and 38.3% were in the various highly specialized areas.

Table 13: Classification and Locus of Practice of U.S. Physicians for 1987

Classification and Locus of Practice	Non-Federal	Federal	All Physicians
Office-based	57.6%	0.2%	57.8%
Hospital-based			
Full Time Staff	6.2%	2.2%	8.4%
Residents	13.6%	0.5%	14.1%
Other[1]	7.9%	0.8%	8.7%
Inactive			8.2%
Unclassified			2.3%
Unknown address			0.5%

[1] Includes medical teaching, administration, research, clinical fellows and others.

IV. AMBULATORY CARE: TRADITIONAL MODELS

A. <u>Introduction</u>: The principal mode of organization of physicians in the United States is synonymous with the term "private practice". Physicians in private practice provide a full range of health care services and are limited or guided only by the laws and licenses of the state in which they practice. The majority of ambulatory patient visits are made to physicians' private offices. In effect, within the confines of the private practice, the physician and the patient enter into a private contract for health care. Traditionally, in the early years of the American health care system, the primary mode of organization was that of solo practice, where one physician in his or her own office provided care to patients who needed his or her services. In recent years however, there has been a gradual shift away from solo practice toward partnerships, small groups, and larger single or multi-disciplinary group practices. The solo practitioner, however, is still a significant part of the American health care system.

B. Traditional Practice Models

1. <u>Solo Practice</u> is an independent practice, in which a physician, usually using his or her own facilities and equipment, works alone. Legally, a solo practitioner is a sole proprietor, one owner of an unincorporated business.

    a. Characteristics

        (1) generally own or rent their office facilities and office equipment

        (2) employ their own nurses and business personnel

        (3) fully responsible for overhead costs

        (4) may share "on call" responsibilities with other solo practitioners in the area and request coverage from other independent practitioners in order to provide for patient coverage during vacations or continuing medical education activities

        (5) tend to be somewhat less satisfied than other physicians when the specifics of private practice are surveyed

        (6) tend to be more satisfied than their counterparts in other types of practices in their overall level of satisfaction

    b. Reimbursement Mechanisms

        (1) fee-for-service is the prevailing method including third-party reimbursement systems

        (2) limited participation in prepaid health plans utilizing a system of capitation and/or prospective reimbursement

    c. Advantages and Disadvantages

        The primary advantage to the solo practitioner is a sense of independence and autonomy allowing more options regarding work and leisure time and enabling them to develop personalized relationships with their patients. The primary disadvantages are the sense of being isolated and possibly, a lack of stimulation from interactions with colleagues.

The primary advantage of solo practice from the patients' perspective is receiving personalized medical care which is unlikely to result in duplication of effort and waste of their time and money. Disadvantages to the patient include becoming too dependent on one doctor's judgment and abilities and a reluctance to seek additional care or opinions even when prompted to do so by their personal physician.

2. <u>Partnerships</u> are legal agreements between two or more physicians to share income and assets in an unincorporated business with each partner legally the agent for the other.

   a. Characteristics

      (1) comprised of two or more physicians representing one or more specialties

      (2) own or rent their facilities and equipment

      (3) share the costs of personnel and overhead

      (4) maintain their own personal panel of patients, (although, they may share the patients openly)

   b. Reimbursement Mechanisms

      (1) fee-for-service is the primary mechanism with dependence on third-party reimbursement systems

      (2) limited participation in prepaid health plans including, Independent Practice Associations, and Preferred Provider Organizations

   c. <u>Advantages and Disadvantages</u>: The main advantage to the physician in a partnership is a built-in coverage system which allows for more control over free time and personal time. In addition, the sharing of costs reduces the percent of personal income spent on overhead. The trade-off comes in a loss of autonomy and a need to engage others concerning both patient and business affairs.

The primary advantage to patients in a partnership setting is that a doctor is more readily available. It is also more convenient to get a second opinion within the partnership than having to travel to another group of physicians with whom the patient has no relationship or knowledge. The primary disadvantage to patients is a potential decrease in the amount of personalized medical care.

3. <u>Group Practice</u> is defined by the American Medical Association (AMA) as "the application of medical services by three or more physicians formally organized to provide medical care, consultation, diagnosis, and/or treatment through the joint use of equipment and personnel and with the income from the practice distributed in accordance with methods previously determined by members of the group." Group practice can be categorized as single specialty groups, multi-specialty groups, or general or family practice groups.

    The first group practice, a multi-specialty group, was founded by the Mayo brothers in the early 1900s and still exists today as the well-known Mayo Clinic, located in Rochester, Minnesota. After 1920, group practices began increasing in numbers. Since World War II they have experienced more rapid growth.

    Single specialty groups constitute the largest proportion of group practices followed by multi-disciplinary groups, and finally general or family practice group practices.

    a. Characteristics

       (1) <u>Single specialty groups</u> are groups of three or more physicians within the same specialty who combine resources to provide medical care to a group of patients.

       (2) The <u>multi-disciplinary group practice</u> is a group of physicians including a primary care specialty such as internal medicine or family medicine in combination with physicians from medical sub-specialists, surgical specialists, and frequently the other major disciplines. Multi-disciplinary groups are usually able to

provide a full range of services within their own group.

  (3) <u>General or family practice groups</u> are large groups of physicians with a specialty in general practice or family medicine.

b. Reimbursement Mechanisms

  (1) Group practices, regardless of the type, derive a significant portion of their income from the traditional fee-for-service mechanism and through reimbursements from third-party carriers.

  (2) More group practices are also entering into the prospective payment market, and some of the larger group practices are associated almost entirely with pre-payment plans. Examples of these larger groups, which are more accurately described as health maintenance organizations, include the Kaiser-Permanente Groups in California, and the Health Insurance Plan of Greater New York.

c. <u>Advantages and Disadvantages</u>: The larger groups build upon the advantages of partnerships. There is frequently more control over personal and leisure time, improved business management strategies by pooling resources, a collegial relationship which results in continued professional growth through sharing ideas and cases with colleagues, a slight financial advantage to physicians in group practices (the average net income per physician is slightly higher in group practices that range in size from three to seven when compared to solo practice or larger group practices), and patient care records as well as financial records can be computerized and the size of the group generally justifies the costs of sophisticated computer technology to manage data. The disadvantages are also extensions of partnerships. There is less autonomy and more need for group decision-making. It is less likely that an individual physician will build the close personal relationships with patients.

The major advantage to patients is the availability of physician and other health care services. Generally, large group practices offer a wider range of health care services than a partnership or solo practice, but this is frequently accompanied with a somewhat less personal touch. The main disadvantage to patients in a multi-disciplinary groups is the potential for decreased personalized care and an increase in duplication of services which may increase health care costs.

4. Conclusions: There are a variety of ways in which private practice can be organized, including solo, partnership, and group practices. Each type has advantages and disadvantages from both the physician and patient perspective. The main advantages of the solo or small partnership is that of autonomy and close personal contact with patients. The main advantages of the larger practices, within certain limits, is a slight benefit in financial rewards and an increased control of free time and leisure time. Current trends are towards partnerships and group practices, and many of these practices are beginning to participate in prospective or capitation reimbursement systems.

V. AMBULATORY CARE: ALTERNATIVE MODELS

A. Historical Background: The term "alternative practice models" generally refers to delivery systems which utilize a prospective or capitation mechanism of reimbursement. As early as 1721, a Boston physician offered a system of paying for health care on a fee-for-service basis or a fixed yearly amount, sick or healthy. A group of doctors in Tacoma, Washington developed a capitation health care contract with a local lumber company around 1910. Another of the early prepaid group practices originated in Elk City, Oklahoma, in 1929.

Alternative practice models or prepaid group practices are among some of the largest growing organizations in the health care industry today. There are estimates that, by the year 2000, approximately half of the people in the United States will receive their health care through some form of a health maintenance organization.

B. Health Maintenance Organizations (HMOs): Recently, the prepaid group practices were reincarnated as health maintenance organizations (HMO), a term that was first used by Elwood in the early 1970s. The concept of the HMO was so attractive, in terms of its potential for controlling health care costs, that the federal government appropriated significant federal funds for the development and promotion of HMOs.

1. The <u>Federal HMO Act of 1973</u> appropriated $325 million over five years for grants and loans to promote HMO plans. To qualify, an organization had to provide or contract for the following services. Basic services had to be available and accessible on a 24-hour-a-day, 7-day-a-week basis:

   a. physician care

   b. inpatient and outpatient hospital care

   c. medically necessary emergency health services

   d. short-term evaluative and crisis-intervention mental health services

   e. medical treatment and referral services for the abuse or addiction to alcohol or drugs

   f. diagnostic laboratory and diagnostic and therapeutic radiological services

   g. preventive health services

2. In 1976, Congress amended the HMO legislation and eased federal requirements to qualify as an HMO. Federal support for HMOs ended under the Reagan administration.

3. HMOs combine insurance and health care delivery into one organization. They can be broadly defined as an organization responsible for providing comprehensive health services to enrolled persons in return for a set monthly fee or premium. The services are provided either directly or by contract with specific providers.

   a. Types of HMOs

      (1) <u>Staff/Group Plan Model</u>: The HMO employs physicians to provide services exclusively to HMO plan enrollees. Staff physicians are usually paid a salary or may receive payment based on a capitation rate.

(2) <u>Closed Panel Model</u>: The physicians actually own the HMO or are paid on a capitated basis. The physicians contract to provide services to the enrollees. HMO enrollees may constitute only a portion of the total patient population in this model.

(3) <u>Individual (Independent) Practice Association Model</u>: Physicians and other professionals work in their own settings where they provide care to both prepaid and fee-for-service patients. Providers contract with the HMO and are paid on a discounted fee-for-service or, especially with primary physicians, on a capitation rate. IPA physicians agree to certain requirements imposed by the HMO in order to be a provider for the organization and thereby increase their patient volume.

b. Characteristics: According to Luft there are four important components embodied in the HMO concept:

(1) HMOs assume contractual responsibility for assuring the delivery of a stated range of health care services, including at least inpatient hospital and ambulatory services.

(2) HMOs serve a voluntarily enrolled population.

(3) The HMO enrollee pays a fixed annual or monthly payment, independent of use of services. In some instances, however, small cost-sharing charges may be used.

(4) The HMO assumes some of the financial risk or gain in the provision of medical services.

c. Reimbursement Mechanisms: Within the pure prepaid group practices, the monies are derived from premiums paid by patients and or employers selecting an HMO option for health insurance and health care. Physicians can be paid a salary, a discounted fee-for-service, or a capitation rate.

(1) Under capitation, the physician receives a fixed sum per patient enrolled in

his/her practice per unit of time regardless of the volume of service provided. The physician shares the risk of health care costs and therefore is encouraged to be maximally efficient. Quality audits protect against skimping on services.

(2) In the group models and IPAs, the HMO still operates on a prospective payment system, but the individual providers derive additional income through their traditional fee-for-service practice.

d. <u>Advantages and Disadvantages</u>: Participation in a prepaid health care plan offers the advantage to a physician or a group of physicians to increase their patient enrollments and to provide a source of constant income. The main disadvantage of these types of organizations is that the physician is sharing some of the financial risk for the patient's health care. Should a catastrophe befall a patient or group of patients within an HMO, a physician could actually stand to lose money. However, there are usually secondary or umbrella insurance policies that can be obtained to decrease this risk.

Prepaid group health practices offer patients a fixed financial financial risk for their health care in most situations. In other words, for a fixed monthly premium, all of their health care needs will be covered. Physician accessibility is another advantage to patients participating in a health maintenance organization. Disadvantages include a decrease in personalized services and a limitation to the physicians from whom patients can seek health care.

4. <u>Enrollment</u>: In 1989, including open-ended and hybrid programs, enrollment in HMOs was nearly 34 million enrollees (13% of the U.S. population). Figures X and XI show the growth in the number of programs and total enrollment since 1976. (Some of the increases seen in 1985 are partly due to changes in reporting methods.)

a. Federal programs: Federal enrollment in HMOs refers to enrollment by Medicaid and Medicare beneficiaries, where the Medicaid and Medicare program contracts directly with the HMO to pay the appropriate annual premium. Medicaid enrollment in 1987 was 811,000 compared to 230,000 in 1978. Medicare enrollment in 1987 was 1,674,000 compared to 376,000 in 1978.

FIGURE X

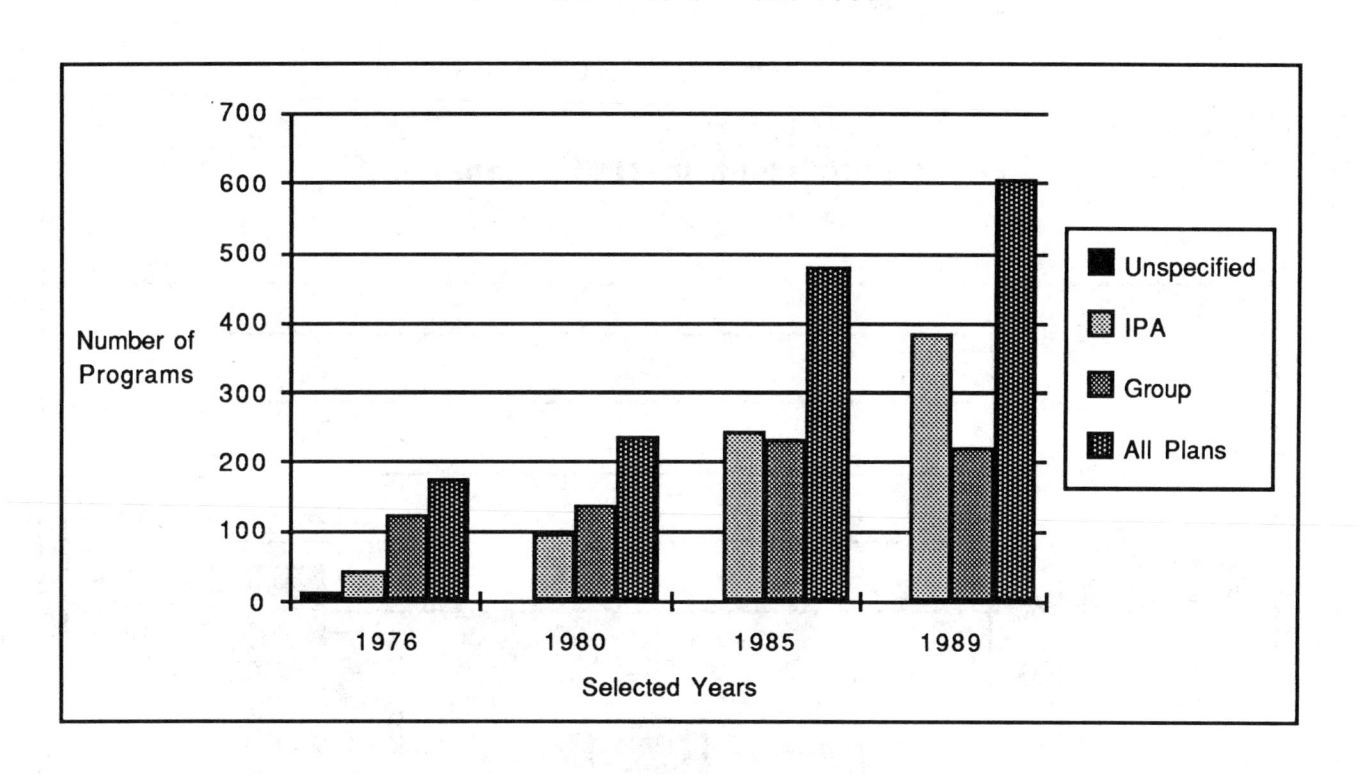

Growth in the Number of HMO Plans
Selected Years 1976-1989

5. <u>Cost containment and quality of care</u>: Several large studies of health maintenance organizations have been undertaken to investigate various aspects of performance. Evidence indicates:

   a. HMOs are able to reduce health care costs primarily by decreasing hospital utilization.

   b. There is a greater emphasis on preventive care in most HMO plans.

   c. Most HMO enrollees are satisfied with the type and quality of care they receive, However the evidence is conflicting and some studies indicate the level of satisfaction may decline over time.

d. Patient outcome studies are more difficult to interpret but when compared to fee-for-service practices HMOs tend to have equally qualified physicians and are more likely to use accredited hospitals. In a review of 25 quality of care studies, Cunningham and Williamson found that the quality of care in HMO plans was better in 19 of the studies compared to fee-for-service practices and at least equal to fee-for-service in the remaining studies.

FIGURE XI

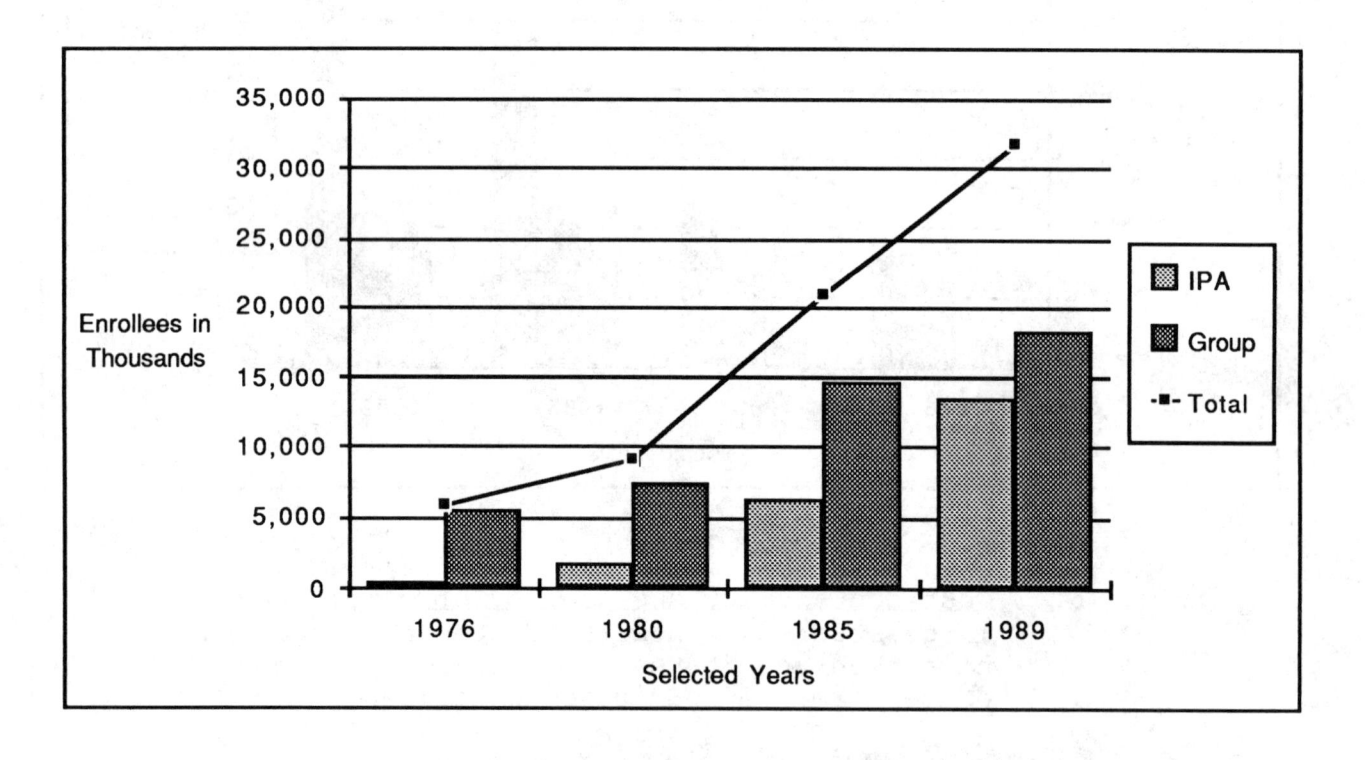

Enrollment in HMO Plans
Selected Years 1976-1989

C. <u>Preferred Provider Organizations</u> (PPOs) are somewhat of a hybrid between a fee-for-service system and a prepaid group health plan. In a PPO, an insurance company contracts with a group of physicians to provide a range of services at a predetermined price. This price is usually somewhat less than usual and customary charges for these services. Patients choosing a PPO have a panel of physicians to consult for health care. They can utilize primary care physicians as well as specialty physicians similar to a straight fee-for-service system. They are limited only by the size of the panel of participating physicians. Once a physician provides a service, the insurance company is billed directly and the prearranged fee is paid promptly without delay. In this sense, a PPO operates as a fee-for-service system, while the prospective payment concept comes from the fact that the fee-for-service schedules are predetermined.

D. Other Private Ambulatory Care Services

1. **Hospitals**: Presently, hospitals are providing ambulatory care services through two major mechanisms. Services are reimbursed through either third-party payers, self payment, or some form of a sliding scale to adjust for a patient's ability to pay. Frequently, patients served by these mechanisms are from lower socioeconomic classes and/or indigent.

    a. **Ambulatory Clinics**: Clinics are either staffed by physicians who are employed by the hospital or by physicians who are donating their time as part of their responsibility to the hospital staff and to the community at large.

    b. **Emergency Room Services**: Emergency rooms provide a significant amount of primary ambulatory care, as well as acute emergency and trauma service.

2. **Urgent Care Centers** or "Doc in a Box" clinics are medicine's answer to the fast food culture in U.S. society. They can be privately owned, hospital sponsored, or franchised as a corporate entity. They usually provide episodic care without an appointment and are reimbursed in the traditional fee-for-service approach. Charges are generally higher than in private offices.

E. Federal Government

The federal government provides ambulatory care basically through three mechanisms:

1. **Uniformed Services and Veterans Administration**: Persons in active service and their families can have their medical care, including ambulatory care, provided through various military bases and military hospitals. The Veterans Administration also has outpatient or ambulatory care services

providing on-going care for veterans with service-connected illnesses and injuries.

2. <u>Indian Health Service</u>: There are numerous Indian Health Service hospitals and outpatient clinics throughout the United States which provide a significant portion of the health care to the American Indian population of this country.

3. <u>Federally Funded Programs</u>: The third mechanism through which the Federal Government participates in ambulatory care is through support for various community programs, including:

   a. Neighborhood Health Centers,

   b. Women, Infant and Children programs,

   c. Renal Dialysis Program, and

   d. Other federally funded programs.

F. <u>State and local governments</u> participate in health care in ambulatory settings through several different systems:

1. Public health departments

2. State and community neighborhood centers (usually in cooperation with federal funding)

3. Municipal and county hospitals

G. <u>Conclusions</u>: Ambulatory care makes up one of the largest sections of the health care delivery system in the United States. Private physicians' have traditionally provided this care and have been reimbursed through fee-for-service mechanisms. Currently, physicians tend to practice in small groups or small multidisciplinary groups which offer the advantage of increased leisure time, slightly higher incomes, and the supportive relationships which facilitate continued professional growth and development.

Alternative delivery systems including HMOs, IPAs, and PPOs are beginning to flourish throughout the United States. Surveys indicate these types of delivery systems are capturing a larger and larger portion of the health care market. They appear to be a cost effective approach to health care primarily by decreasing hospital days and possibly by emphasizing a preventive approach to health care.

VI. INSTITUTIONS FOR HEALTH CARE

A. Hospitals

1. Historical Notes

Hospitals are the institutional centers for health care delivery in the United States providing a complex assortment of health services including acute inpatient services, ancillary services such as respiratory therapy, physical therapy, pharmacy, emergency room services, and ambulatory services. Hospitals have expanded into the areas of health promotion and health prevention and have developed services such as wellness centers and alcohol rehabilitation units.

Historically, hospitals developed as a health care service for the poor and medically indigent and were primarily places where the poor could die with some degree of comfort. In colonial days, the earliest hospitals were actually infirmaries in poor houses. Private hospitals were also primarily institutions for the sick poor. Since they had little to offer in the form of care, there was little reason for the self-supporting sick to utilize these facilities. The first voluntary hospital in the American colonies was the Pennsylvania Hospital in Philadelphia, founded in 1751.

It was not until the twentieth century that a patient admitted to a general hospital had a better than even chance of being discharged alive. The increased survival rate were primarily due to improvements in general hospital hygiene, asepsis, and surgical anesthesia. Further developments in drug therapy, such as insulin and antibiotics, increased the chances that hospitalized patients would improve and benefit from their stay. Continued advances in anesthesia and surgical techniques and technological advances in diagnostic and therapeutic modalities have contributed to the fact that most people admitted to hospitals are discharged alive and improved.

The technological advances and the increased benefit from hospitalization, created an increased demand for hospital services. Until the 1940s, a shortage of hospital beds and supplies existed; but in 1946, the federal government enacted a generalized health planning program by passage the

Hospital Survey and Construction Act, otherwise known as the Hill-Burton Act. The Hill-Burton Act was intended to improve the hospital bed-to-population ratio in rural areas and to upgrade facilities and standards. Federal funds were made available to help construct and equip public and voluntary non-profit general, mental, tuberculosis, and chronic disease hospitals, as well as public health centers. The Hill-Burton legislation was a landmark program because it provided the stimulus and the means for a much needed building and reconstruction program It also introduced new approaches for the planning and development of health care facilities.

To some extent, the Hill-Burton legislation led to an over-abundance of hospital beds. The present bed utilization statistics run far below capacity on a nationwide basis. (See Table 14.) The oversupply and maldistribution of beds, coupled with the cost reimbursement strategy of the initial Medicare and Medicaid legislation, tended to promote over-utilization of beds. The popular formulation of the relationship between the availability of beds and a mechanism of guaranteed reimbursement promoting their over-use is known as Roemer's Law which states "a built bed is a filled bed."

Hospitals now account for the single largest portion of health care dollar expenditures. The combination of hospitals and nursing homes accounts for nearly fifty percent of personal health care expenditures, with hospitals accounting for about forty percent.

2. Classification Schemes: Hospitals can be classified by service rendered, size, location, governance, economic policies, and ownership or sponsorship. A common division between hospitals is short-stay versus long-term hospitals. The typical community hospital is an example of a short-stay hospital.

   a. Long-term hospitals include a few general hospitals, psychiatric hospitals, and hospitals for tuberculosis and other chronic respiratory diseases.

      (1) In 1987 there were only three tuberculosis hospitals in operation and a total of 536 long-term hospitals compared to 5,967 short-stay hospitals.

(2) Beds: The 536 long-term hospitals accounted for 188,369 beds with an average occupancy rate of 87%.

b. **Short-stay or acute care hospitals**: The following classification based on sponsorship is generally applied to short-stay or acute care hospitals and is a particularly useful and common way to classify and group hospitals.

   (1) *Public sponsorship*: These types of hospitals tend to have lower total expenditures, provide better access to low-income persons, and are accountable to publicly elected or appointed officials. On the other hand they do not provide personalized care and tend to be inefficient and bureaucratic.

   (a) Federal government

   Department of Defense Hospitals serve active and retired members of the seven uniformed services and their dependents. *Veterans Administration Hospitals* serve veterans who have left the services largely with some service-connected disability.

   Department of Health and Human Services: The *Bureau of Medical Services* operates eight (8) public health hospitals and 26 clinics which are gradually being turned over to local communities or other governmental departments. *The Indian Health Service* provides care for about 500,000 American Indians and Alaskan natives.

   The *Department of Justice* owns and operates the federal prison hospitals.

   The *Department of Transportation* operates facilities for the U.S. Coast Guard.

   (b) State and local governments own and operate short and long term hospitals, mental institutions, university teaching hospitals, prison hospitals, and city, county and district hospitals.

(2) <u>Voluntary or not-for-profit sponsorship</u>: Most of these hospitals are privately owned and provide a wider range of services than other hospitals and seem to provide higher quality care to more people. They are somewhat inefficient and tend to respond to the demands of private physicians in practice to acquire the latest technology, at times to the detriment of personalized care. Typical ownership includes:

   (a) religious hospitals

   (b) independent hospitals (non-profit hospitals formed by public-minded citizens as corporations, for the sole purpose of providing hospital care for their community)

   (c) HMO hospitals

   (d) Shriners' hospitals

   (e) industrial hospitals

(3) <u>Propriety, for-profit or investor owned hospitals</u> offer better service and provide more services to patients with the ability to pay. They tend to be more efficient and responsive to market pressures and selectively provide services to achieve profitability. They are frequently criticized for over charging, providing unnecessary but profitable services and not offering care to uninsured or under-insured patient's. The major corporations include:

   (a) Hospital Corporation of America is the largest organization with approximately 300 hospitals.

   (b) American Medical International

   (c) Humana

Table 14: Short-Stay Hospitals, Beds, and Occupancy Rates By Type of Ownership for Selected Years 1960-1987

Type of Ownership	1960	1970	1980	1987
Number of Hospitals				
All Ownership	5,678	6,193	6,229	5,967
Public				
Federal	361	334	325	308
State-Local	1,260	1,704	1,835	1,542
Private				
Nonprofit	5,407	5,859	5,904	5,659
Proprietary	856	769	730	828
Number of Beds				
All Ownership	735,451	935,724	1,080,164	1,046,013
Public				
Federal	96,394	87,492	88,144	84,523
State-Local	156,275	203,556	212,058	182,436
Private				
Nonprofit	445,753	591,937	692,929	673,308
Proprietary	37,029	57,739	87,033	105,746
Occupancy Rate				
All Ownership	75.7%	77.9%	75.6%	65.5%
Public				
Federal	82.5%	77.55	77.8%	71.8%
State-Local	71.6%	73.2%	70.7%	63.1%
Private				
Nonprofit	76.6%	80.1%	78.2%	67.6%
Proprietary	65.4%	72.2%	65.2%	51.1%

3. <u>Structure and Organization</u>: The most common hospital in the United States is the voluntary, or non-profit general hospital, which may vary in size, complexity, and services offered. The section which follows describes the organizational structure of the voluntary hospital.

    a. <u>Governance</u>: The governing and legally responsible body of the hospital is the Board of Trustees, sometimes called the Board of Governors or Board of Overseers. The Board is generally made up of a number of publicly-spirited members of a community. The Board of Trustees is governed by a set of by-laws and regularly meets to oversee the operation (governance) of the hospital. There are a variety of subcommittees of the Board of Trustees, but the Executive Committee typically has the bulk of the responsibilities. The Board of Trustees appoints the Chief Executive Officer (CEO) of the hospital. The CEO is primarily responsible for the day-to-day operation of the hospital, and through the administrative organization of the hospital, interfaces with the other major divisions of the general hospital. These include the medical staff, nursing services, medical departments, patient support services, and general administrative and supportive services.

b. <u>Medical Staff</u>: The medical staff of a hospital is made up of the physicians and other health professionals, including dentists, podiatrists, psychologists, etc., with doctoral degrees who provide patient care within a given hospital. The medical staff is subject to the medical staff by-laws which form the rules and regulations that govern the physicians of the medical staff.

(1) Open staff model: An open staff permits any licensed physician to admit and care for patients.

(2) Closed staff model: This more common model permits only those physicians, whose applications for staff membership have been reviewed and approved by the hospital's governing body, to admit and care for patients.

(3) Medical staff organization: Frequently, the medical staff is divided into a number of committees which oversee or direct the activities of the staff. The principal committees usually include the:

(a) Executive Committee (chief decision making body for the medical staff),

(b) Credentials Committee (reviews applications for staff membership),

(c) Utilization Review Committee (monitors the use of health care services and patient care), and

(d) other committees (Medical Records, Pharmacy and Therapeutics, Tissue, and Infection Control).

c. __Internal Organization__: Internally, a hospital is organized through two different methods simultaneously.

(1) Structural organization: The services and nursing units are arranged according to specialty and accessibility. For example, the operating rooms, recovery rooms and intensive care units are generally in proximity to each other. Administrative services are organized in one area and ancillary services in another.

(2) Departmental organization

(a) The __administrative branch__ of the hospital usually has divisions for administration, financial affairs, public relations, admissions, and medical records.

(b) __Supportive services__ include pharmacy, social services, dietary services, physical therapy, the medical library, personnel, purchasing, communication, central supply, housekeeping, nutritional services, maintenance, and security.

(c) The __medical departments__ include the major specialities and their respective subspecialties.

(d) __Nursing services__ include administration, in-service training, and patient care services.

(e) __Ancillary departments__ include radiology, anesthesiology, and pathology and diagnostic laboratory services.

B. Nursing Homes

1. Definition: In many ways, nursing homes are a continuation of hospitals. There are no mutually exclusive definitions to truly differentiate a hospital from a nursing home, but in general, nursing homes provide a less acute form of care, have long-term as opposed to short-term occupants, and care for a more elderly population.

2. Classification: Nursing homes can be described in a variety of ways and can be categorized as diversely as hospitals.

    a. The National Center for Health Statistics classification:

       (1) Nursing care homes are institutions whose primary function are to provide nursing care.

       (2) A personal care home with nursing is a facility whose primary function is to provide personal care with some nursing care.

       (3) Personal care homes function, primarily, to provide personal care.

       (4) Domicillary care homes function, primarily, to provide domicillary care and some personal care.

    b. Medicare and Medicaid Classification

       (1) Skilled nursing facilities must provide 24-hour nursing services, including at least one registered nurse on each day shift. The emphasis is on restorative nursing care and rehabilitation with the availability of physical, speech, and occupational therapies.

       (2) Intermediate care facilities primarily provide services to persons who do not require hospital or skilled nursing facility care, but whose mental or physical condition require services beyond the level of room and board. Frequently, one institution may provide skilled and intermediate care within the same physical structure.

3. Nursing home care is becoming an important part of the health care industry in the United States. With the trend toward an aging population, it is anticipated that the proportion of health care dollars for nursing home care will continually increase. There is considerable need for new nursing homes and for increasing the services rendered through existing facilities. In addition, the health care system is faced with the challenge of providing care for the elderly in a more cost effective manner than through skilled or intermediate care facilities. Today there are numerous programs which are being designed to address this issue by providing care through home care organizations, supported by federal, state, and local funds, and through other public works, such as housing for the elderly, geriatric centers, and respite programs.

C. Mental Health Services

1. <u>Historical Perspective</u>: Historically, the mentally ill enjoyed somewhat better care in America than they did in Europe. Many were cared for at home; while others wandered from town to town and were cared for through the jails and workhouse system of the early colonial days. In the early 1800s, mental illness was looked upon as a treatable disorder to be treated with kindness and sympathy. Many mental hospitals were built, but due to overcrowding and poor care, compassion and sympathy did not exist.

In 1908, Clifford Beers, a former mental patient, exposed the cruel conditions in public and private asylums. Through his efforts and those of others, the National Committee for Mental Hygiene was founded. World War I also helped focus the nation's attention on mental illness due to the number of veterans returning with war neurosis and other "shell shock" conditions. Advances in psychoanalysis and psychiatry throughout the world helped to continue the focus on treating the mentally ill. World War II again helped bring public attention to mental disorders.

In 1955, Congress established the Joint Commission on Mental Illness and Health, whose charge was to examine American mental health care. Through this commission the emphasis shifted toward community mental health centers. Progress was made during the 1960s and 70s in developing community mental health clinics and alternative approaches to mental problems, such as those provided by private psychiatrists, psychologists, and other mental health workers.

Today, expenditures for mental health services account for approximately 10-15% of the national expenditures for health care.

2. <u>Organization</u>: The public component of the mental health system is a layered system. It is anchored by the community mental health centers, established as a result of legislation in the late 1950s and 60s to improve the delivery of mental health services to the entire U.S. population. These centers are responsible for providing services to ambulatory patients and, in some instances, have short-term in-patient care services. One effect of the community centers has been to unload the burden from the state and county mental hospitals which form the second layer of care in the public sector.

State and county mental hospitals still exist and tend to care primarily for the chronically mentally disturbed patient who is unable to maintain an existence in the general population and who requires a highly structured, protected environment for continued existence. In addition, private institutes or hospitals for mental illness continue to provide care for psychiatric disorders such as schizophrenia and depression, alcoholism and drug abuse, and problems of the mentally retarded.

VII. FINANCING PATIENT CARE

A. <u>Introduction</u>: Perhaps the single greatest challenge facing the American health care system today is controlling health care costs. The costs for providing care in this country have dramatically increased since 1960. Growth in personal health care expenditures can be attributed to three factors: price, population growth, and intensity of usage. From 1965 through 1975, increases in prices and increases in intensity of usage contributed nearly equally to the continued increased cost of personal health care expenditures. Since 1975, price increases have consistently out-stripped increases in intensity of usage as a major contributing factor to increasing health care costs. From 1975 to 1985, prices averaged approximately 66.6% of the increase expenditures, while intensity of usage averaged 24.9% of the increase. Population changes averaged only 8.7% of the increases in personal health care expenditures during this same time period. However, for the most recent data available for 1985 through 1987 price has accounted for 53% of increased expenditures, intensity of usage for 37% of increased expenditures, and population growth for 10% of increased expenditures.

The increases in health care costs began to escalate with the passage of the Social Security Amendments of 1965, which created a cost-reimbursement system to pay for health care for the elderly and medically indigent through the Medicare and Medicaid programs. Until recently, all attempts to control health care costs have been directed at regulating the utilization of health care services. More recently, however, attempts to control health care costs have been directed at pricing. The most dramatic change has been the introduction of the prospective payment system for Medicare hospitalization based on the Diagnostic Related Groups (DRG). Effective 1 January 1992 price controls for physician services for patients insured through Medicare will be regulated by the Resource-Based Relative Value Scale system. It is expected that private insurers will follow the governments lead to prevent cost shifting similar to the actions they took in response to implementation of DRGs.

B. <u>Reimbursement and Financing Mechanisms</u>: The mechanisms for financing health care in the United States are perhaps the best examples of the pluralistic organization of the American health care system. The various partnerships which exist between federal, state, and local governments, private enterprise, and consumers are numerous and complex. Generally speaking, health care services are financed or produced from monies which originate from the following:

1. Direct or out-of-pocket payment by the patient

    a. An example is the common situation where a patient visits his or her physician and pays for the services rendered, directly out-of-pocket, with cash or credit.

    b. Direct or out-of-pocket payments are the backbone of the fee-for-service system. Historically, nearly all health care costs were financed through this mechanism. Today, only about 30% of the health care dollar is derived from direct payment sources. The major reasons for this shift in payment source has been the development of private health insurance programs and government sponsored health insurance programs. Presently, the services which are primarily financed through direct payment mechanisms include the following.

    (1) Most dental services

    (2) Drug and pharmaceutical services and supplies

    (3) Eyeglasses and other appliances

    (4) A significant portion of the ambulatory care provided by private practicing physicians

  c. It is projected that the portion of health care services financed through this mechanism will continue to gradually decrease, especially with the increase in capitation and prospective payment organizations and with the prospect of universal or national health insurance.

2. Indirect patient payments

  a. Indirect patient payments are essentially synonymous with health insurance premiums. Private health insurance is usually purchased through a combination of consumer and corporate dollars to cover health care costs which may be incurred at some future time. In turn, when the patient uses a covered health care service, the insurance premium dollars are used to pay for that service. Government health insurance is financed primarily from Social Security taxes with lesser contributions from general revenues and from eligible patients.

  b. Health insurance carriers are frequently referred to as third party payors. Third party payors can be broken down into four basic types:

    (1) Commercial carriers (frequently for-profit corporations): Commercial carriers are usually stock or mutual insurance companies that operate for profit. Premiums paid to commercial carriers are intended to not only cover benefits, but also to make a profit for the parent corporation. Health insurance is only one of the many types of insurance offered by the insurance company. Fraternal societies are another

type of commercial carrier, and are usually non-profit corporations that are basically organized for the mutual benefit of their members to whom they offer life and health insurance coverage.

(2) Blue Cross and Blue Shield (non-profit or not-for-profit corporations): Blue Cross and Blue Shield plans represent the non-profit service benefit approach to health care protection. They are distinguished from private carriers in that they do not operate with a profit motive. Blue Cross and Blue Shield use premiums to cover benefits, administrative costs, and to support a catastrophe loss fund. The premium is not intended to produce a profit. Blue Cross covers hospital related costs and Blue Shield covers physician services.

(3) Government programs

    (a) Medicare is the largest of the federal health benefit programs and finances health care benefits for persons over 65 and for persons under 65 who are permanently disabled.

    (b) Medicaid is a program that is sponsored jointly by federal and state government and provides benefits for persons who low incomes qualify them for public assistance.

    (c) The Federal Employee Program is a health insurance program sponsored by the federal government for federal employees.

    (d) CHAMPUS is a health care program which provides benefits for health care services provided to military personnel and their dependents outside of government health care facilities.

(4) <u>Capitation or pre-payment programs</u>: Health Maintenance Organizations (HMOs) are the primary example of this type of a health insurance program. In this type of program, a portion of the health

insurance premium is paid prospectively to the provider. The provider then becomes a financial manager for these funds as he or she provides health care services to the HMO recipients. The major difference between this system and the systems described previously is that the provider shares a significant portion of the financial risk of providing health care instead of the third party payor assuming the risk for health care costs.

3. <u>Non-patient dollars</u>: A third source of funds to finance health care comes from dollars that are not paid directly or indirectly by consumers for health care services they receive. The services funded through this mechanism include:

   a. <u>Government-related programs</u>: The services to the uniformed services, Veterans Administration, Indian Health Service, and other federally funded and operated programs are provided through this mechanism. The funding source actually comes from general tax revenues, which are then appropriated for use by programs such as the Veterans Administration.

   b. At the <u>state and local level</u>, various types of health care services are provided out of general tax revenues to patients who otherwise cannot pay for health care services.

   c. <u>True charity health care services</u>: The extent and nature of these are generally both unknown and unquantifiable. Virtually all physicians in private practice provide some care to patients under various conditions at no charge to the patient. The costs are absorbed as part of the operation of practice. There are also more sophisticated forms of charity services which take the form of free clinics and other types of voluntary health care activities.

C. Private Health Insurance

1. <u>Historical Notes</u>: Insurance is not a new concept, but has developed into a major industry since World War II. Health insurance in America first began in the 1800s, primarily as a mechanism to replace lost income due to sickness or injury. To this extent, it was more accident insurance than health

insurance. In the early 1900s, there were a variety of private or individual arrangements which began to cover health care costs through payment of insurance premiums for health care costs. In 1929, at Baylor University in Texas, a plan was developed to cover hospital costs for the teachers and eventually to other groups of employees. This was the forerunner of the Blue Cross program. In 1933, Kaiser developed an industrial group practice plan to provide medical services for its workers. In 1942, this concept included the Permanente groups and gave rise to the Kaiser-Permanente Medical Care Program, which was the forerunner to the modern HMOs.

During World War II, when wages and prices were frozen, employers began to cover employee health care costs through insurance programs as a way of increasing the employees' overall wages and benefits. This concept caught on rapidly and health care benefits are now one of the major bargaining points between most corporations and unions. In fact, as stated earlier, rising health care costs and employee health care benefits are a major problem facing American industry today.

Private companies now fund about 30% of the health care dollar and government programs fund about 40% of the health care dollar. Health insurance programs have grown rapidly in the last forty years, and are a major source of funding for health care services. They have also contributed to the expansion of health care costs by making health care readily available to consumers while taking the "sting" out of the cost. Despite the success of the health insurance industries, there is an increasing number of uninsured and under-insured Americans. This creates a situation where people are confronted with financial barriers to access to essential health care services. This has prompted renewed political interest in universal or national health insurance.

2. <u>Scope</u>: In addition to Blue Cross and Blue Shield, there are approximately 1,000 private insurance companies writing health care service insurance, using thousands of different policies. Some of the major private companies include Prudential, Equitable, Aetna, Metropolitan, and Connecticut General. In 1977, as many as 9 out of 10 people under age 65 had some form of non-governmental health insurance. The coverage and adequacy of such policies varied greatly. In response to the

increasing expense of providing health care benefits through Blue Cross/Blue Shield or private carriers, several large corporations are experimenting with self-insured programs. Basically, these large corporations have developed their own health insurance fund and when employees use insured services, the services are paid for by the corporate insurance fund.

3. Common terms and concepts

   a. Coverage

   Health insurance programs or policies provide wide ranges of services and numerous types of coverages. Some may be as simple as to cover only hospital costs, while others cover hospital costs in addition to certain outpatient diagnostic procedures, outpatient laboratory tests, and other ambulatory or outpatient procedures. The most common forms of coverage are:

   (1) hospital (pays hospital bills),

   (2) surgical (pays for surgeon's fees and related costs),

   (3) regular medical (pays for non-surgical doctors fees in hospital and for non-hospital physician care),

   (4) major medical (pays for all expenses with co-insurance and deductible), and

   (5) disability (covers lost income)

   b. Benefits

   (1) Service benefits pay the provider of care for the specific health services rendered. This is the mechanism utilized by Blue Cross, Blue Shield and Medicare.

   (2) Indemnity benefits pay the insured a predetermined amount of money for any covered health care costs which the insured patient incurs.

   c. Rate setting

   (1) Community rating is a process by which all of the insured groups participating

in a plan, share equally the total costs of the plan. This has been a method traditionally utilized by Blue Cross/Blue Shield. Initially, it provided health insurance at a reasonable cost to the consumer. Under community rating procedures, the premium paid does not reflect the coverage utilized by members of the group. In a community rating system, the costs incurred by the "sickest" members are distributed or shifted, to some extent, to the "healthiest" members of the plan.

(2) <u>Experience rating</u> is a mechanism by which health insurance premiums are based on a group's previous claims history. In this setting, higher risk groups pay a higher premium and low risk groups pay a lower premium. Experience rating has been a competitive strategy used by private carriers to compete with Blue Cross/Blue Shield plans. Due to this competitive pressure, Blue Cross/Blue Shield plans are utilizing experience rating more extensively.

(3) <u>Variable cost rating</u> is an alternative method of determining premiums. Basically, it is intended to shift some of the financial risk of health care away from the third party carrier and toward the group or corporation which is purchasing the health insurance plan.

d. <u>Cost management</u>: Health insurance companies are facing the pressure of cost containment to a greater extent now than at any other time in the past. Cost management methods help contain coverage rates by limiting the risk assumed by the third party payor. The savings resulting from these and other mechanisms can then be passed along to the consumer in the form of lower rates. Commonly used methods of cost containment include:

(1) <u>Deductibles</u> are specified amounts that are to be paid by the consumer before the third party payor begins to pay. The purpose of deductibles is to lower costs by insuring only larger claims. Deductibles hopefully prevent unnecessary use of health care benefits.

(2) Co-payments are another form of deductibles under which the insured is responsible for paying a fixed dollar amount for covered services rather than a percentage.

(3) Co-insurance is an arrangement under which the third party pays a fixed percentage of the total health care bill, while the insured pays the remaining portion out-of-pocket.

(4) Indemnity benefits pay a specified dollar amount for services rendered rather than the actual cost or charge for those services. With indemnity benefits, any difference between the actual charge for services and the indemnity amount must be paid by the insured. The result is similar to co-payment. In traditional Blue Cross/Blue Shield plans, the provider (hospital or physician) absorbs the uncovered costs.

(5) Benefit maximums are the maximum amount the third party payor will pay under a certain contract in a given calendar year or for a certain person, illness, or service.

D. Government Programs: Medicare and Medicaid

1. Historical notes: The Medicare and Medicaid programs represent the largest federal programs for financing patient care. Medicare and Medicaid originated out of amendments to the Social Security Act. In 1935, the Social Security Act was established and represented the first major entrance of the federal government into social insurance. Subsequent amendments to the Social Security Act have had significant effect on health care funding and financing patient care. Some of the more significant amendments and legislation affecting Medicare are summarized below.

In 1950, amendments to the Social Security Act created federal aid to states to match funds for medical assistance to help provide for medical services for the medically indigent.

In 1960, the Kerr-Mills Amendments created funding to support medical aid to the medically indigent over age 65 and were the forerunners of the Medicaid programs.

In 1965, the amendments to the Social Security Act created the Medicare program, which is national health insurance for the aged. It also expanded the Kerr-Mills Amendments and helped to create the Medicaid program. Both of these programs were financed through increases in the payroll tax for Social Security benefits.

In 1972, extensive amendments were made to address the issue of cost containment. These amendments basically prevented federal funds from being utilized to support capital expenditures which were not approved through Health System Agencies or by the Certificate of Need procedures at the state level. In 1972, amendments also established the Professional Standards Review Organizations and strengthened the process of utilization review. The amendments throughout the remainder of the 1970s were aimed at cost containment and crackdowns on fraudulent activities.

In 1982, the Tax Equity and Fiscal Responsibility Act (TEFRA) was passed, which has been the most significant cost containment legislation in the history of the Social Security Act, and in the history of Medicare and Medicaid. The TEFRA legislation focused on in-hospital patient costs. This legislation discouraged payment for hospital-based services and limited the reimbursement to hospital-based physicians. The major changes to come out of the TEFRA legislation was the establishment of a prospective reimbursement system based on Diagnostic Related Groups, or DRGs.

In 1984, the Deficit Reduction Act was passed. This act also focused on cost containment, but primarily affected Part B of the Medicare program and restricted payments to physicians and laboratories and froze physician payments. A physician, under the Deficit Reduction Act, could choose to participate or not participate in Medicare reimbursement. If the physician chose to participate, he/she accepted assignment of Medicare benefits. If he/she chose not participate, the physician could not raise charges to Medicare beneficiaries above the April, 1984 levels.

Through a provision in the Consolidated Omnibus Budget Reconciliation Act of 1985, Congress created the Physician Payment Review Commission (PPRC) and called for that commission to study physician reimbursement. In 1988 the PPRC's role was expanded to include consideration of policies to slow the rates of increase in expenditures and utilization of physician services. In 1989 the PPRC recommended the implementation of a fee schedule based on resource consumption by 1992. The Resource-Based Relative Value Scale went into effect 1 January 1992.

In summary, Medicare and Medicaid were initially established to provide adequate health care services to the elderly and the medically indigent. Initially, it was a cost reimbursement program. The cost reimbursement approach was utilized to provide an incentive for physicians and hospitals to provide the care to those people over 65 and those who were medically indigent and would not otherwise be able to afford quality health care. The incentives worked extremely well and resulted in tremendous increases in the health care expenditures through the Medicare and Medicaid programs. In the past ten years, amendments to the Social Security Act have been aimed at decreasing costs through regulating services. Since 1982, however, legislation has been directed at regulating prices.

2. Medicare

   a. Medicare Part A: Hospital Insurance

   All patients over age 65 are eligible for Part A of Medicare and pay no out-of-pocket expenses for the basic coverage. However, as with other insurance programs, there are limits of benefits and deductibles associated with Part A. Patients under 65 years of age who are permanently disabled are also eligible for coverage under Part A. This program provides basic protection against the cost of hospital and related post-hospital services. Benefits include:

   (1) inpatient hospital services,

   (2) post-hospital extended care services,

   (3) post-hospital home health services, and

   (4) hospital outpatient diagnostic services.

   b. Medicare Part B: Supplemental Medical Insurance

This is a voluntary insurance program which is financed through premiums paid by the Medicare enrollees with some matching funds furnished through general federal tax revenues. Benefits include:

(1) physician services and related services, such as x-rays and laboratory tests, supplies, and equipment, and

(2) home health services

c. Claims management: Claims and payments through the Medicare program are handled through fiscal intermediaries for Part A and insurance carriers for Part B. At times, the fiscal intermediary and insurance carrier are one and the same. The Health Care Finance Administration is the federal governmental agency which is responsible for the administration of the Medicare and Medicaid programs.

3. Medicaid

a. Description: The Medicaid programs are federal/state assistance programs. The Medicaid program establishes a single program for medical assistance and public assistance recipients, and establishes extended eligibility to medically indigent persons not on welfare. Under this program, in order to qualify for matching federal funds, a state must provide at least some of each of the five basic services.

b. Basic services

(1) inpatient hospital services

(2) outpatient hospital services

(3) laboratory and x-ray services

(4) skilled nursing home services

(5) physician services

c. Optional services: In addition to these basic five services, a state may provide a wide range of additional services at the state's discretion.

(1) prescription drugs

(2) dental care

(3) eyeglasses

(4) diagnostic screening

(5) rehabilitation

d. <u>Claims management</u>: Reimbursement through Medicaid program is handled through fiscal intermediaries. Providers are paid directly and must accept Medicaid payment as payment in full on mandatory services; however, on optional services, the beneficiary can be required to share a part of the cost.

e. <u>Revenue sources</u>: The revenues for the Medicaid program come from general tax revenues at the federal, state, and local levels. The federal contribution can range anywhere from 50-80%. The federal government will match different programs within the Medicare system at different levels.

f. <u>Administration</u>: The administration of the Medicaid program is the responsibility of the state, but the federal government provides technical support and oversees the operation of the program.

E. Medicare Prospective Payment and Diagnosis Related Groups

1. <u>TEFRA Legislation</u>: The prospective payment system for hospitals under Medicare legislation, which utilizes the Diagnosis Related Group (DRG) system to determine payment, was established in 1982 with the passage of the Tax Equity and Fiscal Responsibility Act. The TEFRA legislation had three major components.

    a. It extended previous legislation designed to limit hospital costs to include costs for inpatient hospital services, not just the per diem costs. The limits were set on a per discharge or per admission basis.

    b. TEFRA required a limit on the overall rate of increase in reimbursement for a hospital's inpatient operating cost per case.

c. It required the development of a prospective payment methodology for Medicare reimbursement to hospitals, skilled nursing facilities, other providers, and physicians as feasible.

2. <u>Purpose</u>: A prospective payment system for hospitals was developed by the Secretary of Health and Human Services. The foundation of the prospective payment system is based on the Diagnosis Related Group (DRG) system. This is a system that was developed by Yale University researchers in the 1970s as an aid to utilization review and is a simple way of classifying patients on the basis of diagnosis. The basic underlying assumption in the DRG system is that patients with similar DRG classification can be expected to have similar clinical conditions and require approximately equal hospital resources. Under the DRG system, if a patient admitted to the hospital who qualifies for Medicare funding incurs costs greater than the DRG allowed rate, the hospital will absorb the loss. If, on the other hand, the patient is admitted and discharged and incurs costs that are less than the DRG assigned rate, the hospital will profit. The purpose of the prospective payment system is to:

   a. establish the government as a prudent purchaser of health care (the prudent purchaser objective is accomplished by paying Medicare providers a pre-determined specific rate per discharge, based on diagnosis, rather than the previous system which was based on reasonable costs) and

   b. maintain the beneficiaries' access to quality care (the access to quality care objective is addressed through the use of Peer Review Organizations).

3. <u>Peer Review Organizations</u>: The purpose of the Peer Review Organization is to:

   a. establish the validity of diagnoses,

   b. review the quality of care, and

   c. determine the appropriateness of admissions and discharges.

4. <u>Hospitals affected</u>: The prospective payment system is limited to hospitals which are reimbursed under Part A of the Medicare services. The following

hospitals receive special exemption and are reimbursed on a cost based formula.

    a. psychiatric hospitals

    b. rehabilitation hospitals

    c. children's hospitals

    d. long-term care hospitals

    e. certain other hospitals with specific waivers

    f. distinct psychiatric, rehabilitation, and alcohol and drug treatment units with eligible hospitals

5. <u>DRG assignment</u>: The DRG for a patient is assigned using five pieces of information.

    a. principal diagnosis and up to four secondary diagnoses or complications,

    b. principal procedures,

    c. patient's age,

    d. patient's sex, and

    e. discharge status.

6. <u>Assignment of reimbursements</u>: Once the DRG classification is established, cost reimbursement is assigned based on a formula which is a function of the DRG weight and a given dollar rate. The dollar rate is determined through a combination of federal statistics and hospital-specific statistics. Over a four-year period, there will be a gradual transition from the dollar rate being determined primarily by the hospital-specific rate to being determined almost entirely by the federally determined rate. There are allowances within this system which take into account exceptional cases. These exceptional cases are called outliers, and if a patient meets the criteria of being an outlier, additional cost reimbursement can be obtained through Medicare.

7. <u>Effect on hospitals</u>: A number of investigators have studied the effect of the MPPS on hospitals and patient care. Several observations and trends are listed below:

a. Hospitals paid through the MPPS had lower increases in Medicare costs compared to other hospitals. Early government studies indicated that overall 81% of hospitals realized profits whereas 19% incurred losses.

b. The system created a fragile hospital system with a significant number of marginal hospitals being forced to close because of deficits.

c. The system may account for the continued decline in utilization and length of stay was started prior to implementation.

d. The locus of death for terminally ill patients shifted from hospitals to nursing homes and some of the transfer may have been medically inappropriate.

e. In the case of patients with hip fractures, the amount of care given has been reduced, much of the rehabilitation has shifted to nursing homes, and an increase number of patients remained in nursing homes suggesting a negative impact on quality of care.

8. Summary: It was hoped that the prospective reimbursement system would force hospitals to conserve resources and indirectly influence physicians to only admit patients who truly require hospital services. The DRG system also forced hospitals to look at their cost effectiveness in treating various diagnostic categories. Overall, the program was supposed to encourage efficiency in certain programs and alter or eliminate programs or services for which the hospital could not provide cost effective care. The risk involved with this process may produce barriers to care which will have an adverse effect on the outcome for patients who health care is funded through the Medicare system.

H. Resource-Based Relative Value Scale

1. Background: Under Medicare Part B, physicians have been paid through a "customary, prevailing, and reasonable" charges method of payment. Part B became a target for controls because it was growing more rapidly than hospital expenditures (Part A) and is financed through politically toxic mechanisms: enrollee premiums and general tax revenues.

a. Attempts in the past to control costs have had limited success and have involved:

   (1) limiting and reducing fees

   (2) implementing capitation payments to private health plans to manage Medicare enrollees

b. In 1986 the <u>Physician Payment Review Commission</u> was established and has been very influential in congressional action on physician payment. In its report to Congress in 1989, the PPRC recommended implementation of a new fee schedule utilizing the resource-based relative value scale developed by Hsiao and co-workers at Harvard.

c. Medicare policies aimed at further control on physician expenditures were incorporated in the Omnibus Budget Reconciliation Act of 1987 and eventually lead to the enactment of the Medicare Physician fee schedule using a resource-based relative value scale (RBRVS) in January 1992.

   (1) The purpose of the RBRVS is to control costs through a uniform fee schedule and reduce inequities in payment between specialties and establish fairer relative prices.

2. Development of the fee schedule consisted of:

   a. a <u>relative value scal</u>e which indicates the value of each service or procedure relative to others

      (1) Hsiao and co-workers at Harvard developed a resource-based relative value scale as an alternative to the system of payment based on charges for physicians' services. Resource inputs by a physician combine to produce a relative-value scale denominated in non-monetary units and include:

         (a) total work input performed by the physician for each service

         (b) practice costs including malpractice

(c) cost of specialty training

b. a <u>conversion factor</u> which translates the relative value scale into a fee or monetary amount for each service

c. a <u>geographic multiplier</u> which indicates how payment for a service is to vary from one geographic area to another

d. Multiplying these three factors together generates a monetary fee for physician services

Fee ($$) = Service Value (RVS units) x Conversion Factor ($$/RVS unit) x Geographic Multiplier

4. Based on projections it is expected that:

a. fees for cognitive services such as diagnosis and treatment of medical conditions will be reimbursed at a higher level taking into account the complexity of the problem

b. fees and surgical and diagnostic procedures will decrease

c. income for primary care specialties such as family medicine and general internal medicine will increase at the expense of decreased income to surgical specialties

G. Capitation or Prepaid Health Plans

1. <u>Historical notes</u>: With the development and success of the Kaiser-Permanente group health plan of California, there has been considerable interest in the health maintenance organization (HMO) as an alternative method for delivering and financing health care. Presently, HMOs finance a very small portion of the health care dollar, but it is anticipated that HMOs will supply a significantly greater portion of health care in the years to come. Recently, HMOs are being tested as a mechanism to administer Medicare funds.

2. <u>Definition of capitation</u>: The reimbursement mechanism, at the heart of HMOs, is the capitation or prospective payment system. In its purest sense, a capitation system is one in which a patient or consumer pays a fixed monthly fee to a provider; in return, the provider provides all of

that patient's or enrollee's health care. In reality, the purchasers pay a monthly premium to the HMO which in turn administers the funds.

3. **Premium distribution**: The monthly premium is distributed, according to the organizational structure of the HMO, to cover costs. Premiums are dispersed for funding,

   a. administrative costs,

   b. emergency or catastrophe funds including, an umbrella insurance policy to cover unexpected or catastrophic costs, and

   c. capitation to health care providers, based on the number of patients in their practice who are members or enrollees in the HMO.

4. Outcomes

   a. Prospective payment or capitation systems are cost-effective by decreasing hospital-related expenses. Several recent studies which have looked at the cost effectiveness of HMOs have confirmed this claim.

   b. Prospective payment systems are also thought to decrease health care costs through a broader, more preventive approach to health care. The underlying assumption is that it is less costly to prevent a disease than to treat an established disease. There is marginal data to support this premise. Physicians working in health maintenance organizations or prepaid group plans seem to spend more time in patient education and in health promotion activities.

   c. Outcome studies to determine the overall effectiveness of these programs in terms of biomedical outcomes are beginning to come forth. There is no evidence that "skimping" is occurring or leading to poor care. On the contrary most all studies support high quality care with good outcomes.

H. **Flow of Health Care Dollars**: The following graphs are presented to pictorially represent the flow of health care dollars. A brief discussion of each graph is presented to highlight the information depicted.

FIGURE XII

National Health Care Expenditures
Selected Years 1929-1987

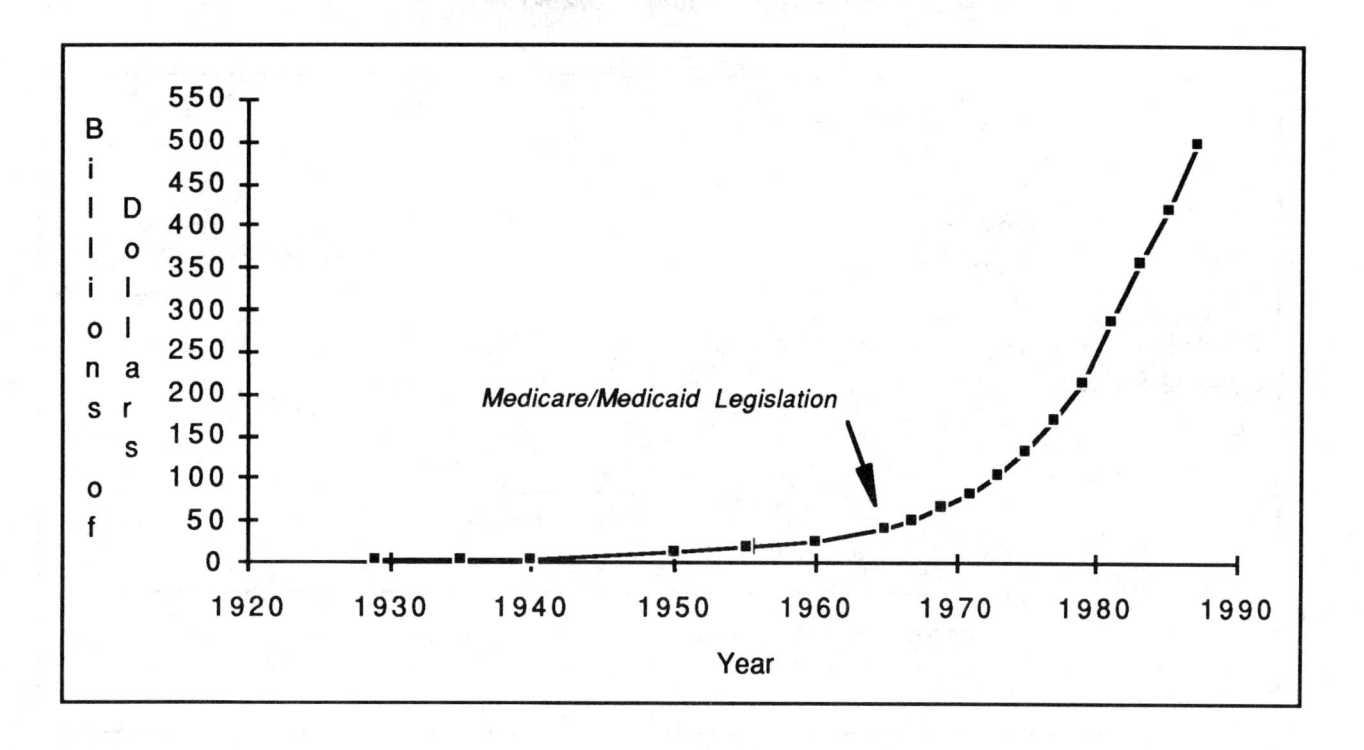

The graph represents national health care expenditures from 1929 through 1987, in billions of dollars. A similar relationship exists when per capita dollars are plotted according to year. The 1987 health care expenditures accounted for 11.1% of the Gross National Product (GNP) and the amount per capita was $1,987.00. In comparison (See Figure XIII), in 1965 health care expenditures accounted for 5.9% of the GNP and the per capita amount was $206.00.

FIGURE XIII

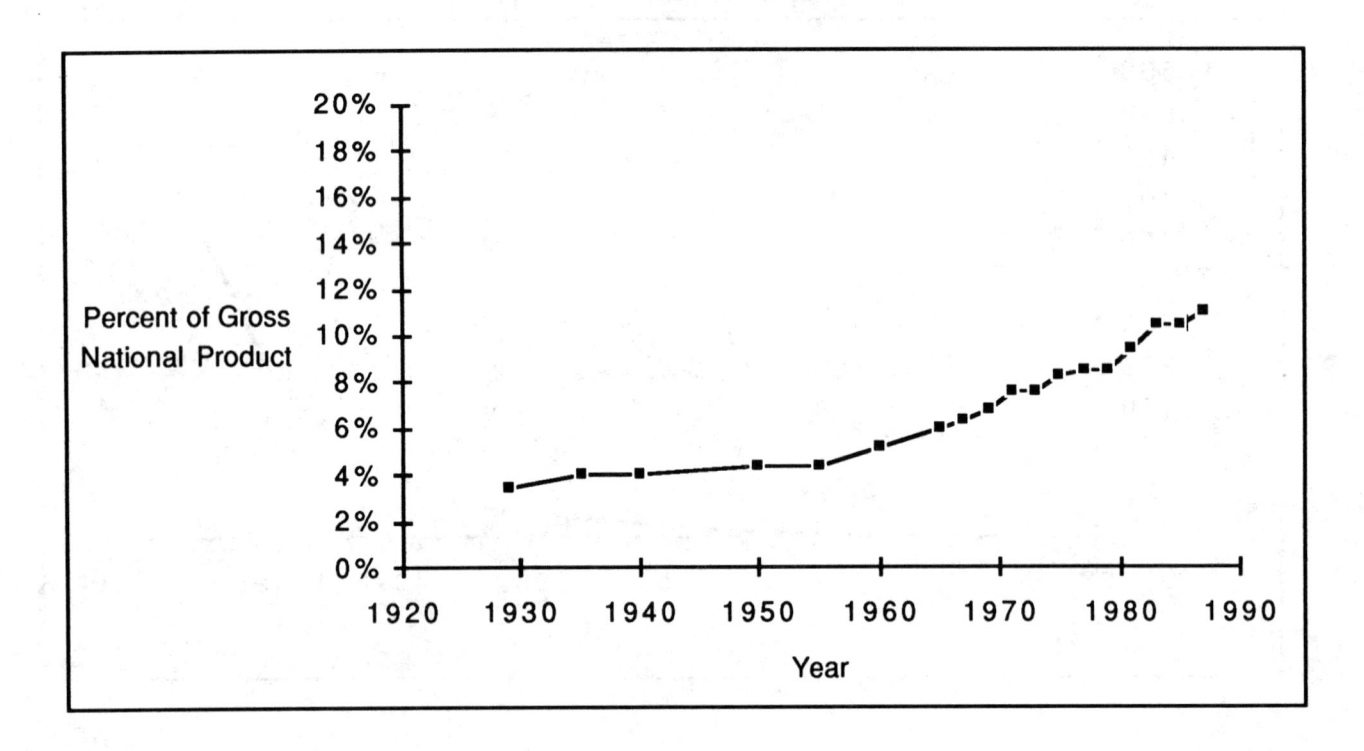

National Health Care Expenditures: Percent of GNP
Selected Years 1929-1987

This graph represents national health care expenditures as a percent of the Gross National Product. The increases here also correlate with the Medicare legislation, but may be leveling off near 11%. In comparison, in 1987 Canada spent 8.6% of its gross domestic product (GDP) on health care and Great Britain spent 6.1% of its GDP on health care without a decline in the health status of their populations as compared to the USA. Total health care expenditures as a percent of gross domestic product for some selected countries for 1987 include: Germany 8.2%, Japan 6.8%, Norway 7.5%, Sweden 9.0%, and Switzerland 7.7%.

Regardless of the way national health care expenditures are expressed, it is obvious that they are increasing at an alarming rate. The increases in health care expenditures began in 1950, and then accelerated in 1965. These two dates coincide with the expansion of private health insurance coverage and the introduction of Medicare and Medicaid legislation, respectively. It is also of interest to note that the regulatory legislation of the 1960s and 70s did not effectively contained health care costs.

FIGURE XIV

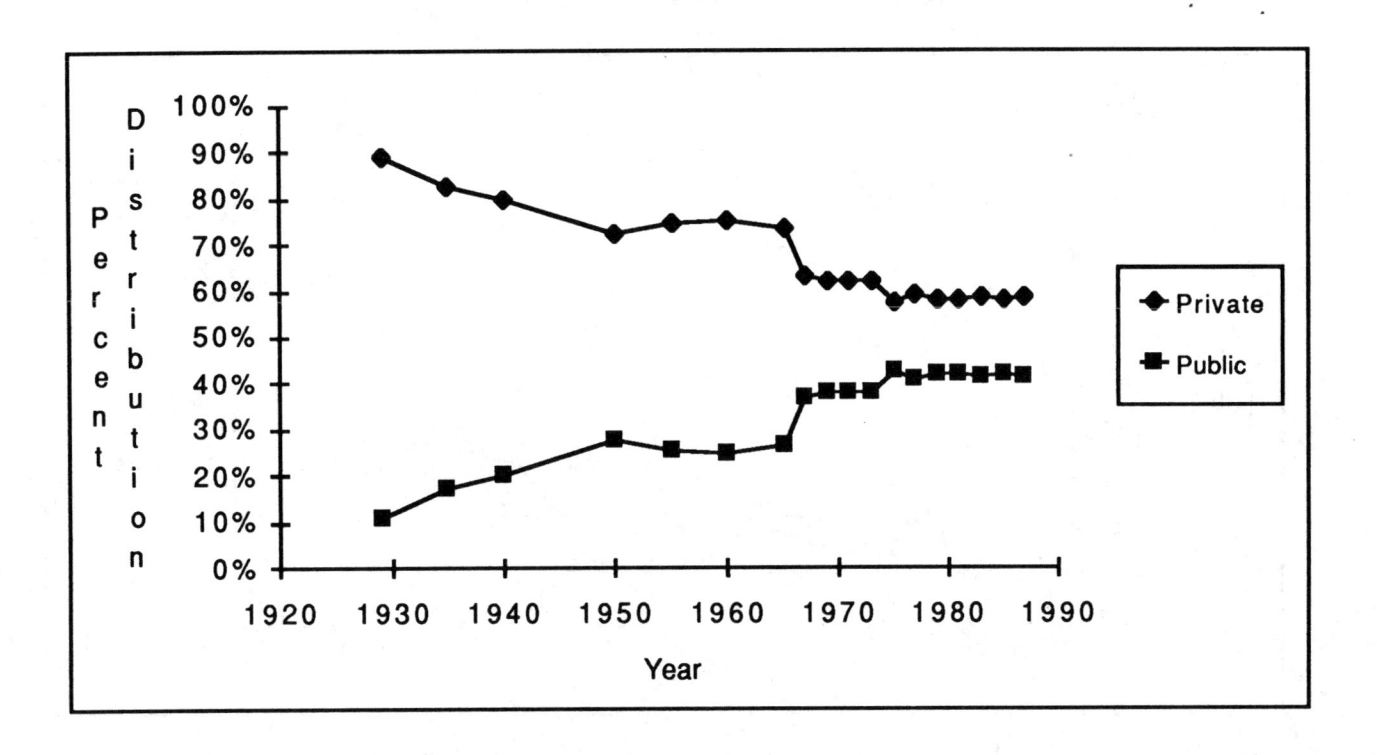

National Health Care Expenditures: Sources of Funds
Selected Years 1929-1987

This graph demonstrates that the funding for national health care expenditures since 1929 has gradually shifted from the private sector to the public sector (government sources). The major shift in funding occurred after the implementation of the Medicare and Medicaid legislation of the mid-60s. Since 1975, the percent of total expenditures has remained relatively constant for both sources. Since 1935, state and local governments have consistently financed an average of 11.5% of the cost of personal health care expenditures. During the same time period, the federal portion for personal health care expenditures has risen from 3.4% to 29.6%.

FIGURE XV

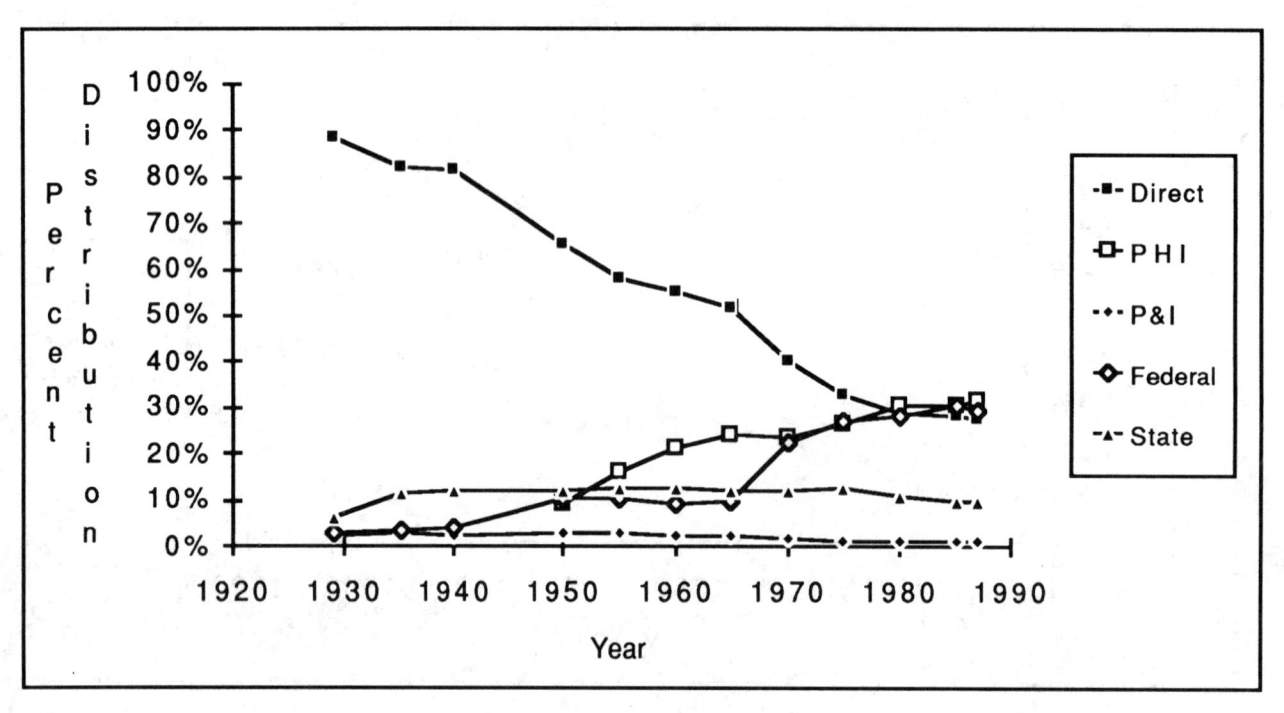

Personal Health Care Expenditures: Sources of Funds
Selected Years 1929-1987

Key: Direct = Direct payment by consumers   State = State and Local Governments
      P H I = Private Health Insurance   Federal = Federal Government
      P&I = Philanthropy and Industry

Personal health care expenditures account for about 88% of the total health care expenditures in the United States (See Figure XVI). This graph shows the gradual shift from direct payments by health care consumers to third party payors including private health insurance and public funds from state and local governments and the federal government. These three major sources have shared the burden of funding personal health care costs. Since 1980 direct payments and private health insurance have shared equally, funding approximately 30% of expenditures while public funding has covered about 40% of the costs.

FIGURE XVI

National Health Care Expenditures - 1987
Percent Distribution by Type of Expenditure

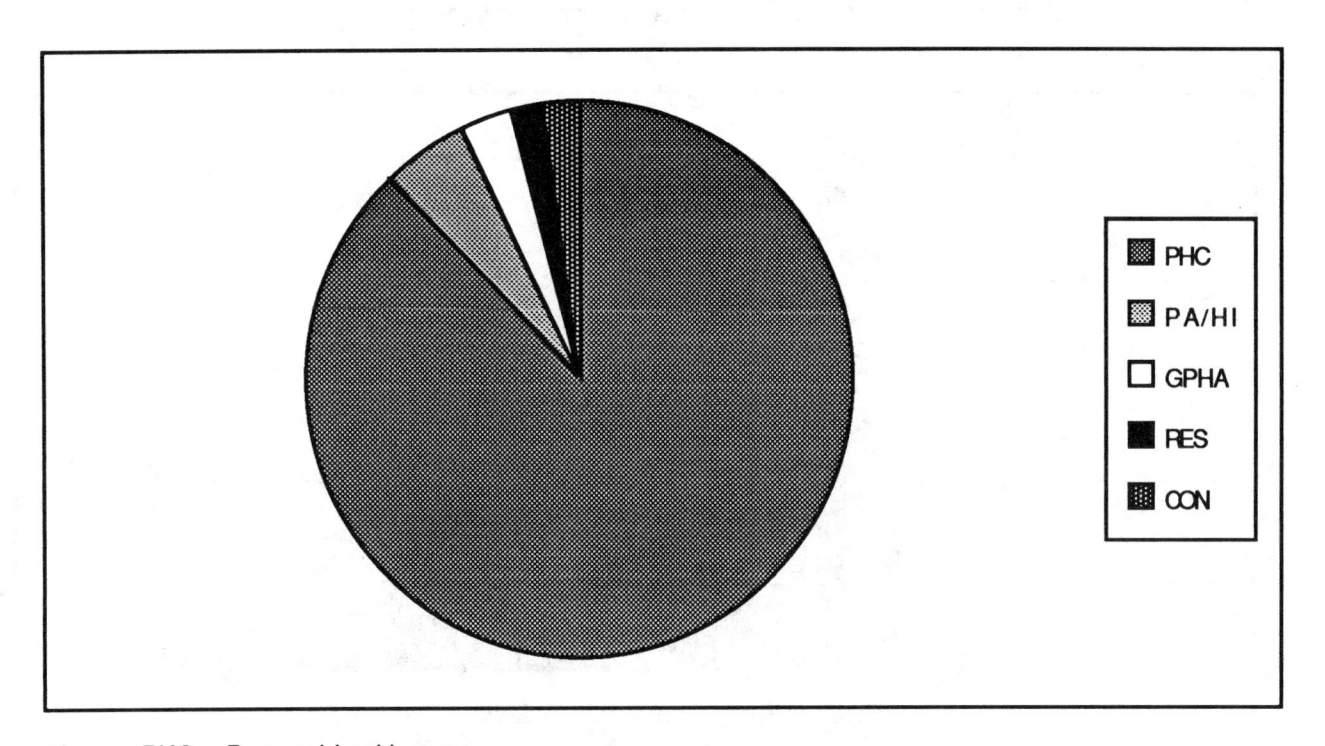

Key: PHC = Personal health care
      PA/HI = Program administration and net cost of health insurance
      GPHA = Government public health activities
      RES = Research
      CON = Construction

The pie chart demonstrates the percent distribution of national health care expenditures according to the type of expenditure. Since 1950, the distribution has remained quite constant with personal health care accounting for 88%, program administration and net cost of health insurance accounting for 5%, government public health activities accounting for 3%, research accounting for 2%, and construction accounting for 2% of total expenditures. Figure XVII shows a further breakdown of personal health care expenditures.

FIGURE XVII

Personal Health Expenditures
Percent Distribution According to Type of Expenditure
Selected Years 1950-1987

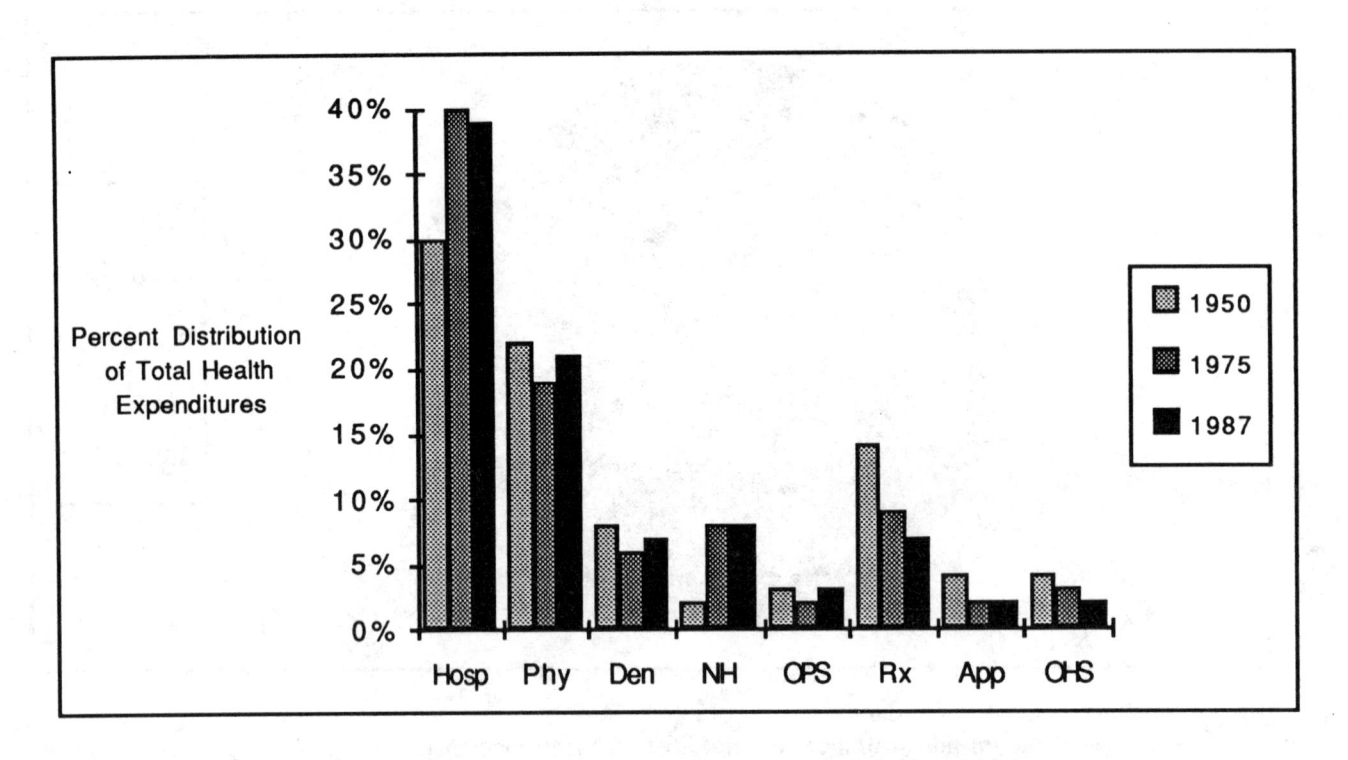

Key:
- Hosp = Hospital care
- Phy = Physician Services
- Den = Dentist Services
- NH = Nursing Home Care
- OPS = Other Professional Services
- Rx = Drugs and Medical Sundries
- App = Eyeglasses and Appliances
- OHS = Other Health Services

In 1987 personal health services accounted for 88% of national health expenditures. Program administration and net cost of health insurance accounted for 5% of total expenditures, government public health activities accounted for 3%, and research and construction each accounted for approximately 2% of the total national health expenditures. This chart depicts the breakdown of personal health services and illustrates some minor changes since 1950. Considering that physicians admit most of the patients to hospitals and nursing homes and prescribe most of the drugs used, directly and indirectly they influence the flow of nearly 75% of all health care dollars.

FIGURE XVIII

Expenditures for Physician Services, Hospital Care, and Nursing Home Care
Percent Distribution by Funding Source - 1987

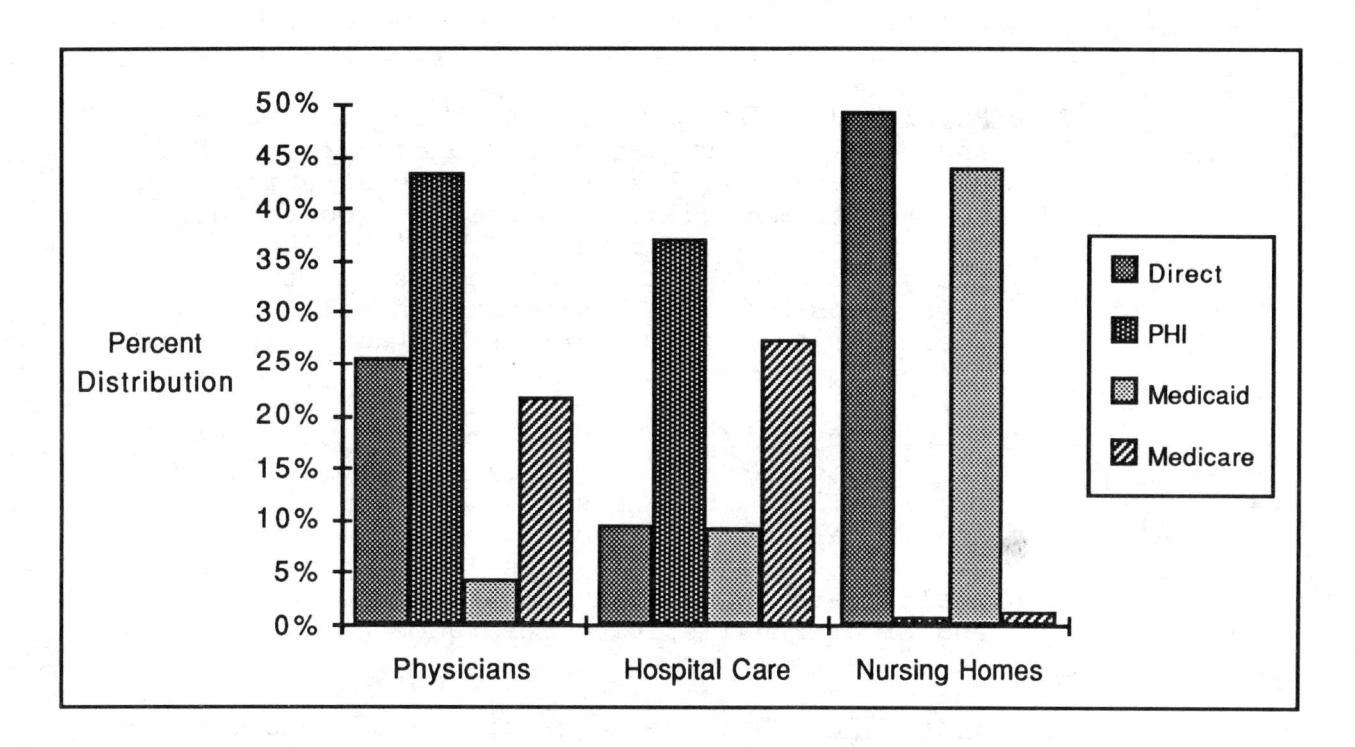

Expenditures for physician services, hospital care, and nursing home care account for nearly 70% of all health care expenditures and are funded through four major sources direct payments, private health insurance (PHI), Medicaid and Medicare. This chart represents the percent distribution according to the source of funds for these personal health care services.

I. Trends for the Future

There is no doubt that controlling health care costs is a prime objective of the federal government, corporate America, organized medicine, and consumers. All segments of health care delivery will be affected. The remainder of the 1990s are likely to produce many new and innovative approaches to health care financing and health care delivery, while at the same time trying to insure access to the highest quality care possible.

1. <u>Physicians</u>: It is also likely that physician fees and services pertaining to Medicare and Medicaid beneficiaries will continue to be scrutinized and come under more direct control by federal and local governments. Private carriers will likely follow the governments lead to avoid cost shifting. More physicians may seek employment in salaried positions to avoid the risks and uncertainty in private practice.

2. <u>Ambulatory care</u>: It is anticipated that health maintenance organizations or other prepaid group plans will begin to finance larger portions of health care services and hospital services. At the same time, slight decreases in the percent of health care costs financed through direct payment and traditional private insurance carriers is expected to occur.

3. <u>Hospitals</u>: During the remainder of this century, hospitals will continue to be the single largest consumer of health care dollars. However, the source of funding for these services will probably change to some extent. It is anticipated that the government systems will not increase their share of reimbursements for these services, but that their overall budget will undoubtedly continue to increase. The rate at which this increase will occur is presently unknown. It is also anticipated that the nature of hospital governance and ownership will change. Projections suggest that the number of investor-owned hospitals will increase, while the number of government and not-for-profit hospitals will decrease (See Table 14). There will undoubtedly be a greater need for cooperation between the chief executive officers and chief financial officers of hospitals and the medical staff of hospitals. The types of services delivered in a given hospital will likely change to some extent. Hospitals may be forced to provide only those services that can be provided in a cost

effective manner. Services which are cost inefficient will probably be eliminated.

4. <u>Commercial insurance carriers</u>: Commercial insurance carriers and Blue Cross and Blue Shield plans will continue to diversify and look for alternative mechanisms for providing health care insurance. The overall trend will be to shift the financial risk of health care costs to the providers and consumers. As a result, the health maintenance organizations and prepaid group plans will continue to capture a larger share of the consumer market.

5. <u>Federal Programs</u>: As health care costs continue to increase at exponential rates and consume larger percentages of the gross national product, the federal government, which has been financing a larger and larger portion of national health care expenditures, will step up regulatory efforts to control costs. The government, like commercial carriers, is beginning to shift the responsibility for health care costs back toward the physician and patients.

6. <u>National or Universal Health Insurance</u> is becoming an increasing important topic on the political scene and will probably be a significant issue in the 1992 presidential race. The increasing number of uninsured and under-insured families has rekindled interest in universal health insurance. The significant issues to be addressed by a national health insurance plan include definition of covered services, description of delivery arrangements, development of plausible financing mechanisms and cost controlling payment strategies, quality assurance, and health care planning. Two proposals were recently published in the New England Journal of Medicine.

   a. A <u>National Health Program</u> was described by the Writing Group of the Physicians for a National Health Program that would:

      (1) fully cover everyone under a single, comprehensive public insurance program

      (2) pay hospitals and nursing homes a total annual or global amount to cover all operating expenses

      (3) fund capital costs through separate appropriations

(4) pay for physicians' services and ambulatory care by:

    (a) fee-for-service based on a simplified universal and mandatory fee schedule for covered services,

    (b) global budgets for clinics employing salaried physicians, or

    (c) capitation payments

(5) be funded initially through current revenue mechanisms, all of which would be turned over to the national plan, including Medicare and Medicaid funds, state and local health care funds, employer contributions in the form of a health benefit tax, pass throughs from private insurance revenues duplicating national health plan services, and an increase in general tax revenues equivalent to health insurance premiums and out-of-pocket expenses

(6) contain costs through savings on billings and bureaucracy, improved health planning, and the ability to establish spending limits by a single plan

b. A <u>Consumer-Choice Health Plan</u> proposed by Enthoven and Kronick is a universal health insurance plan based on managed competition with a mixed public and private sponsorship. Essential components of the plan include:

(1) continuation of current public insurance programs such as Medicare and Medicaid providing benefits to eligible persons

(2) affordable health insurance for everyone not covered by an existing public plan through

    (a) employers in the case of full time employees

    (b) "public sponsor" in the case of part-time employees and all others

(3) creation of sponsors as institutions that ensures each member of its sponsored

group financial coverage of health care expenses at a moderate price (Sponsors serve as a broker, negotiate and contract for health care services and manage the health care benefits for beneficiaries.)

- (a) individuals may contract with a sponsor for health insurance coverage

- (b) small business may contract with sponsors when unable to provide coverage and thereby achieve economies of scale

(4) continuation of employment-based health care coverage requiring all employers to cover all full-time employees and their dependents, to offer a choice of qualified plans, and to pay 80% of the weighted average

(5) subsidizing premiums for families below 150% of the poverty level and for small businesses

(6) establishment of qualified plans which must meet basic benefit packages

(7) creation of an environment of cost-conscience choice by limiting tax deduction incentives to business and industry for health care costs

(8) financing subsidies and public sponsors through the payroll tax paid by employers, taxes paid by self-employed and others eligible to purchase subsidized health insurances, and additional revenues created by restricting tax deductions by employers for health benefits

(9) broad based programs in technology assessment and monitoring and evaluating health outcomes

VIII. REGULATION AND QUALITY ASSURANCE

A. <u>Introduction</u>: The laws which regulate health care and the programs designed to assure high quality health care are taking on more significance in today's marketplace.

The public has mandated access to high quality health care and at the same time, together with industry and government, has mandated cost containment. At times, these two mandates seem to be in opposition. Through the regulatory and quality assurance processes these two objectives can be kept in balance. The regulatory and quality assurance programs serve four basic purposes.

1. They maximize high quality care while simultaneously minimizing substandard care and provide mechanisms to remediate substandard care practices.

2. Since increasing portions of the gross national product are being devoted to health care costs, these processes are directed at holding down costs and encouraging efficient expenditures of the health care dollar.

3. They foster an attitude of professionalism among health care providers and help the medical professions police their own ranks.

4. The processes and programs provide guidelines and critical feedback to the health care system to guarantee that the social ethic to do good work is realized.

B. Licensure

1. <u>Historical Notes</u>: Medical licensure dates back to the thirteenth century, when the first medical practice act required a scientific education and a one-year apprenticeship for practicing physicians. This act also set fees and required free care to be given to the poor. It set forth a code of ethics and forbid physicians from running for-profit practices. The original medical practice act in North America was written in Virginia in 1639, but the first modern medical practice act in this country did not go into effect until the later 1800s in Texas.

2. <u>General Characteristics</u>: Each year the American Medical Association publishes a report which outlines most of the requirements of individual states with regard to medical licensure. The following are general requirements which are common to most of the states' medical practice acts.

    a. The physician is required to be of high moral and ethical character.

      b.   The physician must provide evidence of successful completion of a medical curriculum in an approved school.

      c.   The physician must successfully pass an appropriate examination. In most states, either the FLEX Exam or the National Board of Medical Examiners exam will suffice.

      d.   The physician is required to pay a fee. These fees vary from $50 to $350.

3. Implementation of Licensure Laws

      a.   State legislatures write the medical practice acts for the states, but frequently delegate the authority for implementing the laws to medical boards that have delegated powers of examination, licensing, and discipline. State boards of medical licensure are primarily made up of physicians.

      b.   A medical license is usually granted once and is retained for life, barring practice of extremely poor quality medicine, moral turpitude, or some similar offense.

      c.   Each state sets forth the reasons and processes through which a medical license can be suspended or revoked. A physician holding a medical license is guaranteed due process if charges or questions are raised regarding his or her practice of medicine. If brought before a licensing board, a full range of actions may occur, the least of which is a simple reprimand. The most severe is a permanent revocation of the medical license.

4. <u>Continuing Medical Education</u>: Some states are beginning to require medical education credits as a requirement for maintaining a medical license. Presently, approximately seventeen states require 50 hours of continuing medical education each year or 150 hours every three years to maintain the medical license.

5. <u>Summary</u>: Medical licensure provides a set of standards which all physicians must meet before being granted a license to practice medicine in that state. The medical practice act, of which the licensure laws are a part, defines the ways by which a state can regulate the practice of medicine within its boundaries.

C. **Institutional Licensure**: Institutions for health care are subject to licensure laws in a parallel fashion to health care practitioners. Hospitals are required to be licensed in all fifty states except in the state of Ohio, where certain general hospitals are excluded from general licensing. In addition, nursing homes and pharmacies are required to be licensed in all fifty states. In order for an institution to qualify for federal funding (Medicare and Medicaid) it must be licensed by the appropriate licensing agency. This type of licensure is another means by which the pluralistic and partnership relationship of the United States health care system operates.

D. **Self Regulation**: In addition to the state-mandated regulatory processes embodied in the medical practice acts, there are several types of self-regulation to which physicians are subjected. These self-regulatory processes are also designed to insure a high level of quality of care. The self-regulatory process is implemented through various professional medical organizations. The principal mechanisms through which medical societies operate are peer pressure and recommendations to the state board of medical licensure.

   1. **Code of Ethics**: The American Medical Association, as well as the state and local medical societies, publish codes of ethics which direct or govern the behavior of their members.

   2. **Impaired Physician Programs**: Most state and local societies have impaired physician programs which help rehabilitate physicians with drug and/or alcohol abuse problems.

   3. **Grievance Committees**: State and local societies also have grievance committees to hear complaints against physicians that come from either other physicians or from the public.

E. Certification

   1. **Definition**: Certification is the voluntary process by which individual health personnel are affirmed to have attained a high level of qualification according to standards and criteria such as education, experience, and examination as set forth by their professional associations. In a sense, certification is a form of self-regulation.

   2. **Board Certification**: There are presently 23 specialty boards which offer board certification in

the United States. In order to be able to sit for Board examinations, a physician must successfully complete a required period of residency training in that specialty. Board Certification is a benchmark of achievement that indicates to consumers that the physician they are seeing has had appropriate training and has been examined for a mastery of knowledge in that area.

    a. <u>Recertification</u>: The American Board of Family Practice was the first specialty board to require recertification. Other specialty boards are beginning to follow this example, at least on a voluntary basis.

3. <u>Professional Specialty Organizations</u>: In addition to specialty boards, there are also specialty colleges or associations. Examples include the American College of Surgeons, the American College of Physicians (the professional organization of internists), the American Academy of Family Physicians, etc. These organizations also provide a quasi-regulatory role by:

    a. describing the principles and philosophy of the specialty,

    b. making recommendations as to standards of care for the specialty, and

    c. providing continuing medical education programs for their members.

F. Accreditation

1. <u>Definition</u>: Accreditation is the institutional counterpart to certification. It is the process by which an institution or an educational program is determined to meet certain generally acceptable standards set forth by an appropriate professional association. It is voluntary and an institution or program must apply to the accrediting agency for the necessary appraisal.

2. <u>Accrediting Organizations</u>: Accrediting bodies are generally composed of representatives of professional organizations concerned with the institutions or programs in questions, and their titles generally reflect their collaborative purpose.

a. Joint Commission on Accreditation of Healthcare Organizations (JCAHO)

   (1) <u>Historical notes</u>: The JCAHO evolved from the Third Clinical Conference of Surgeons of North America which convened in 1912. At this conference, the surgeons called for some degree of standardization of equipment on wards in hospitals throughout the country. In 1918, the newly formed American College of Surgeons conducted a nationwide survey. These efforts, in the early part of the 1900s, led the way to the formation of the Joint Commission for the Accreditation for Hospitals in 1951. The name was changed to the Joint Commission on Accreditation of Healthcare Organizations in the late 1980s when the organizations services expanded beyond hospitals.

   (2) <u>Membership</u>: The JCAHO is made up of members from the American College of Surgeons, American Hospital Association, American College of Physicians, American Medical Association, and American Dental Association.

   (3) <u>Criteria and standards</u>: The JCAHO develops standards or criteria which hospitals must meet in order to be accredited. These criteria are not outcome-based, but rather are organizational and processes oriented. For example, a hospital must have a quality assurance process and publish a list of drugs available for use in the hospital. The JCAHO also sets standards for the structure and function of nursing services and other services in the hospital.

   (4) Accreditation process

      (a) The hospital must be accepted for registration by the American Hospital Association.

      (b) The hospital must request and purchase the services of the JCAHO.

      (c) The JCAHO sends a team of reviewers to the hospital and if criteria and standards are met, accreditation is granted.

  (5) <u>Regulatory role</u>: JCAHO accreditation is another example of the pluralistic nature of the health care system, because Medicare and Medicaid funding is dependent upon a hospital having JCAHO accreditation.

 b. <u>Liaison Committee on Medical Education</u>: Committee membership comes from the American Medical Association, and the Association of American Medical Colleges. Its primary purpose is to review and accredit medical schools throughout the country.

 c. <u>Accreditation Council on Graduate Medical Education</u>: This committee is charged with the responsibility of reviewing and accrediting residency training programs.

 d. <u>Accreditation Council for Continuing Medical Education</u>: This committee is responsible for accrediting sponsors of continuing medical education programs.

G. Audit Systems

 1. <u>Medical audit and quality assurance</u> are frequently combined together in hospital administrative organizations under the title of risk management. Medical audits are frequently accomplished through subcommittees of the medical staff which review patient care by diagnosis and make recommendations to eliminate problems which identified. Virtually all hospitals monitor the quality of care and the utilization of health care services through two mechanisms. The structure and function of these two quality assurance programs are closely linked to federal funding.

  a. Utilization Review (internal audit)

   (1) <u>Historical Notes</u>: The utilization review process resulted from the explosive increase in health care costs through the Medicare and Medicaid programs. The government initially funded Medicare and Medicaid services on a cost reimbursement basis. This provided an incentive for practitioners and hospitals to provide care to the medically indigent and

elderly. The incentive nature of this program worked all too well, and within the first few years of the program, budgeted amounts were being exceeded by claims. Through amendments to the Social Security Act governing Medicare and Medicaid disbursements, provisions were made for the development of Professional Standards Review Organizations (PSRO), and hospitals were encouraged to have Utilization Review committees. Accreditation by the JCAHO requires the presence of a utilization review process.

(2) **Purpose**: Utilization review assures proper allocation of hospital resources while endeavoring to provide high quality patient care in the most cost-effective manner. Its primary objectives are to review:

    (a) the appropriateness of admissions,

    (b) continued hospital stay,

    (c) use of ancillary services, including delays in service, and to

    (d) facilitate efficient discharge planning.

(3) **Membership**: The utilization review committee is generally made up of members of the medical staff, nursing personnel, and hospital administration. A utilization review coordinator oversees the working staff of the utilization review committee.

(4) **Process**: Briefly, the utilization review process consists of reviewing all patient charts on admission. The admission is justified based on the intensity of care criteria, i.e. what is being done for the patient, and on severity of illness criteria which assesses the severity of illness on admission. The chart must be reviewed by a physician advisor other than the attending physician at least once within the first fifteen days of hospitalization.

Under the present prospective payment system of the DRGs, utilization review assists in justifying the admission based on severity of illness and intensity of care and continues to monitor hospital stays which lie outside of expected norms. Many utilization review committees also do reviews for private insurance carriers.

b. Professional Review Organizations (external audit)

(1) <u>Historical Notes</u>: In 1972, amendments to the Social Security Act mandated the development of Professional Standards Review Organizations (PSROs) which were to be developed nationwide and were charged with the purpose of monitoring the utilization of hospital resources and assuring they were appropriately utilized. The PSROs frequently operated through the utilization review committee system. In 1982, with the passage of the TEFRA legislation the PSROs gave way to federally mandated Peer Review Organizations, or PROs. The federal government contracts with PROs nationwide to monitor the use of hospital and health care resources.

(2) <u>Function and authority</u>: The PROs have the ability to recommend withdrawal of federal funding to hospitals which do not comply with certain guidelines regarding the hospitalization and care of patients. Hospitals are first advised of their shortcomings and encouraged to correct them internally. If the hospital is unable to do this or refuses to comply, the PRO then has the authority to conduct the review themselves and make recommendations to the federal government, which could result in loss of federal funds.

(3) <u>Cost</u>: Initially PROs were funded by the federal government at a cost of 4.7 million dollars. It was projected that within two years that over 40 million dollars would be saved. Similar to the utilization review committees, PROs contract with private insurance companies

to conduct utilization review within the private sector to continue to assure cost effective care and prevent cost shifting from losses from Medicare and Medicaid patients to those covered by private insurance policies.

H. Health Care Planning

1. <u>Introduction</u>: Perhaps the highest level of regulation and quality assurance within the health care system is the process of health care planning. The Hill-Burton Act, which created a process for increasing hospital beds and improving current facilities, had a mechanism built into the legislation requiring a review of plans for expansion and improvement of hospital structures and services. Health planning is designed to control capital expenditures.

2. Health Systems Agencies and Certificate of Need

   a. <u>Historical Notes</u>: The most common system in place today to monitor capital expenditures is the Health Systems Agencies. These are generally non-profit corporations set up on a state-wide basis for health care planning and coordinating of health care facilities. The system was established under the National Health Planning and Development Act of 1974 and superseded the previous health planning agencies established in 1966, which had likewise replaced those established under the Hill-Burton Construction Act.

   In 1974, wholly state-defined Certificate of Need programs came to an end with the passage of the National Health Planning and Resource Development Act. This law requires that all states institute a Certificate of Need program which meets federal regulations or risk losing federal support for health planning efforts on a state-wide basis. Part A of this legislation mandated that the Secretary of the Department of Health, Education and Welfare (now the Department of Health and Human Services) establish national health care planning goals. Part B of the title created the Health Systems Agencies.

(1) Health Systems Agencies were charged with:

    (a) gathering and analyzing data,

    (b) establishing long-range health systems plans and short-term annual implementation plans,

    (c) providing technical or financial assistance to those seeking to implement provisions of the plan,

    (d) coordinating activities with the PROs,

    (e) reviewing and approving or disapproving applications for federal funds for health care expenditures,

    (f) assisting states in the performance of capital expenditure reviews or granting certification of need,

    (g) assisting states in reviewing institutional health services with respect to appropriateness of such service, and

    (h) recommending annually to states projects for the modernization, construction, and conversion of medical facilities in the area.

I. **Summary**: There are four basic regulatory mechanisms which are utilized to improve quality of and access to health care and control cost of health care and capital expenditures. These include licensing, certification or accreditation, medical audit systems, and health planning systems. The Health Systems Agencies and the Certificate of Need process is a cooperative effort between the federal and state governments to insure appropriate use of funds for capital expenditure.

Regulatory systems are a mixture of state and federal regulations and a prime example of the pluralistic and partnership arrangements within the American health care system. Many of the reviewing agencies are private organizations which are federally approved and funded. They serve as a liaison between the private sector, state and local governments, and the federal government.

Compliance with the regulations and suggestions of these agencies is closely tied to approval and eligibility for federal funding. Since up to 60% of a hospital's costs may come from federal dollars, there is a significant motivation to comply with these regulatory systems and agencies.

IX. **COMPARATIVE MODELS OF HEALTH CARE SYSTEMS**

As the American health care system moves into the twenty-first century change is inevitable. Some are calling for sweeping change others for incremental change. In considering change it is important to learn from other healthcare systems. To accomplish this, it is useful to have a model to compare and contrast characteristics of different systems. Light has proposed a model which uses eight characteristics to compare systems and has developed four basic types of delivery systems.

A. Key elements for comparison include inherent values and goals, organization, key institutions, power, finance and cost, image of the individual, division of labor, and medical education. The four basic models are briefly summarized below and adapted from Light's description. Combination or hybrid models can exist.

B. Health Care System Models

1. Mutual Aid Model

    a. Inherent Values and Goals: to improve the health of fellow members, educate and prevent disease, minimize health care costs, and be sure no outside force (state, profession) controls the health care system

    b. Organization: a loose federation of member groups with egalitarian services with an emphasis on preventive and primary care organized around epidemiological patterns of illness

    c. Key Institutions: Mutual Benefit associations

    d. Power: local control within common rules where the state and profession are relatively weak and play a facilitative role

    e. Finance and Cost: members contribute to an insurance fund which contracts with physicians and facilities for services; expenditures are a relatively small proportion of GNP and the doctors' share of all cost is relatively low

  f. <u>Image of the Individual</u>: active, self responsible, informed member of the group

  g. <u>Division of Labor</u>: egalitarian with more teams and delegation and fewer physicians and specialists

  h. <u>Medical Education</u>: favors cooperative, egalitarian training of health care teams

2. State Model

  a. <u>Inherent Values and Goals</u>: to control the health care system, provide good accessible care to all sectors of the population, minimize health care costs to the state, and strengthen the state via a healthy population

  b. <u>Organization</u>: national, integrated system with decentralized administration organized around primary care

  c. <u>Key Institutions</u>: Ministry of Health and regional or district councils

  d. <u>Power</u>: state is the sole power in an autocratic model, but in democratic models power rests with tiers of representative councils and partnerships with medical associations

  e. <u>Finance and Cost</u>: all care is free to the patient with monies derived from taxes

  f. <u>Image of the Individual</u>: a member of society and thus a responsibility of the state, but also responsible to stay healthy

  g. <u>Division of Labor</u>: relies on mid-level providers with fewer physicians and specialists

  h. <u>Medical Education</u>: a state system for all providers and extensive continuing education

3. Professional Model

  a. <u>Inherent Values and Goals</u>: to provide the best possible clinical care to every sick person, develop scientific medicine to its highest level, promote the medical profession in prestige, wealth, and influence

b. Organization: loose federation with decentralized administration, organized around hospitals and private practices with an emphasis acute, hi-tech interventions and specialty care

c. Key Institutions: physician organizations and autonomous hospitals and physicians

d. Power: sole power rest with physicians who try to prevent state intervention

e. Finance and Cost: direct payments by individual consumers or through private health insurance plans

f. Image of the Individual: private individual who chooses how to live and when and how to use medical care

g. Division of Labor: proportionately more physicians with an emphasis on specialty care

h. Medical Education: private autonomous schools and universities with tuition, loosely coupled continuing education

4. Corporatist Model

a. Inherent Values and Goals: to bring together consumers, employers, and providers in administering the health care system, minimize conflict between consumers, providers, and payors, balance costs against providers

b. Organization: numerous funds by occupation and geography with administrative boards, citizens join the fund, physicians and health facilities are autonomous and negotiate and bargain with the funds for services

c. Key Institutions: sickness fund boards and physicians' associations, state plays a role as rule maker and referee

d. Power: countervailing power structure subject to imbalance, statutory power to set financing, mix, and range of services, regulatory power by state

e. <u>Finance and Cost</u>: employers and employees contribute premiums, costs dependent on balance of interest in negotiations but tend to favor the profession

f. <u>Image of the Individual</u>: private individual who chooses how to live and when and how to use medical care

g. <u>Division of Labor</u>: physician dominated

h. <u>Medical Education</u>: no inherent structure though can be a point of focus

C. The British System

1. The British system is an example of a <u>democratic state model of a health care system</u> and has as its central delivery system the British National Health Service. Principles of a national health service include:

   a. universal deliver of health care to all persons at zero cost at the point of entry

   b. quality of medical services available is uniform across the system

   c. public accountability

2. <u>Development</u>: The system developed in a synchronous manner with the historical, political, and social development of Great Britain and continental Europe which emphasized social welfare above individual rights. This led to nationalization of the hospitals in 1948. Eventually the entire system became nationalized with the establishment of the British National Health Service.

3. <u>Administration</u>: Budgets and expenditures are set by the central government but are administered by regional health authorities and district authorities and boards.

   a. A form of rationing exists in the system but creating waiting lists for elective services and setting stringent criteria to qualify for services such as renal dialysis.

   b. Approximately 6% of the GNP is spent on health care.

c. Recent reforms are introducing more autonomy into the system.

4. <u>Hospitals</u>: The hospitals were nationalized in 1948 and are managed by the National Health Service. They are the centers of specialty care and training. New reforms may allow some hospitals more autonomy.

5. <u>Physicians' services</u> form a two level network.

   a. Regional health care is provided by general practitioners, who make the majority of physicians in the system, and coordinated teams of health care workers.

      (1) Patients are enrolled in a given practice and must use their local services.

      (2) General practitioners contract with the National Health Service and receive a capitation fee based on the number of enrollees. Reforms may allow larger practice to apply for a separate budget.

   b. Specialty services are organized within the hospitals. Specialists or "Consultants" as they are known accept referrals from the general practitioners.

6. <u>Private insurance</u>: Private insurance is gradually increasing in the British system. Most of the private practice is provided by the consultant segment of the profession who have been powerful enough to maintain a small private practice which accounts for 5 to 10% of all care.

D. The Canadian System

1. The Canadian system is an example of a <u>corporatist model of a health care system</u> and has is organized around a centrally subsidized but provincially administered National Health Insurance program.

   a. The <u>primary goal</u> of the system is to eliminate any and all financial barriers to basic health care for the Canadian people.

   b. Approximately 8 to 9% of the Canadian GNP is spent on health care.

2. <u>Development</u>: The system is relatively new compared to other industrialized nations. Key events include:

   a. enactment of a federal hospital-insurance program in the late 1950s

   b. enactment of a federal medical-insurance program in the mid 1960s covering physician and related services

   c. adoption by the provinces of health insurance programs which met standards of universality, coverage, and administration making the provinces eligible for federal cost sharing by 1972

   d. 1977 establishment of federal caps on cost sharing creating incentives for the provinces to contain expenditures

3. <u>Administration</u>: Each province is responsible for its own program within federal guidelines, receiving heavy subsidies from the central government. Provinces are responsible for administering the program and monitoring utilization and quality of care.

4. <u>Hospitals</u>: Annual prospective budgets for hospitals are negotiated on an annual basis. The central government sets limits on the percent increase in budgets it will pay leaving the province and the hospital responsible for budgeted expenses above the federal subsidy level.

5. <u>Physicians' services</u> are provided on a fee for service basis. Fee schedules are negotiated and are uniform on a province wide basis.

6. <u>Private insurance</u> is allow but restricted to cover only additional services not provided by the national insurance such as private rooms in the hospital. A number of Canadians cross into the United States to purchase services that are either not covered or difficult to obtain because of waiting lists for elective services.

E. Comparative studies

As U.S. policy makers consider alternatives to improve health care delivery, maintain quality care, and curb escalating health care costs, it is important to critically review other health care delivery models. It is difficult to conduct cross national studies of health care systems and health outcomes because of the differences in the ways statistics are collected and reported, different political philosophies, and heterogeneity of the populations to be studied. Recently Starfield provided some insight into this important problem with a cross national study of ten industrialized nations.

1. <u>Design</u>: Ten industrialized nations were compared using indices and scales that characterized the standing of each country relative to the other countries on the basis of three characteristics:

   a. the extent of their primary care services in terms of related to the overall system and those related to the mode of practice

   b. their levels of 12 health indicators (eg, age-adjusted death rates, infant mortality, life expectancy)

   c. the satisfaction of their populations in relation to overall costs of the system

2. <u>Results</u>

   a. <u>Primary care</u> scores ranged from a low of 0.2 in the United States to a high of 1.7 in the United Kingdom. Canada and the Scandinavian countries also achieved relatively high scores.

   b. Health indicator rankings

      (1) The Netherlands and Sweden were in the top third for all 12 indicators

      (2) Canada ranked in the top third for 5 indicators and along with Australia, Netherlands, and Sweden had no indicators in the bottom third.

      (3) The United States had only one indicator in the top third and ranked in the bottom third for seven of the indicators. The United Kingdom also performed poorly on health indicators.

   c. The <u>satisfaction-expense ratio</u> ranged from a low of 0.2 for the United States to a high of 9.0 in the Netherlands. Canada achieved a relatively high rating of 7.6.

3. <u>Conclusions</u>: With the exception of the United Kingdom, there was general concordance for primary care, the health indicators, and the satisfaction-expense ratio. In other words nations who achieve a high degree of primary care services and limit financial barriers to access to health care tend to be healthier as determined by the health indicators surveyed and more satisfied with their health care.

X. FINAL COMMENTS

The American health care system has sometimes been called a non-system. More precisely, it is a system characterized by pluralism and partnerships. Over the past fifty years, public demands for access, technology, and quality have led to exponential increases in costs. All components of the health care system, including government, consumer, and provider are faced with the challenge of meeting these public demands while, at the same time, controlling costs. The health care system in this country will undoubtedly meet this challenge but, in the process, we are likely to see changes in distribution and utilization of health manpower, innovative change in health care delivery systems, and new and creative approaches to financing health care. The challenges of the future are of no greater magnitude than the challenges of the past. It is only the focus and the emphasis of the challenges which are changing.

XI. SELECTED BIBLIOGRAPHY

Boring CC, Squires TS and Tong T: Cancer Statistics, 1991, Ca-A Cancer Journal for Clinicians 41:19-36, 1991.

Case Watch, AIDS Clinical Care 4:1, 1992.

Donabedian, A., Axelrod, S.J., Wyszewianski, L. Medical Care Chart Book, 7th Ed. AUPHA Press, 1980.

Diagnostic-Related Groups and the Prospective Payment System: A Guide for Physicians. American Medical Association, 1984.

Ellsbury KE, Montano DE and Parker JJ: Preventative Services in a Hybrid Capitation and Fee-For-Service Setting, J of Fam Prac 28:540-544, 1989.

Enthoven A and Kronick R: A Consumer-Choice Health Plan for the 1990s: Part 1, N Engl J Med 320:29-37, 1989.

Enthoven A and Kronick R: A Consumer-Choice Health Plan for the 1990s: Part 2, N Engl J Med 320:94-101, 1989.

Epstein AM et al.: The Use of Ambulatory Testing in Prepaid and Fee-For-Service Group Practices, N Engl J Med 314:1089-1094, 1986.

Feder J, Hadley J, and Zuckerman S: How Did Medicare's Prospective Payment System Affect Hospitals, N Engl J Med 317:867-873, 1987.

Fitzgerald JF, Moore PS, and Dittus RS: The Care of Elderly Patients with Hip Fracture, N Engl J Med 319:1392-1397, 1988.

Gill D: A National Health Service: Principles and Practice, in The Sociology of Health and Illness-Critical Perspectives, 3rd Ed., Conrad P and Kern R, (eds.), St. Martin's Press, New York, 1990, pp. 474-487.

Hayward RA, et al: Inequities in Health Services Among Insured Americans, N Engl J Med 318:1507-1512, 1988.

Health Care in the 1990s: Trends and Strategies. Arthur Anderson Co., 1984.

Himmelstein DU et al.: A National Health Program for the United States, N Engl J Med 320:102-108, 1989.

Hsiao WC et al.: Estimating Physician Work for A Resource-Based Relative-Value Scale, N Engl J Med 319:835-841, 1988.

Inglehart JK: Health Policy Report: Early Experience with Prospective Payment of Hospitals, N Engl J Med 314:1460-1464, 1986.

Inglehart JK: Health Policy Report: Payment of Physicians Under Medicare, N Engl J Med 318:863-868, 1988.

Jonas S: Health Manpower, in Health Care Delivery in the United States, Jonas S (ed.), 3rd Edition, Springer Publishing Co., New York, 1986, pp. 54-89.

Lee PR et al.: The Physician Payment Review Commission Report to Congress, JAMA 261:2382-2388, 1989.

Light DW: Comparing Health Care Systems: Lessons from East and Wear Germany, in The Sociology of Health and Illness-Critical Perspectives, 3rd Ed., Conrad P and Kern R, (eds.), St. Martin's Press, New York, 1990, pp. 449-463.

Lister J: Proposals for Reform of the British National Health Service, N Engl J Med 320:877-880, 1989.

Luft H: Health Maintenance Organizations: Dimensions of Performance, New York, John Wiley, 1981.

Manning WG et al.: A Controlled Trial of the Effect of a Prepaid Group Practice on Use of Services, N Engl J Med 310:1505-1510, 1984.

Marmor TR: Canada's Path, America's Choice: Lessons from the Canadian Experience with a National Health Insurance, in The Sociology of Health and Illness-Critical Perspectives, 3rd Ed., Conrad P and Kern R, (eds.), St. Martin's Press, New York, 1990, pp. 463-473.

McCarthy CM: DRGs: Five Years Later, N Engl J Med 318:1683-1686, 1988.

Menck HR, Garfinkel L and Dodd GD: Preliminary Report of the National Cancer Data Base, Ca-A Cancer Journal for Clinicians 41:7-18, 1991.

Murray JP: A Follow-up Comparison of Patient Satisfaction Among Prepaid and Fee-For-Service Patients, J of Fam Prac 26:576-581, 1988.

National Center for Health Statistics: Health, United States, 1989, Hyattsville, Maryland, Public Health Service, DHHS Pub. No. (PHS) 90-1232, 1990.

Sager MA et al.: Changes in the Location of Death after Passage of Medicare's Prospective Payment System, N Engl J Med 320:433-439, 1989.

Starfield B: Primary Care and Health, JAMA 266:2268-2271, 1990.

Thorpe KE, Thorpe JL and Barhydt-Wezenaar N: Health Maintenance Organizations, in Health Care Delivery in the United States, Jonas S (ed.), 3rd Edition, Springer Publishing Co., New York, 1986, pp. 166-182.

Wilson, F.A., Neuhauser, D. Health Services in the United States, 2nd Edition. Ballinger Publishing Co., 1982.

Winkenwerder W, Kessler AR and Stolec RM: Federal Spending for Illness caused by Human Immunodeficiency Virus, N Engl J Med 320:1598-1603, 1989.

Whitcomb ME: Health Care for the Poor: A Public-Policy Imperative, N Engl J Med 315:1220-1222, 1986.

STUDY QUESTIONS

DIRECTIONS (Items 1-30): Each of the questions or incomplete statements below is followed by four or five suggested answers or completions. Select the **ONE** that is **BEST** in each case and completely fill in the circle containing the corresponding letter or number on the answer sheet.

1. The U.S. Health Care System can best be categorized as a(n):

    A. institutional care system
    B. national health insurance program
    C. pluralistic system for health care
    D. corporatist health care system
    E. mutual aid model of health care

2. Currently, the leading cause of death in the U.S. is:

    A. diabetes mellitus
    B. motor vehicle accidents
    C. AIDS
    D. cardiovascular disease
    E. cerebrovascular disease

3. Which of the following can best be described as funded by a federal-state matching grant program?

    A. Medicare - Part A
    B. prepaid group health plans
    C. Blue Cross/Blue Shield programs
    D. Medicare - Part B
    E. Medicaid

4. A single specialty group of family physicians, who have a large portion of their practice based on fee-for-service, have agreed to accept patients who are insured by a prepaid health plan in order to stay competitive with other physicians in the community. The term which best describes this arrangement is:

    A. independent provider organization
    B. group model health maintenance organization
    C. preferred provider organization
    D. staff model health maintenance organization
    E. exclusive provider organization

5. The classification of nursing homes is generally based on:

   A. levels of care
   B. profit structure
   C. patient demographics
   D. geographic location
   E. number of beds

6. Which of the following were enacted as amendments to the Social Security Act?

   A. Medicare
   B. Hospital Survey and Construction Act of 1946
   C. Public Health Service Act
   D. Comprehensive Health Manpower Training Act
   E. Federal Food, Drug, and Cosmetic Act

7. Which of the following accounts for the largest percentage of health care expenditures in the United States?

   A. physicians
   B. hospitals
   C. research
   D. construction
   E. nursing homes

8. The reimbursement plan by which the physician receives a flat annual fee for each person who agrees to be under his/her care regardless of the frequency with which the physician's services are utilized is known as:

   A. fee-for-service
   B. salaried employment
   C. indemnity insurance
   D. retrospective payment
   E. capitation

9. A Board of Trustees, as the source of responsibility for the operation of a hospital, is typical of:

   A. private community hospitals
   B. VA hospitals
   C. state hospitals
   D. Department of Defense hospitals
   E. state mental hospitals

10. The GMENAC report projected that by the year 2000 there would be:

    A. a shortage of women physicians
    B. a significant surplus of physicians
    C. a shortage of physicians in the primary care specialties
    D. an optimal geographic distribution of most specialties
    E. a surplus of psychiatrists

11. The highest percentage of ambulatory health care is delivered by physicians in:

    A. industrial occupational medicine clinics
    B. public health clinics
    C. hospital outpatient departments
    D. private medical practices
    E. student health services

12. The final authority for granting staff membership to the closed medical staff of a voluntary general hospital rests with the

    A. Chief Executive Officer
    B. Qualifications and Credentials Committee
    C. Chief of Staff
    D. Board of Trustees
    E. Executive Committee of the Medical Staff

13. "The amount of money paid by health insurance policies for a type of illness or treatment", best defines the term

    A. exclusions
    B. coverage
    C. benefits
    D. rider
    E. waiver

14. The single largest factor influencing the increase in total health care expenditures in the past ten years has been

    A. population growth
    B. price of services
    C. intensity of usage
    D. expansion of hospitals
    E. quality assurance

15. Which of the following funding sources has decreased the most during the past 50 years?

    A. state and local governments
    B. direct out-of-pocket payments
    C. private health insurance
    D. philanthropic contributions
    E. federal government

16. Which of the following is expected to consume an increasingly larger percentage of the health care dollar in the future?

    A. hospital construction
    B. physicians
    C. research
    D. nursing homes
    E. dental services

17. The most common type of hospital in the United States is the

    A. federally owned general hospital
    B. investor owned short-term general hospital
    C. voluntary long-term general hospital
    D. proprietary psychiatric hospital
    E. not-for-profit short-term general hospital

18. Blue Cross/Blue Shield plans differ from other private health insurance plans because they:

    A. are organized on a not-for-profit basis
    B. offer only indemnity benefits
    C. provide coverage for physician services
    D. are exempt from regulation by insurance commissions
    E. are restricted from participation in preferred provider organizations

19. The medical staff of a hospital is

    A. governed by a set of approved bylaws
    B. usually organized into departments according to specialty
    C. organized into committees for decision making purposes
    D. more commonly organized as a closed staff
    E. all of the above

20. Hospitals covered by the Medicare prospective payment system regulations include:

    A. alcohol treatment centers
    B. sole community hospitals
    C. psychiatric hospitals
    D. general hospitals
    E. children's hospitals

21. In Canada, physicians are paid primarily by

    A. capitation fees
    B. federal salaries
    C. fee-for-service
    D. mutual aid societies
    E. provincial salaries

22. The definition of "principle diagnosis" in relation to DRGs is

   A. the condition which, after appropriate studies, caused the patient's admission
   B. the diagnosis that yields the lowest reimbursement
   C. the admitting diagnosis
   D. the condition that is likely to require the longest length of stay
   E. the diagnosis which is likely to consume the greatest number of resources

23. Research comparing HMOs and fee-for-service practices indicate that HMOs:

   A. provide less preventive care
   B. utilize hospitals to the same degree as fee-for-service practices
   C. provide comparable care for less money
   D. underutilize modern diagnostic technology
   E. achieve a higher level patient satisfaction

24. The current Canadian health care system was developed around the desire to:

   A. recover from the aftermath of World War II
   B. effectively compete with the United States
   C. provide access to care without economic barriers
   D. generate enthusiasm and admiration for the medical profession
   E. reduce the utilization of hospitals

25. Health care services covered by Part A of Medicare include all of the following **EXCEPT**

   A. inpatient hospital services
   B. physician services
   C. post-hospital extended care services
   D. post-hospital home health services
   E. hospital outpatient diagnostic services

26. DRGs are assigned on the basis of all of the following **EXCEPT**

   A. patient age
   B. sex
   C. marital status
   D. principle diagnosis
   E. discharge status

27. Changes in medical education attributed to the Flexner Report include all of the following **EXCEPT**

    A. a four year medical school curriculum
    B. an increase in full time faculty
    C. centering medical education in universities
    D. the emergence of proprietary schools
    E. addition of laboratory teaching exercises

28. All of the following statements about the JCAHO are true **EXCEPT**

    A. accredits psychiatric facilities
    B. accredits short-term acute care hospitals
    C. develops standards and provides advice to hospitals about meeting them
    D. accredits ambulatory care programs
    E. enforces Medicare regulations

29. The resource based relative value scale developed by Hsiao and his colleagues defined total work input by the physician by all of the following **EXCEPT:**

    A. time
    B. mental effort and judgement
    C. length of specialty training
    D. technical skill and physical effort
    E. psychological stress

30. Direct out-of-pocket payments (synonymous with self pay) usually include all of the following **EXCEPT**

    A. insurance deductibles
    B. payments for eyeglasses
    C. co-insurance payments
    D. health insurance premiums
    E. prescription charges

DIRECTIONS (Items 31-50): Each group of questions below consists of four to five lettered headings followed by a list of numbered words or phrases. For each numbered word or phrase, select the one lettered heading that is most closely associated with it and fill in the circle containing the corresponding letter on the answer sheet. Each lettered heading may be selected once, more than once, or not at all.

    A. Voluntary hospitals
    B. Proprietary hospitals
    C. Both
    D. Neither

31. Usually enjoy tax exemptions

32. Owned, operated, or owned and operated by religious groups such as the Roman Catholic Church

33. Provide primary, secondary, and tertiary care to patients

34. Owned and operated by state or local governments

35. Investor-owned and operated hospitals

    A. Medicare - Part A
    B. Medicare - Part B
    C. Both
    D. Neither

36. Primarily pays for physician services

37. Provisions for deductibles, co-insurance, or premiums are included in funding mechanisms.

38. Payment is primarily determined by DRGs (Diagnosis Related Groups)

39. Enacted as an amendment to the Public Health Service Act

    A. Diagnosis Related Groups
    B. Resource-Based Relative-Value Scale
    C. Both
    D. Neither

40. Part of legislation enacted as cost control measures to reduce federal health expenditures related to Medicaid

41. Applies primarily to hospital reimbursement for service provided to beneficiaries covered by Medicare Part B

42. Basis of a uniform fee schedule for physician services

43. Emphasizes payment for the cognitive component of evaluation and management of as opposed to the technical services

    A. Public Health Service Act
    B. Kerr-Mills Act
    C. Hill-Burton Act
    D. Tax Equity and Fiscal Responsibility Act

44. Forerunner of the Medicaid legislation of 1965.

45. Mandated the development of the Medicare prospective payment system.

46. Funded construction and renovation of hospitals.

    A. Medical audit
    B. Quality assurance
    C. Utilization review
    D. Peer review

47. Analysis of individual cases based on defined criteria for diagnosis and management

48. A program of assessment designed to alter professional and organizational behavior so as to remedy deficiencies and improve performance

49. The assessment of the necessity for medical services usually directed to controlling costs

50. A method to evaluate the medical care rendered by reviewing the patient's medical record

ANSWER SHEET

1.	C	21.	C	41.	A
2.	D	22.	A	42.	B
3.	E	23.	C	43.	B
4.	A	24.	C	44.	B
5.	A	25.	B	45.	D
6.	A	26.	C	46.	C
7.	B	27.	D	47.	A
8.	E	28.	E	48.	B
9.	A	29.	E	49.	C
10.	B	30.	D	50.	A
11.	D	31.	A		
12.	D	32.	A		
13.	C	33.	C		
14.	B	34.	D		
15.	B	35.	B		
16.	D	36.	B		
17.	E	37.	C		
18.	A	38.	A		
19.	E	39.	D		
20.	D	40.	D		